Grounds for Cognition

How Goal-Guided Behavior Shapes the Mind

Radu J. Bogdan

LAWRENCE ERLBAUM ASSOCIATES, PUBLISHERS
1994 Hillsdale, New Jersey Hove, UK

Lawrence Erlbaum Associates, Inc., Publishers
365 Broadway
Hillsdale, New Jersey 07642

Cover design by Kate Dusza

Library of Congress Cataloging-in-Publication Data

Bogdan, Radu J.
Grounds for cognition : how goal-guided behavior shapes the mind / Radu J. Bogdan
p. cm.
Includes bibliographical references and index.
ISBN 0-8058-1591-0 (alk. paper). — ISBN 0-8058-1592-9 (pbk. : alk. paper)
1. Cognition. 2. Goal (Psychology) 3. Teleology. 4. Philosophy of mind. I. Title.
BF311.B5774 1994
153—dc20 93-50126
CIP

Books published by Lawrence Erlbaum Associates are printed on acid-free paper, and their bindings are chosen for strength and durability.

Printed in the United States of America
10 9 8 7 6 5 4 3 2 1

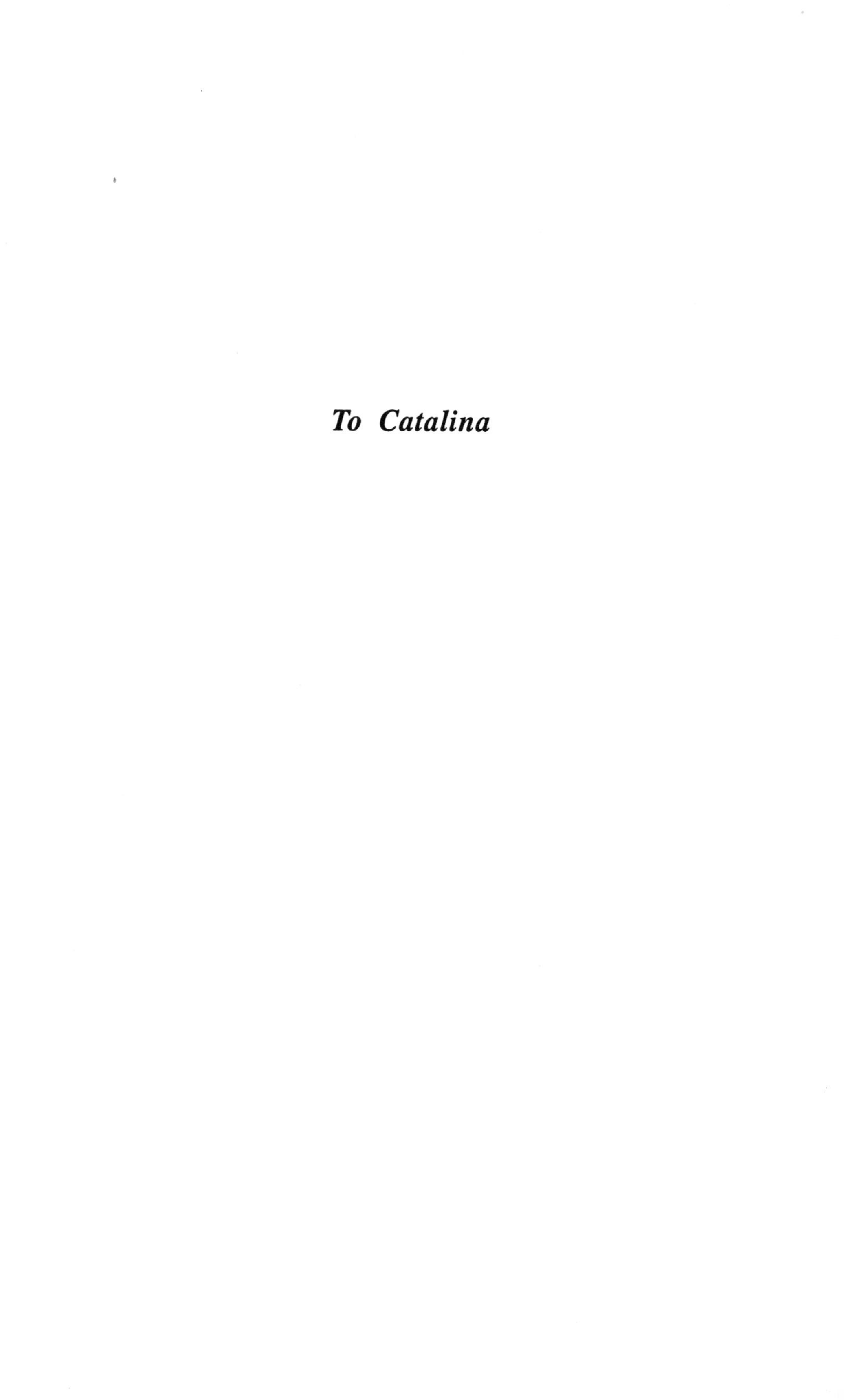

To Catalina

Contents

PART II FORMS OF GUIDANCE

Acknowledgments

This book has been slow in taking shape. New versions buried earlier ones in archeological layers that my memory is hard pressed to retrieve. Each layer has its deposits of queries and reactions. I do not recall too well who said what, when, and particularly why. Many people, I fear, would inevitably be overlooked, but some I recall well, with warmth and gratitude, for they made this project worthwhile, and in many ways so much better than it would otherwise have been.

My advanced undergraduate and graduate students in philosophy of mind and the foundations of cognitive science were almost always the first to bear the brunt of my inspiration. Over the last few years, their questions and objections have helped me very much. The most vivid in my memory are Eric Lormand, Jack Crumley, Brian Harrison, Ernie Edmundson, and, currently, Tian Ping.

Another, much cherished, layer of memory covers my French interludes. Since the early 1980s, I have regularly tried my ideas on a group of faithful hexagonal friends, splendid thinkers, and critics. During the spring of 1987, under their fire, I assembled the first core of this book by writing a longish paper on "Information and Semantic Cognition," published (with commentaries by Fred Dretske and David Israel) in *Mind and Language* in 1988. My warm thanks go to Daniel Andler, Pascal Engel, Pierre Jacob, François Recanati, and Dan Sperber. Their support and interest in my work means a lot to me. *Salut les copains!* I also thank Lucien Sfez and Daniel Parrochia for following my work and publishing fragments of it, and the participants at several Cerisy-la-Salle colloquia in Normandy, and one (unforgettable) in Corsica, where I sketched some of the arguments pursued here. I also developed ideas in other places, most memorably in my native but renewed Romania where, since 1990, I have presented almost yearly still other fragments and versions at the University of Bucharest to an assortment of students, teachers, and researchers in philosophy and other disciplines. For that opportunity I owe thanks to my good philosophical and personal friends Mircea Flonta, Adrian Iliescu, Ilie Parvu, and Sorel Vieru; also to Alexandru Valentin for making it possible; to Cornel Popa for lively and stimulating discussions; and to the researchers at the Institute of Psychology in Bucharest, always curious about my philosophical speculations on matters they think they know better.

But, of course, the bulk of the work and of the reactions to it belong to my home base in New Orleans. Our regular Friday seminars have been a testing ground for most of the ideas presented in or removed from this book. My friends at Tulane University and the University of New Orleans have helped in so many ways. I am thinking, in particular, of Graeme Forbes, Harvey Green, Carolyn Morillo, and Norton Nelkin. Harvey, Carolyn, Norton, and I have been discussing the mind for years. My own mind is so much richer for that. Carolyn and Norton read, patiently and carefully, an earlier version of the entire manuscript and made a lot of good observations. Thanks also to Carol Jobtansky who surely lost count of, but did not mind too much, the many piles she had to print, copy, and mail.

Reaching further back in time, a few people were there when it mattered. This project owes a lot to them. My heartfelt thanks and gratitude go to Keith Lehrer, a dear friend and philosophical companion, who has followed my work since my student years in Romania. I also bow, with fond memories, to Ian Hacking and Jaakko Hintikka for guiding my first academic steps in this country and encouraging some of my earliest ideas on the topics presented here.

Over the years I have discussed aspects of this project with many people. Some not only influenced my thinking but also took the time to comment verbally or in writing, publicly or privately, on various bits and pieces. My warm thanks go to Paul Churchland, Rob Cummins, Dan Dennett, Fred Dretske, Jerry Fodor, and Zenon Pylyshyn. I want also to thank David Israel, Marcelo Dascal, and Amir Horowitz for stimulating published comments on my papers and Dan Lloyd and Amy Pierce for their support and good suggestions.[1]

Not the type to be easily fooled by articles, rejoinders, talks, or edited collections, my parents waited patiently for this book. Here it is, as a modest way to say thank you for everything. Catalina, always warm, radiant, and good-hearted, made the entire effort so meaningful and worthwhile. She is my light, and this book is dedicated to her, as is my heart.

[1]During the gestation of this work I have benefited from, and am grateful for, several research fellowships provided by Tulane University and the hospitality of CREA in Paris and the University of Bucharest. Early versions of some parts of this work have been published before but almost never in the form found here. The most extensive literal inspiration from an earlier work (Bogdan, 1986a) occurs in chapter 7, section 5. Also chapter 5, section 4 is based in part on Bogdan (1989b), and chapter 10, section 2 builds on some notions first developed in Bogdan (1988c). Permission to draw on these works here is gratefully acknowledged.

1 The Project

1. THE ARGUMENT

Questions and Answers

Why do organisms cognize? That is, why do they process and store data, form concepts, or solve problems? To obtain behaviorally relevant information about their environments. Why would they need such information? Because organisms must guide themselves to their goals. Why guidance to goal? Because goals must be satisfied, and for that, organisms must locate and identify their goals. But why would organisms have goals in the first place? Because they are material systems or complexities that are genetically programmed to maintain and replicate themselves by engaging their worlds in goal-directed ways. That is the trick of life. These, essentially, are the questions this book asks, and the answers it proposes, as prerequisites for understanding what cognition is and how it works. The order of the questions suggests the order of grounding and explanation. Goal-directedness grounds and explains guidance to goal, and the latter in turn grounds and explains the design and operation of cognition.

Methodological Stance

This construal of cognition relies on a certain methodological stance. We are not viewing the cognitive mind merely as a complex physical system reacting mechanically to stimuli. Life and cognition are not solely particles or molecules bouncing around under causal pressures. Life and cognition also display functional properties whose rationale and work cannot be reductively explained by their physical composition. The cognitive mind is a tool with a job to do. The question is: What is that job? The assumption behind this question is that a description of the job would reveal the nature and operation of the cognitive mind.

This is the methodological stance of evolutionary biology. It recommends, first, figuring out the program or modus operandi of an organ from a reconstruction of the task or job for which the organ was naturally selected and then explaining the functional mechanism or architecture of the organ in terms of its program.[1] The explanatory sequence, thus, goes from task to program to mechanism. (This, as is seen later, is also the explanatory policy adopted recently in the foundations of cognitive science.) Evolutionary biologists use this approach for every organ and capability. When they ask, for example, why skunks smell bad, the immediate causal answer is that skunks secrete chemical substances whose molecular structures result in bad smells. This answer bears on the program and mechanism involved. But when the question turns to why skunks smell bad in the first place, the inquiry must probe the deeper and historically more distant reason for having smelling programs and mechanisms at all. That reason defines the task those programs and mechanisms have evolved to handle. The answer is that smelling bad is a good defense, and natural selection favors those organisms with the worst smells, who survive to produce the most babies. The specific molecular structure of the bad smelling mechanisms is an accident; any other chemical structure or any other defense mechanism programmed in some other way to spread bad smells could have had the same results by handling the required defense task.

This is the familiar distinction between proximate and ultimate explanation. Proximate explanations are about mechanisms, their programs, and the surrounding external conditions (inputs, contexts) of operation. I lump all these factors under the notion of proximate arrangement. Proximate explanation, then, is about proximate arrangements, as it proceeds from functional mechanisms and programs (as explanantia), and their contexts of operation as boundary conditions, to particular organ performances (as explananda).

Ultimate explanations are about the evolutionary shapers that configure the proximate causes (functional mechanisms and their programs) in the first place. The direction of the ultimate explanation is from evolutionary shapers (genetic variations, natural selection, guidance to goal) to the tasks or jobs to be accomplished and then to the programs carrying out the tasks and the functional mechanisms running the programs in specific proximate arrangements. Proximate explanations are causally or functionally subsumptive, whereas ultimate explanations are typically

[1]It is important to insist, even at this early stage, that a mechanism or architecture must be construed functionally, as material bits and parts organized and sequenced so as to carry out the functions of the program, and not merely physically, as a description of the inert composition of the organ under analysis.

reconstructive.[2] Our first explanation of the skunk's smell was proximate, the second ultimate. In the psychological domain, the explanation of an inference or behavior in terms of some program is proximate, whereas an evolutionary explanation of why the program was first naturally selected, for what task, is ultimate.

The Genetic Grounding of Goal-Directedness

Our teleological approach takes *goal–directedness* as the ultimate evolutionary reason for guidance to goal and the latter as the ultimate evolutionary shaper of the cognitive mind. Guidance to goal defines the information tasks that cognitive programs and their mechanisms evolved to handle.

This is the overall direction of our project. For the project to take off, it must first establish that goal-directedness itself, the ultimate explainer, is a respectable and scientifically intelligible material phenomenon in the world, a property of biomatter, indeed, the key property of life. This is the aim of chapter 2, in which I argue that goal-directedness characterizes the generic form in which genes program the design and behavior of living beings. Organisms are genetically primed to pursue goals. Although natural selection eventually decides which goal-pursuing policies work as adaptations, it is goal-directedness that ultimately explains the most general and systematic pattern that all adaptations, including the cognitive ones, display in their relations to environments. As Lynn Margulis is reported to have said, natural selection is the editor, not the author. The author is the genetic code. Chapter 2 shows that, fundamentally, genetic writing is teleological. When we set aside the richness of variations spawned by evolution, goal-directedness appears as the fundamental property of life, the systematically recurrent theme underlying all the variations.

From Teleology to Cognition

The next step in our project is to bring this genetically grounded teleology to bear on our understanding of cognition. Its aim is to connect goal-directedness (the evolutionary reason) to cognition (the family of programs) by way of guidance to goal (the family of tasks the programs had evolved to execute). We need, therefore, an analysis that effects the transition from the ultimate to the proximate explanation of cognition. The basic insight behind the analysis is the following: We noted that goal-directedness captures the

[2]See Mayr (1982). Plato, of course, was the first to articulate the proximate-ultimate distinction clearly, as he reacted against (what we may call) the proximate materialism of immediate causes and material compositions entertained by his predecessors (in *Phaedo*, especially 98c to 99d). A bit later, after providing a clear (and possibly first) statement of the hypotheticodeductive method, Plato also suggests that the most explanatory hypotheses must be ultimate (99e to 100c).

general patterns of all organism–environment interactions. Guidance to goal is one family of such patterns, those characterizing the informational transactions between organisms and environments. Cognition is the overall adaptation (or family of adaptations) evolved to instantiate such patterns of informational transactions.

To understand the programs of cognition and their proximate operation is to understand that the information tasks facing these programs eventuate in guidance to goal. Guidance to goal describes the systematically recurrent pattern that all cognitive adaptations display in their informational relations to their environments. The reason for this simple, fundamental, but often overlooked truth is that to pursue goals, organisms evolve ways to guide themselves to goals, and to do that, they come to exploit systematically pervasive and recurrent patterns of information relations available to them. The exploitable information patterns (tasks) in turn select for appropriate (adaptive) cognitive programs and functional mechanisms. How this selection works and its real life outcomes are the business of evolutionary psychology. Although my discussion often points at cognitive adaptations, its direction is more ultimate and concerns guidance to goal and its information tasks.

To effect the proposed transition from goal-directedness to cognition by way of guidance to goal and the information relations that secure it, we need a suitable methodological framework. This is the object of chapter 3. Guidance to goal defines the sort of knowledge that goal-directed systems or organisms need to manage in their worlds. Guidance to goal is secured by patterns of information relations that must be in place among an organism, its goals, its behaviors, and its ecology. Finding the goal-guiding patterns of information relations constitutes the information tasks facing an organism's cognition. The environmental opportunities exploited by the organism and the cognitive programs that do the exploiting can be regarded as the executors of the information tasks. Inside the organism, the program execution is implemented by appropriate functional mechanisms (the operating system). The grounding and explanatory order thus goes top–down from goal-directedness to guidance to goal to information tasks to cognitive programs (and ecological opportunities) to functional mechanisms. We can call it the *KICM* method of analysis: from Knowledge to Information to Cognition to Mechanism.

Forms of Guidance

I have noted that my focus is on the first two and most ultimate components of the KICM framework: knowledge as guidance to goal and the information patterns that make it possible. Given the account of knowledge and information offered in chapter 3, the next questions I ask are how many and what forms of guidance are possible, and what it takes informationally (i.e., what tasks must be executed in what configurations) to effect guidance in each of these forms. Put plainly, the question is: How many ways are there to spot and track a goal? These are not bioevolutionary questions about specific cognitive adaptations (programs and mechanisms) that have evolved in specific species. Our questions are more fundamental and speculative. And their answers, suggested in chapters 4–8, sketch the teleoevolutionary profiles of possible forms of guidance. These profiles offer theoretical guidelines and heuristic hints to the more proximately and empirically oriented cognitive sciences whose job is to confirm (or not) which of the suggested forms of guidance and types of information tasks are embodied in the biological (or computer) world, in what ways, and why. With that empirical confirmation, the information tasks that passed the test of natural selection can be mapped into causal–functional analyses of the successful cognitive programs and their mechanisms. The latter in turn can proximately explain particular program applications. Our project, however, does not go so far and proximately. How the forms of guidance and their information tasks are empirically fleshed out by natural selection theories and specific cognitive sciences is a matter well covered in the recent literature and about which I have little to say in this volume.

The following are the principled forms of guidance I examine. When goals are gross, diffuse, and normally proximal, and the behaviors directed at them simple, reflexive, and indiscriminate, the guidance is managed by simple information tasks whose execution relies heavily, rigidly, and almost exclusively on laws of nature and ecological cooperation. Guidance, in this case, is parasitic to the ways of nature with little functional initiative on the part of the organism's cognition. This is the *teleonomic guidance* discussed in chapter 4. Finely individualized goals, which are revealed by specific and distal properties and satisfied by complex and delicate behaviors, normally require a systematic targeting by means of discriminating information tasks able to triangulate the goal-revealing properties from the internal encodings left by the sensory inputs. This is *teleosemantic guidance.* When the triangulation in question is primitive, in the sense that the semantic information tasks range over simple signs or presentations of external correlations and are not executed in terms of simpler semantic information tasks, we have guidance by *primitive semantics* (chap. 5). A semantics that secures guidance through a flexible and combinatorially versatile triangulation of goal-revealing properties from internal signs or presentations of other such signs or presentations, with the effect that complex semantic tasks are executed in terms of simpler such tasks, is *re-presentational.* Human vision appears to be an instance of the transition from a primitive to a re-presentational semantics, as chapter 6 argues.

Together with other program developments, re-presentation in turn facilitates a massive internalization of guidance through conceptualization and the mental ability to model goal situations (chap. 7). Besides being goal-directed, re-presentational systems that model goal situations are also goal directors. They create goals by means of desires and plans, and anticipate their guidance to these goals mentally. Chapter 8 briefly discusses the social form of guidance. Mental modelers of goal situations, as we are, can spontaneously conceive of each other as goal-directed agents, pursue their goals by knowing those of others, and use each other as sources of information in guidance and as tools in the pursuit of goals. In so doing, such goal directors and modelers develop a conceptual framework in which they think of each other and figure each other out. That is commonsense psychology.

Reasons for Speculation at the Top

Although this discussion and particularly the illustrations of each form of guidance tentatively address real-life programs and the mechanisms likely to instantiate them, the emphasis of our discussion is consistently on the two top levels of analysis—guidance and the information relations that make guidance possible. There are two good reasons for this division of labor, with guidance and information on one side and cognitive programs and mechanisms on the other side, and for the speculative exercise of profiling possible forms of guidance solely in terms of theoretically plausible configurations of information relations. The first reason has to do with the ultimate–proximate distinction and the resulting top–down analysis now prominent both in evolutionary biology and cognitive science. It is almost a logical point that if the proximate is explained by the ultimate, then, given sufficiently realistic although not necessarily biological constraints, the possible scenarios of guidance through information patterns envisaged at the top levels of analysis must have a bearing on the particular, often deviant and messy program and mechanism instantiations in the real world. The converse perhaps makes the point better: If the speculation on possible forms of guidance have no bearing on understanding real cognitive adaptations, then it is hard to see the point and usefulness of the ultimate–proximate or top–down analyses. Indeed, one would expect those who deny the antecedent to deny the consequent as well.

The second reason for playing our theoretical game at the speculative heights of guidance and information, far from their biological instances, is that the cognitive and all other biological adaptations installed by natural selection are provincial relative to how goal-directedness and guidance to goal are construed. Biological life is not the only form of life and biocognition not the only form of cognition. This is true in principle and may become an empirical truth in a few decades. Although I take the genetics of goal-directedness very seriously, I regard it merely as a biological expression of the more general phenomenon of goal-directed self-organization and self-reproduction. Although this book does not explore this more general phenomenon, I think its scientific analysis may one day ground biogenetic goal-directedness, as one of many forms of goal-directedness displayed by self-organizing and self-reproducing systems. So, althought I take goal-directedness seriously, I am liberal about its worldly and specifically biological incarnations. This is why my teleoevolutionary stance is generic, does not entail biology, and is necessarily hybrid by combining bioevolution with abstract speculations about alternative forms of goal-directedness.

The reason for my position is simple. There is an objective sense in which goal-directedness obtains whenever certain teleological constraints (specified in chap. 2, section 5) are met by some form of matter or another. Goal-directedness need not be intrinsic to any particular form of matter and is not necessarily biochemical. If other forms of matter (e.g., mineral, plasmatic, robotic) organized in functional configurations other than biological (e.g., synthesized on a computer, embodied in a robot, or manufactured in some other artificial manner), run means–ends programs that maintain and replicate an internal structure in some environment, then, according to the argument of chapter 2, these forms display goal-directedness. This means that the bioevolutionary constraints on DNA-run life on earth need not be the same as the teleoevolutionary constraints operating on other forms of goal-directed life.

This angle on goal-directedness explains why the forms of guidance and the information tasks examined in this work are not intended to match real biological taxonomies and at times may even fail to have any biological counterparts. This is acceptable, as long as we recall that the biological taxa are but one version of goal-directedness among the multiplicity of versions abstractly contemplated by our story. This approach is not new. Decades ago, general system theorists and cyberneticians made similar proposals, and some (Wiener, 1948, 1950) grounded teleology in a comparative analysis of brains and servomechanisms.[3] Without the teleology, I find the same spirit in Braintenberg's (1984) splendid essay on synthetic psychology, and I expect the von Neumann-inspired views of artificial life to rehabilitate and further develop these early and good insights (Levy, 1992).

This generic and hybrid stance on goal-directedness should also allay the misgivings of those skeptical of evolutionary accounts of cognition and of top–down reconstructions that derive biological features, including real cognitive programs, from rational models (Lewontin, 1990; Pinker & Bloom, 1990). These skepticisms draw on the idea that bioevolution is too messy and opportunistic, biocognition too complex, and its rational models too rarefied and abstract to allow for a neat and enlightening fit. I agree. This volume does not offer an

---

[3]I think that the early work in cybernetics is out of favor today for two main reasons. One is that its models of cognition were too general, coarse, and too indifferent to how information runs cognition to map intelligibly into the finer grained preoccupations (specific tasks and computational programs) of current cognitive science and philosophy of mind. The other reason is the strong antiteleological bias still formidable in the latter fields. In this last respect, cybernetics was ahead of its time.

evolutionary account of biocognition, nor does it reconstruct biocognition from rational models.[4] Although my project is inspired by genetics and bioevolution, its focus is on guidance and its possible forms and implications, not on biological embodiments. Evolutionary teleology, as stated earlier, need not be only biological, and evolution need not be reducible to bioevolution. To the extent that cognitive science generally and psychology in particular concern themselves with the information tasks and cognitive programs involved in guidance to goal, it follows that neither can be reduced to or exclusively grounded in biology.[5]

2. CRITICAL TARGETS

Most of this book is dedicated to the constructive argument just previewed. Occasional criticisms and exegetical analyses intrude (as in chap. 6) solely to support the ongoing argument. Yet throughout this work, and notably in its third part, there are two critical and related targets that are pursued and contended with systematically. Dominant in current cognitive science and philosophy of mind, these targets are major obstacles to a teleological understanding of cognition. Let me introduce the first target, and the most relevant to our project, by contrasting the standard and the teleological styles of top–down analysis of cognition.

Psychosemanticism

Knowledge, almost everybody agrees, is information about the world on which organisms act. An ancient, popular, and implausible view, which has become standard, sees knowledge in two dimensions. One dimension is the hook-up relation to the world, the other the causal or functional impact of this relation, once cognized, on behavior. To simplify, I label the first dimension

---

[4]Clark (1989) provided a good account of the messiness and evolutionary opportunism present in biocognition.

[5]For an analogy, think of the grammar program in humans. It may appear that the program is essentially biocognitive, but that is not so. Any successful form of language processing, natural or artificial, whatever its form of implementation, is bound to have the recursive and constructive features of generative grammar, if it relies on finite resources to handle indefinitely many and combinatorially explosive structures. This is a point of principle, concerning the computational problems faced, not the biological implementation of the solutions. In this sense, Chomsky's theory of grammar is an exercise in generic psycholinguistics, not in the descriptive biology of language processing, in psychology rather than biopsychology. The same is true of goal-directedness and guidance to goal. If we consider dynamic arrangements between self-organizing systems and their environments, whereby the systems maintain and replicate their organization in means–ends forms, then we must consider generic problems faced by the systems, irrespective of the specifics of the implementation of the solutions.

in terms of its most prominent version, the semantic form of hook-up, although the force of my critique extends to any form of hook-up, whether (strictly) semantic or nonsemantic. So construed, the semantic dimension takes the job of cognition to be about, or indicate, or refer to, or reflect, or picture, or represent, or covary with, aspects of the world of interest to the organism and its behavior; the causal dimension indicates that, once encoded and processed, the information is *causally–functionally efficacious* in virtue of its hook-up relation to the world, of what it represents. This is to say that the forms in which information is encoded and processed as data have causal or functional efficacy in virtue of how the data hook up with the world.

Working top–down now: To yield semantic knowledge, cognition must provide the organism with information that causes behavior in virtue of what it represents. Cognition causally converts semantic information into behavior; the semantics runs the psyche. The form and function of the cognitive programs are psychosemantic because they reflect this semantics-to-causation conversion. The operating system running such programs must be a semantic mind. Evolution, therefore, must have installed a cognitive mind whose rationale and role is to map semantic information into behaviors. The view committed to this top–down analysis and its implications is *psychosemanticism*.[6] It is the main and explicit villain of our story.

The spirit of psychosemanticism is aptly encapsulated by Ramsey's notorious metaphor of belief (cognition, generally) as a map by which we steer. This metaphor begins to tell us what is right and wrong with psychosemanticism. It is right that maps have the job of causally steering travel in virtue of what they represent, just as cognitive programs have the job of causally steering behavior in virtue of the information they make available to the organism. Right but incomplete. Steering is not by maps only, nor does a map steer merely in virtue of what it represents. A map must be used to yield information, and the context and purpose of its use make a vast difference to the steering. The map user has access to information that the map does not provide (starting points, destinations, difficulty of access, various other values, and so much more). The use of a map relies on and exploits but does not represent the contexts, assumptions, limitations, and choices associated with its use. The same, I argue, is true of guidance and cognition. The guiding knowledge is the information that gets us from our current condition to our goal by means and under assumptions that are not represented (cognized) at all; at the same time what is represented, or generally linked up with, often has little if anything to do with goals pursued. The information cognized is only part of the total information that guides to goals, and the semantic informa-

---

[6]Fodor's book *Psychosemantics* (1987), which inspired this "ism," portrays one version of psychosemanticism. There are others, too. Yet, as noted, psychosemanticism also applies to forms of hook-up that (according to chap. 5) are not strictly or technically semantic.

tion itself (when available) often is only part of the information cognized. A semantic mind would be a very narrow and unadapted mind.

My criticisms of psychosemanticism surface often but are brought together in a focused and integrated form in chapter 9. The limitations of psychosemanticism are symptomatic of a narrow view of the tasks of cognition and of the resulting failure to see the wider arrangements in which, and the deeper reasons for which, organisms have knowledge. This narrow view is encouraged not only by the standard account of knowledge, but also is a symptom of a deeper conceptual ailment. This brings us to our second critical target, which I call *Psychological Newtonianism.* Unlike its psychosemantic version, which bears the brunt of our critique, psychological Newtonianism is mostly in the background, the implicit villain. Whereas psychosemanticism obscures the phenomenon of guidance to goal and thus the teleological determination of cognition, deeper down in the order of theorizing, psychological Newtonianism is inimical to the more fundamental phenomenon of goal-directedness itself.

Psychological Newtonianism

This is the view that psychology ought to be a sort of physics functionalized. It is a view animated and held together by several doctrines: that the cognitive mind is a complex body subject to external and internal causal interactions (physicalism) that have been functionalized (functionalism) either by accident or deliberate design or natural selection (historicism). Physicalism assigns the mind to the physical order of nature, whereas functionalism redescribes the causal work of the cognitive programs as patterns of input-internal states-output functions. In the domain of cognition, psychosemanticism legitimizes these functions as mappings of semantic relations into cognitive and behavioral causation. Historicism is a recent and not always welcome addition to psychological Newtonianism. When adopted, typically in the form of natural selection, historicism tells us which task-specific psychosemantic functions have prevailed over time and why. The explanatory policy of psychological Newtonianism, both in the ultimate and proximate domains, is that of causal–functional explanation: Ultimately, natural selection causally shapes the mind's programs; proximally, their psychosemantic applications can be explained functionally, in terms of the rules of the programs and the causal push of the sensory inputs.[7]

[7]There is a long and distinguished tradition, going back to Plato and Aristotle, which argues that there are objective patterns and regularities in the world, particularly in the domain of life, which cannot be reduced and explained by their physical components and causal interactions. This work is inspired by that tradition and its quest for the objective (here, genetic) grounds of goal-directedness.

To follow the contours of my critique of psychosemanticism and psychonewtonianism, I should mark the areas where teleology does not make a difference to my view of cognition, and so where nonteleological accounts are legitimate and useful. One such area is that of the proximate analyses of dedicated cognitive programs (vision, language, sensory–motor), which handle domain-specific tasks, often psychosemantic in nature. Teleology is also unimportant in the evolutionary psychology that explains more ultimately, by natural selection, such tasks and programs. In neither of these areas does teleology make a difference, not because goal-directedness is not present (it is), but because what is examined are its partial embodiments that can be explained ultimately and causally by natural selection, and proximately by the causal–functional work of dedicated programs. It will be a constant tactic of my argument (a) to note the mutually reinforcing links between psychosemanticism, domain-specific tasks, and dedicated programs, on the one hand, and their ultimate yet causal explanation by natural selection, on the other hand; (b) to acknowledge the validity of these links within definite (normally, modular) limits; but (c) to challenge the links outside those limits, where teleology makes a difference, both ultimately and proximately.

The Teleological Difference

As the preview of my argument indicates, there are two areas of explanation where teleology does make a substantial difference, and where, therefore, the conflict with psychological Newtonianism and psychosemanticism is bound to be the sharpest. These areas form the object of this book. One concerns the grounding and ultimate explanation of cognition in terms of guidance to goal, and the grounding and ultimate explanation of the latter in terms of goal-directedness. In this area psychological Newtonianism fails to recognize the teleological patterns that the genes (or other shapers of life) cast around to organize their products (organs, functional capabilities, behaviors) and thus pursue their maintenance and replication policies. This is why psychological Newtonianism looks like a reform Cartesianism that views the cognitive mind as a functionally autonomous unit whose design and operation owes nothing essential to how it engages the world and why. The historical appeal to natural selection (when attempted) probes only the pedigree of individual and task-specific functions and never inquires into the larger picture that gives reason and rhyme to the overall interplay of these functions.

The second and proximate area of explanation where teleology matters (literally) and where psychological Newtonianism and its psychosemantic cousin again fail is thinking. In simpler forms of guidance, the cognitive component is typically a rigid cog in a larger arrangement, and instantiates evolutionarily preassigned and fixed functional paths that lawfully connect with inputs, ecological accidents, and natural regularities to provide guidance to goal. By contrast, in mental guidance, the cognitive component itself, in the form of thinking, is intrinsically teleological because its design has evolved to posit and flexibly script its own goal models before action is initiated. The intrinsic teleology of thinking simply eludes the causal–functional style of explanation so dear to psychological Newtonianism and psychosemanticism; like any goal–directed activity, from metabolism to escape behavior, mental goal scripting is systematically and irremediably underdetermined by its causal and functional implementations. So argues chapter 10.

3. RESPECTS AND DEMARCATIONS

This book approaches the cognitive mind in terms of its natural properties and evolutionary history, an approach we might call *mind naturalization.* To naturalize the mind is to determine its origin, place, and role in nature in: (a) the metaphysical terms of *materialism*, that everything exists in space and time, as some form of matter, at some level of complexity; (b) the logical terms of *noncircularity*, that the analysis should not employ the notions to be naturalized; (c) the methodological terms of *intelligibility and explanatoriness*, that the analysis should make intelligible and explain the properties of its object; and (d) the ideological terms of *scientific respectability*, that the analysis must be compatible with science.

In recent years a good number of works have significantly advanced the cause of mind naturalization (Churchland, 1989; Cummins, 1983, 1989; Dretske, 1981, 1986, 1988; Fodor, 1975, 1983, 1987, 1990a; Pylyshyn, 1984; Quine, 1960; Searle, 1983; Stich, 1983; as well as influential papers by Davidson, Putnam, and many others). Many of these works are committed to a proximate and often psychosemantic mind naturalization. A more ultimate and natural selection-based mind naturalization, with faint teleological echoes, has been attempted most notably by Dennett (1969, 1978, 1987, 1991a) and Millikan (1984, 1986,1989) and anticipated in earlier and important works of evolutionary epistemologists like Piaget, Popper, Campbell, and of cyberneticians like Wiener, Ashby, Somerhoff, and others. I have learned very much from these works and developed my views in constant and fruitful dialogue with them.

It has been widely assumed that mind naturalization is incompatible with teleology. This book shows not only that there is no such incompatibility but also that the mind naturalization project cannot be completed without teleology. In pushing for this line of argument, I have benefited considerably from a number of works on mind naturalization that have shown a lively and systematic interest in teleology. Among them are Bennett (1976, 1991), Collins (1984. 1987), Lycan (1981, 1989), Matthen and Levi (1984), Matthen (1988), McGinn

(1989), and Papineau (1984, 1987). My project is intended to fortify and extend this common enterprise. Yet there are differences, often important. I find some of these teleological analyses too indebted to the psychosemanticist agenda. Instead of being primarily puzzled, as most teleoevolutionary psychosemanticists are, by the narrower question of how cognitive programs link up with the world in ways that steer behavior, I am more puzzled, antecedently, by the deeper question of how self-organizing systems such as organisms enter in complex, dynamic, and evolving arrangements with their natural and social ecologies, and manage to settle into ecological–cognitive patterns of informational transactions that instantiate guidance to goal. Also, unlike most of my teleological colleagues, I take genetics very seriously and use it to ground goal-directedness, while at the same time remaining open to forms of goal-directedness which are not biological.

Finally, I hope that the novel methodological approach to goal-directedness and guidance taken in this book can bring teleology in line and in communication with the top–down analyses practiced in evolutionary biology, the emerging theory of self-organized and self-replicating systems, and cognitive science. If I were to capture the methodological spirit of my enterprise in a simple formula, I will choose, with some trepidation, the inelegant notion of transcendental naturalism—in a modest and unusual form. Kant's notorious transcendental question was, given that we have knowledge, how is it possible? To simplify enormously, Kant's view was that knowledge results from and encompasses the application of concepts to sensory experiences. So, when he asked his transcendental question about knowledge, his interest was in what the human mind must be like in order to know what it does.

I share neither the narrow psychological scope of Kant's question nor the idealist and a priori answer to it. For my notion of knowledge is so much different from his. I think of knowledge in terms of guidance to goal by way of information. Kant's notion covers only the cognitive leg of the guidance journey; Kant's notion is exclusively human, in most respects, while mine isn't. I would go even further, and say that Kant and those who followed him have not been radical enough in their transcendentalism. The most radical question is not what the human mind must be like, in order for it to cognize as it does and know what it does. For me, a deeper foundational question, the question of this book, is how knowledge and cognition are possible at all, and why, in the larger scheme of matter and evolutionary history, so that simple and then complex minds evolve to embody various forms of cognition and have various forms of knowledge.

Because I propose a more comprehensive story of knowledge, I also have a wider framework in which to examine its possibility. That examination will be modestly transcendental, as opposed to empirical or historical. For I think that the notions of guidance to goal and information tasks—not just cognitive tasks, for that would be more like Kant's angle—explicate the general conditions in which knowledge and cognition are evolutionarily possible, and even suggest some general constraints on, and forms of, their possibility. Therefore, prior to the empirical details of cognitive science and the historical details of evolutionary biology, the notions of guidance to goal and information tasks, which will be the key notions of my analysis, characterize the logic of the cognitive situation in general—indeed, the very conditions for the possibility of cognition.

A good deal of work in cognitive science, artificial intelligence, artificial life, evolutionary biology, and the design of self-maintaining and self-replicating systems is modestly transcendental, in my sense. People in these fields ask what a system (biological, robotic, whatever) must be like to interact successfully with the world; what its interaction tasks must be like to account for this success; and what the executing programs must be like to carry out the tasks. The transcendental stance is compatible with and can be very useful to scientific naturalism in its many forms. I think that stance needs a place in mind naturalization. It is also great fun.

The language of this work is going to be neither ordinary nor elegant. It is largely technical. Its basic vocabulary is made of notions such as guidance, information task, program, assumptions, goal situations, and others. Most of my analysis is in such terms. To help keep track of these notions and the places where they are first explicated, the reader can consult a short glossary at the end of the book.

This terminological decision was not taken lightly. There are several reasons for it. One is that readers are going to cross many disciplinary boundaries, with their own vocabularies and habits of thinking and explaining. A single frame of terminological and conceptual reference can only help. Another reason is that in philosophy, a discipline with a very long and unforgiving memory, such concepts as knowledge, belief, goal, intentionality, representation, and the like, carry associations and implications that one has to track and fight for, or against, constantly. This is not what I want to do here. As a result, I have either abandoned these standard philosophical notions or else, as in the case of knowledge or goal-directedness, re-explicated them in terms of my technical vocabulary.

The final reason has to do with commonsense psychology, which implicitly defines understanding of such widely used notions as belief, desire, goal, thinking, and the like. In recent years, grand doctrines and research programs have analyzed the commonsense wisdom for what it can reveal about the mind, and enlist it in the service of scientific theorizing, or else try to prove it false of the mind and hence detrimental to cognitive science. I happen to think and argue a little in chapter 8 and other works that these are the wrong ways to look at commonsense psychology, and that, in particular, its notions have little to say about the matters discussed in this book. Pending a clarification of what the commonsense notions are all about, their uncritical use could only obscure my inquiry. So, again, I try either to avoid using the commonsense notions or, as in the case of some, such as goal, desire or belief, redefine them in our technical vocabulary. I can only hope that what is lost in agreeableness and familiarity is compensated for by some uniform precision and focus.

Part 1

THE TELEOEVOLUTIONARY STANCE

2 By Way of Means and Ends

This chapter provides the teleological foundations for my analysis of guidance to goal. Its objective is to ground goal-directedness genetically. The basic suggestion is this. Organisms are small things, with few energy resources and puny physical means, battling a ruthless physical and biological nature. How do they manage to survive and multiply? Cleverly, by organizing themselves to engage and exploit a user-friendly ecological niche in a goal-directed manner. Organisms evolve structures capable of coopting and directing causal processes originating internally and externally so as to engage their habitat and bring about specific, limited, and attainable end states as goals. Goal satisfaction allows organisms to maintain and replicate their basic design by doing certain things in and to an environment. This explains how goal-directedness came about, as an instrument and modality of maintenance and replication of design, and why it was naturally selected as a successful policy.

Our hypothesis presupposes that evolution precedes and is more general than biological life. There are nonliving and nonteleological systems that evolve by natural selection. So the latter cannot explain or reduce goal-directedness. In its biological form, natural selection works precisely because and to the extent that its targets, the organisms, are already goal-directed systems whose interactions with the environment are themselves goal-directed. Goal-directedness and its tools, such as guidance to goal, do not reduce to their biological implementations. Yet, because these implementations alone have evolved programs causally capable to shape goal-directed processes, including those of guidance, our naturalization of goal-directedness and guidance to goal must necessarily appeal to and find illustrations in genetics and bioevolution. The chapter has no ambition beyond providing a pragmatic and limited exposition and defence of goal-directedness sufficient to establish its materialist credentials and legitimize the notion of guidance to goal.[1]

1. AN UR ROLE FOR GOALS

To flesh out our hypothesis, let us regress to ur and speculate. To survive and propagate, organisms must be able to husband their energy resources by generating or encountering states of affairs that help maintain their internal design, service its needs, and reproduce it. Organisms that fare better over time are those lucky to evolve internal structures and processes that reliably identify the beneficial states of affairs and guide the behavior to them. I call such structures and processes means–ends (or *m–e*) structures and processes.

The ability to pursue specific ends by specific means enables an organism not only to specialize and focus its efforts but also to terminate them at some opportune point, thus saving energy and wear when the results are good or to continue its efforts or try something else when they are not. The more efficient an organism's ability to identify and get beneficial results and the more accurate the information gained from the results, the better off the organism and its ability to spread its genetic heritage will be. We can think of the m–e structures and processes that accomplish these things as strategies by which organisms maintain a stable internal organization and replicate it. It is a clever evolutionary ploy to do that by way of pursuing finite and specific states of affairs in a means–ends format. Having and satisfying goals is the strategy of life. Life is maintaining and replicating an internal structure *by means of doing* something or other. Life is *a manner* of maintaining and replicating internal organization (the goal-directed manner) but not the only one. There are other forms of such maintenance and replication. This distinction is important to my argument because, by disengaging goal-directed life from other and simpler forms of maintenance and replication of internal organization through natural selection, the exclusive explanatory grip of natural selection is weakened, thus providing room for goal-directedness and its (more ultimate) explanatory constraints on life and cognition. The disengagement argument goes as follows.

Simply maintaining and replicating an internal structure without doing anything else is not yet life. There are nonbiological forms of matter (for instance, crystals) and concoctions (computer programs, for example), which mutate, develop, maintain, and replicate their internal organization under

---

[1]For comprehensive and sustained defenses of teleology, see Taylor (1964), Bennett (1976), and Woodfield (1976) for an early survey of the debates about teleology.

the ax of natural selection. Crystals mutate, develop, maintain, inherit, and replicate their organization because their organization comes in the form of repetitious physical patterns. The patterns give crystals their structural integrity and allow them to grow by incorporating atoms from the surroundings. Because in many crystals the atomic bonds between layers are weaker than those within a single layer, it is easy for layers to shear along the natural crystalline planes, thus replicating their internal organization (Cairns-Smith, 1985; Casti, 1989, chap. 2; Dawkins, 1986, chap. 6).

It is significant that crystals enjoy both random mutation of structure and the natural selection of the reproductive effects of such mutations and so are subject to a prebiological evolution. Crystals often mutate structural defects that can be passed on to successors as their layers grow and replicate. When the newly formed mutant crystals happen to survive longer and replicate faster than older versions (because of better sticking to the surrounding rocks, for example), thus displacing the latter and coming to dominate their corner of the world, we have a case of genuine crystalline evolution.

For a materialist this is as it should be, if both the emergence and properties of life are to be understood in prebiological yet evolutionary terms. The key parameters of systems that evolve—that is, (a) the maintenance and (b) replication of internal organization by means of (c) random mutation (but not sexual recombination) and (d) natural selection—antecedently characterize nonliving systems. It follows that these four parameters are not definitive of life and hence cannot be invoked to explain its goal-directedness, or explain it away. Mere evolutionary explanations in terms of structural mutations and natural selection cannot account for biological systems generally and for their conative and cognitive programs in particular. This creates elbow room for the teleological difference in life's earliest and most fundamental form. Life is teleoevolution.

What is specific of life is the form in which it instantiates the evolutionary parameters (a)–(d). *Goal-directedness* offers an opportunity for bioevolution. The maintenance and replication of internal design are attained by specialized mechanisms. It is these mechanisms that genetic mutations and recombinations modify, and it is upon the functional effects of these modifications that natural selection acts. Because organisms, being goal-directed, do things functionally, not just physically or chemically, bioevolution can do its job.[2]

Bioevolution could not have a grip on crystals precisely because they lack

[2]This difference between doing things functionally as opposed to physically or chemically is manifested theoretically in the types of properties and laws that characterize and explain the doings. The difference is not one of material composition or causation, for everything in our world is compositionally physical or chemical and causally happens. The difference is that some material structures underly causal processes that have dedicated effects whose impact on a larger system of such structures and processes warrants their categorization as functional. The biochemstry of organisms is already functional in this sense.

specific means–ends processes whose functionally dedicated effects on the ecology and crystals themselves could be selected for or against. A mutation of crystalline structure is replicated directly as a matter of physical law. Crystals do not do anything intermediate that could be one day modified by mutation and hence naturally selected for or against. Crystals evolve by virtue of what they are physically, whereas organisms evolve by virtue of what they do, goal-directedly.

The growth, maintenance, replication, and inheritance of internal structure by crystals are the result of mere instantiation of physical properties and laws. Although crystal mutation and replication may be implemented by means of intermediate physical processes as anything in nature is, the implementation itself is not functional. No intermediate functional processes, which are served by specialized structures, operate in crystals or other nonbiological forms to generate sequences of outcomes whose final effect is to maintain and replicate an internal structure. The same is true of self-replicating organic molecules artificially synthesized,[3] and also of computer programs that replicate themselves by passing their own spontaneous internal changes on to their offsprings.[4] Neither crystals nor synthesized molecules nor self-replicating computer programs maintain and multiply their organization by doing something else, not just physically, but in ways whose

[3]The MIT chemist Rebek synthesized an organic molecule that replicates itself. Its constitution and shape are different from those of the biomolecules of life. The molecule is made of an amine (containing nitrogen) and an ester (acid and alcohol), and reproduces in chloroform and not, as biomolecules do, in water. In a solution of like esters and amines, the synthetic molecule's ester will seize a free amine, and its amine a free ester. The loose ends of the captured compounds then fuse in an exact copy of the parent molecule that brought them together (*Discover*, December 1990, p. 28). This, I humbly opine, is more than what crystals appear to do but less than what the molecules of life do. The synthetic molecule needs specific ecological assistance (the right solution, like compounds) and some simple functions (recognizing and capturing like compounds) to replicate, which is part of what life is. Yet the molecules of life do more than that, as they build cells and bodies, which they must nourish and service and also replicate. The two tasks are connected because it is the bodies thus built and serviced that participate in replication. This is why life is maintenance and replication of something (the ur molecules) by doing something else (i.e., building bodies and having them reproduce in an environment by means of development and behavior). More recently (*New York Times*, August 27, 1991), Rebek's group was reported to have installed occasional errors that are passed on to the descendant molecules. Again, this is not goal-directed life, not because it does not involve the biomolecules typical of life, but because the replication itself does not require pursuing and satisfying intermediate goals by specialized functions other than the copying functions.

[4]I find the concept of artificial life coherent and instantiable. I also think that programs other than genetic, once installed in appropriate systems, can display nonbiological goal-directedness. Nevertheless, I find the current computer programs, for example, that of Thomas Ray, falling short of goal-directedness, hence life. Like the crystalline and organic replicators, Ray's computer program replication is not goal-directed because it does not rely on intermediate specialized functions targeted on states of affairs that secure their maintenance and replication.

functional specialty is to have such effects. This is the key difference, the key to goal-directedness.

It does not mean, however, that goal-directedness could not emerge from forms of matter other than biological or be programmed other than genetically. On the contrary, this possibility is assumed and exploited by our inquiry. Computer programs could one day build and animate active, gregarious, autonomous, and goal-directed robots the way genes animate bioorganisms as program replication machines. Guidance to goal and its cognitive realization would then be part of the system, sharing many of the constitutive and regulative properties of their biological counterparts. This was the leading insight of cybernetics and of von Neumann's theory of cellular automata, now revitalized by work on artificial life (Levy, 1992). But artificial goal-directedness is only a promise, which is why a naturalization of goal-directedness is still bound to biolife. This is why the generality of my discussion must constantly bow to the specifics of biolife. This is also why, as noted in the next section, we must understand the limited role of bionatural selection very carefully, because inevitably it tends to portray misleadingly the ecological and competitive coordinates of biolife and hence the reasons for bioadaptations as the only shapers of the cognitive and behavioral design of self-reproducing systems.

In its biological embodiment, goal-directedness is a natural product of evolution. It probably emerged as an accidental sequence of processes improvised by the organic compounds that must have exploited crystals into becoming genetic formations.[5] Because goal-directedness turned out to have adaptive results, it must have been naturally selected. Our analysis maintains, without circularity, that the evolution that initially generated and selected goal-directed organisms is prebiological; it is the same evolution that acts on crystals and organic molecules. Once goal-directedness got into the picture, evolution took a biological turn, playing a new natural selection game. In this new game bionatural selection acquires a grip on organisms in virtue of their being goal-directed, hence functional, and not merely in virtue of their possessing mutating structures that replicate.

Our evolutionary approach to goal-directedness clarifies another fact often used against teleology. Prebiological evolution shows that the maintenance and replication of internal structure are not the goals of anything. This applies to the genes, too. Far from being genetic goals, structural integrity and replication are physical dispositions whose exercise has no rationale and no

[5]Cairns-Smith (1985, chap. 14) told a story about crystals binding organic compounds, which helped them survive and replicate. At some point, some of the organic structures managed to replicate faster than their crystalline hosts and became dominant by the rules of natural selection. See also Dawkins (1986, chap. 6).

goals of its own. That is true of genes as of crystals. It is the form of the exercise of those dispositions that differentiates genes from crystals or current versions of artificial life. DNA replication, unlike the crystalline or artificial ones, is mediated by concrete end states, involving substance and energy, which are attained by the functional means of m–e structures and processes. Likewise, the RNA and proteinic processes involved in this functional mediation do not have their own goals either and certainly not the goals of preserving and replicating DNA; the RNA and the working proteins have only specific functions to run causal processes with dedicated effects, which consist in building and servicing particular organs or in running particular types of behaviors.

Still, one may ask, as properties of biological matter, aren't the integrity and replication of internal organization the goals of a large variety of m–e structures and processes? Yes, they are, but no longer in a pure, ur, inert, nonfunctional, and merely physical form. This is a crucial difference. In their biological version, the stability and replication of internal organization acquire specific and diversified expressions as (mainly) so many forms of metabolism and reproduction. The maintenance and replication of internal organization become goals by taking the particularized form of substances to be recognized and digested as food, of colorful and smelly conspecifics to mate with, of situations to avoid, and opportunities to encourage, and so on. The specific goals of life and the strategies to satisfy those goals are the biological implementers of the maintenance and replication of internal organization. Goal-directedness is an instrumentality, a clever strategy fortuitously evolved to maintain and replicate the design of some classes of physical systems. Biosystems are a subclass of self-organizing and self-reproducing physical systems with the differentiating property of having goal-directed processes, not just physical or chemical laws, doing the work of securing the integrity and replication of their design.

To summarize, in the beginning there were funny physical propensities for maintenance and replication of internal structure. These are the propensities manifested by any self-organizing and self-reproducing physical system, whether biological or not. Then there was biomatter exercising these physical propensities by way of means and ends or goal-directedly. Finally, there was bioevolution working on particular biomatter–ecology arrangements. In their exclusively physical form, the maintenance and replication of internal structure are not the goals of anything, since they are not brought about by any functionally specialized instruments; when, however, such instruments, as goals and ways to satisfy them, evolve and become operative, the maintenance and replication take the specific forms of metabolism and reproduction associated with concrete designs in concrete interactions with concrete substances found in concrete environments. Biolife is crystallization metabolized and reproduced with the help of amino acids, dirt, water, sun, sex, and so much more.[6]

2. NATURAL SELECTION

Goal-directedness is the result of prebiological evolution and is constantly reshaped by natural selection. This relation between goal-directedness and natural selection is a complex and delicate one, which is why we have to work hard constantly to keep it in the right perspective. There are two related reasons that the explanatory limitations of natural selection matter to our argument. One (as explained in section 7) is that biologists and cognitive scientists are uncomfortable with the notion of goal-directedness and hopeful that natural selection alone could explain ultimately what goal-directedness does. What they hope for is either a reduction or an elimination of goal-directedness. I do not think this is either possible or desirable. It is not possible because natural selection presupposes goal-directedness. It is not desirable because, without a teleological frame of explanation, we are bound to miss some pervasive and systematic patterns governing life and cognition which are not visible from the vantage point of natural selection. The second reason is that, intrinsically, the explanation by natural selection is narrow since it is limited to specific mechanisms and programs that operate in a corner of the

---

[6]It is not yet clear how metabolism and reproduction came about, nor which came first. It does not much matter for my speculative story how these issues are going to be settled. Dickerson (1978) summarized the issue:

> A living cell has two central talents: a capacity for metabolism and a capacity for reproduction. The cell survives in the short run by rearranging the atoms of the compounds it ingests into molecules needed for its own maintenance. It survives vicariously over the long run by being able to reproduce itself and give rise to offspring with similar biochemical talents. Which came first, a functioning metabolism, protected by some kind of membrane against dilution and destruction by its surroundings, or a large molecule that survived by making copies of itself from materials in its surroundings? In other words, which is older, the "protobiont" or the "naked gene"?

Neither Dickerson nor anyone else seems to have provided an answer. Once the life forms come into being, their metabolic and reproductive functions appear complementary: the instruments of reproduction (the nucleic acids) cannot replicate without the instruments of metabolism (the proteins), and the latter cannot be manufactured without the former. It is reasonable to think of metabolism and reproduction as continuous with and parasitic to the more basic physical propensities (like those attributed to crystals) for maintaining a stable organization and replicating it under exclusively physical constraints. There are, of course, many hypotheses about these matters, some quite fascinating. The one I find attractive is the mineral–crystal hypothesis sketched many years ago by Bernal (Dickerson, 1978) and originally developed by Cairns-Smith (1985).

environment and propagate in a specific population. On some issues, where the tree–forest difference matters, this limitation encourages either tree, rather than forest, viewing or else encourages modeling the forest in the image of particular trees. Guidance to goal turns out to be one such issue.

Before I unpack this theme, let me note vigorously that I am concerned only with the explanatory limitations of natural selection in relation to goal-directedness and its subordinate phenomena such as guidance to goal. Natural selection has other limitations as well, for which it has taken a domestic beating in evolutionary biology and a foreign beating in cognitive science. The general charge has been that the explanatory range of natural selection has important limits because not all biological phenomena are touched by its shaping hand. There are forces other than natural selection that drive bioevolution, such as random genetic drift, meiotic drive, exaptation which occurs when old adapted structures develop new functions, and accidents, which may isolate organisms in an adaptive ecology. Also, various properties may spread in a population not because of their own adaptive value but because they are by-products of other adaptive structures; there may be a selection for the latter but only of the former, to use Sober's distinction (Sober, 1984a, pp. 100–101). Finally, as advanced organisms and their social and cultural habitats become more complex and versatile in their mutual interactions, it becomes harder to explain their current patterns of performance in terms of the architectures originally sanctioned by natural selection.[7]

These explanatory limits of natural selection bear in many ways on the evolutionary story of cognition. (For a sample of the debates, see Dennett, 1983 and ensuing commentaries; Dennett, 1987, pp. 277–286; Lewontin, 1990; Pinker & Bloom, 1990 and ensuing commentaries; Stich, 1990, chap. 3). Yet all the forces of evolution, including natural selection, cannot fail to design organisms that operate goal-directedly and guide their behaviors to goals. My argument is not contingent on the kind and number of evolutionary forces historically and causally responsible for the design of cognition, nor on how adapted that design is. My question centers on what it takes for a system to exercise guidance, given general constraints on its goals, design, behavior, and habitat. My answer sketches several possible versions of guidance. How real organisms manage their guidance in real habitats becomes a question of

[7]Think of the fact that when last naturally selected (more than ten thousand years ago) the key cognitive programs of humans were not acquainted with either writing or mathematical figures and symbols. Then think how much your thought, consciousness, and memory every minute depend on these relatively recent accessories. Although a natural selection account could reveal what programs are used in thinking or memorizing based on systematic tendencies and biases—which is no small accomplishment—it is quite unlikely that the account could identify and explain a variety of patterns of performance that the programs had picked up only later when hooked up to the new accessories (for a stimulating review of these matters, see Donald, 1991).

which of these possible versions or which mixture of versions they instantiate and why.

Natural selection theories can answer this latter question most of the time. It was Darwin's revolutionary insight to construe natural selection as the causal shaper and optimizer of functional design. Far from excluding genetic goal-directedness, as is often assumed, Darwin's insight about natural selection presupposes it. Darwin's view and the entire "evolutionary synthesis" of the 1930s and 40s, which is still its most popular reading, were completed before major advances were made in genetics, and prior to the realization that there is prebiological and molecular evolution (Eldredge, 1985, chap. 1; Mayr, 1982, chap. 13; Dawkins, 1986, chap. 6).

These advances and realizations begin to suggest that goal-directedness, genetic programming, and natural selection are compatible (Mayr, 1982; Granit, 1977), and that their compatibility has explanatory value. Both the work of natural selection and that of the genes are causal, although at vastly different scales of space and time. What goal-directedness brings to this causal picture is the format of functional configurations in which the genetic instructions are executed. In causally shaping genetic programs, natural selection is bound to act on their goal-directed policies already in place. Natural selection works on fully developed individuals and their reproductive capabilities. As Trivers (1985, p. 20) noted, "[i]t is individuals that are purposively organized, and they are organized to leave surviving offspring." Therefore, the purposive organization of individuals, including their propensity to reproduce, must be presupposed by the work of natural selection. Because, as noted previously, natural selection also works on self-maintaining and self-replicating but purposeless crystals or current computer programs, we must infer that natural selection is both blind and indifferent to how and by what means the individuals subject to its attentions maintain and replicate themselves. This explains why natural selection cannot account for goal-directedness, which, we argue, is precisely a matter of the means by which organisms maintain and replicate themselves.

In the biological world, unlike that of crystals, natural selection designs programs good at doing something. Because the functional character of being-good-at-doing-something is, on the present account, a consequence of goal-directedness, the outcome of natural selection must be constrained by the antecedent goal-directed format and exercise of the programs in question. The constraint goes as follows: Being good at doing something means being capable of discharging a function; being capable of discharging a function means being capable of having a causal process yield a specific type of effect with certain implications for the system's well being and operation. For reasons to be explored shortly, some of these types of effects can be best characterized as goals. This is why genes can be regarded as causally executing sequences of functions with goals as their end effects. This is also why natural selection can be regarded as causally designing genetic programs that execute their goal-oriented functions adaptively. Nothing in this story puts goal-directedness and natural selection on a collision course.

3. TELEOGENETICS

The next step in my argument on behalf of genetic goal-directedness is to show that genes do operate goal-directedly. Think of DNA as a programming architecture and of RNA, the functional proteins it transcribes from DNA instructions, and the proteinic outputs (i.e., tissues, organs, processes, behaviors) as an executive architecture. The genes are of two sorts, structural and regulatory. The former work in development and behavior, the latter in timing and regulating the developmental and behavioral expression of the structural genes.

Together the structural and regulator genes and the transcription controls are responsible for configuring the goal-directedness found in organisms. The configuration of goal-directed mechanisms and processes emerges from a vast and intricate functional interaction initiated at the genetic and transcriptional levels (Beardsley, 1991). There are no individual "master genes" for any particular goal-directed processes just as, and because, there are no individual master genes for anything significant in an organism, whether tissue, organ, function, or behavior. The latter are all the cumulative outcomes of numerous interactions among genes, input signals, and transcription proteins; so is goal-directedness itself, given that the developmental goals are nothing but specific types of tissues and organs, and the behavioral goals emerge only from the execution of various functions and behaviors relative to ecological opportunities.

The configuration of goal-directedness is material and causal by virtue of the nature and organization of the chemical elements involved. The notion of configuring identifies the formation of a mechanism or the deployment of a process through the execution of genetic instructions. Goal-directedness is a matter of genetic and transcriptional programs causally–functionally configuring structures and processes along certain dimensions (the teleological parameters are described in section 5).[8] The causal configuring along teleological dimensions takes place in several stages during gene expression: A DNA structure is copied or transcribed into a messenger or mRNA structure; the mRNA structure is translated into particular proteins, which then form

---

[8]Mayr (1982, especially pp. 48, 56, 68) is the biologist perhaps most clearly committed to the notion that genetic programs work goal-directedly. He has taken the view, which I share, that the goal-directedness of genetic programs offers the ultimate evolutionary explanations of why organisms are configured as they are and operate as they do.

tissues and organs, and run the organism. In the DNA to mRNA transcription the causal direction is to, not from, the DNA. It is not a DNA structure that is being produced as a causal effect. A DNA structure is already in place, but not in a form propitious for transcription and forward-looking causation. So processes must be marshalled to open up the DNA structure and ready it for transcription.

This is a critical point in my case for genetic goal-directedness. The DNA is not a causal initiator. It is a shaper, a configurer, in the guise of a set of instructions about what to do when a causal initiative is taken by the environment or by other genes or internal processes.[9] The program instructions have effects in configurations that render biological causation goal-directed.

Here is an example of teleogenetic configuration that yields guidance to goal: Plants live on solar energy. To satisfy its metabolic goals, a plant must grow in the direction of metabolically helpful conditions. Solar light is both an input to photosynthetic metabolism and an informational guide to growth. Photomorphogenesis is the process by which solar light acts on the genes and guides plant growth. Photomorphogenesis has three parts: registration of light by means of pigments; transduction of the light signal from pigment to gene; and induction of development through genetic regulation. The gene activation involves the usual transcription of DNA into an mRNA, which is then translated into proteins. It is through the modulation of the mRNA transcription that the light input guides the growth process by affecting both the choice of the goals of development (e.g., leaves, stem) and their actual form and size. The proteins executing the genetic instructions can become either structural parts of the plant or perform functions that organize the form of the plant. This is how the DNA configures the whole process and its products.

The registration phase marks the beginning of guidance. It involves a pigment, called phytochrome, which activates the genes controlling development. The phytochrome operates as a sensing device that allows the plant to detect and measure variations in the quality, intensity, and duration of the light input. The light acts as a stimulus on the regulatory ambiance of a light-responsive gene, governs the expression of the gene, and modulates its transcription into mRNA. The pigmental guidance (i.e., registration and transduction) by the phytochrome steers the developmental functions to

[9]Intuitively, the DNA may be likened to the laws of, say, physics which, to indulge in a Platonic fancy, are "consulted" or "read" as instructions by physical interactions as they shape themselves one way or another. The physical laws themselves are not causal in any sense; they are a blueprint for causation. It is the physical elements and structures in interaction, organized and animated by the laws, which have real causal potency. Just as the character of physical causation resides in the laws governing it, so the character of genetically controlled causation resides in the program instructions coded in the organism's DNA.

their goals. In so doing, the pigmental guidance aligns development to the relevant variables of the environment (Moses & Chua, 1988).

The process just sketched is both causal and goal-directed. It is causal because it displays the right physical interactions in the right order; it is goal-directed because the functional interactions that are genetically configured, converge in a dedicated and terminal fashion in an end state. This means that only certain types of causal processes—those functionally dedicated—execute genetic instructions and that the processes are called off—are terminal—when the end state obtains. The causal interactions involved can be said to implement a goal-directed configuration, as (2.1) reveals:

(2.1) environmental conditions $\rightarrow$ light input $\rightarrow$ registration (by phytochrome) $\Rightarrow$ transduction (phytochrome conversion) $\Rightarrow$ genetic induction (activation of developmental genes) $\Rightarrow$ developmental processes by proteins under pigmental guidance $\Rightarrow$ part developed (goal).

The occasion for the genetic processing is provided by an external (light, in this case) input. This is a triggering causation symbolized with simple arrows. Although the input triggers the internal causal processes resulting in the development of some part or in other organisms in behavior, it does not configure these processes. The latter task belongs to the genetic program. The DNA is a causal configurer by virtue of its structure and functional consequences. Its role consists in organizing the causal processes in certain structural and functional formats.[10] This role of configurational causation is symbolized above with double arrows.

4. TELEOLOGICAL PARAMETERS

What is goal-directedness? What are its dimensions? The teleological literature has identified a few that will do for my purposes.[11] I call them teleological parameters. I do not mean them to *explain* goal-directedness. That explanation must emerge from an evolutionary theory of the genetic expression,

---

[10]In the mind naturalization literature, the distinction between triggering and configurational causation has been evoked by Dretske (1988, pp. 42–43) and Fodor (1987, chap. 2; 1990a, chap. 5).

[11]See, in particular, the comprehensive surveys by Nagel (1961, 1977) and Woodfield (1976, p. 40). The latter mentioned E.S. Russell (who in turn inspired Braithwaite) as the biologist who treated bioprocesses as goal-directed and analyzed goal-directedness in terms of terminality of effect, cessation of process when goal is achieved, persistence when it is not, and of alternative causal–functional routes in achieving the goal. These are key parameters of goal-directedness. None of these writers, with the exception of Mayr (1982), grounded goal-directedness in genetics, although Nagel (1977) considered yet rejected this possibility.

transcription, and control in the biological domain and from a more general theory of self-organizing and self-replicating systems in other domains. Rather, the teleological parameters should be construed as jointly characterizing a type of program expression, genetic or of some other sort. Nor do I see the teleological parameters as jointly constituting goal-directedness because there are goal-directed organisms or systems generally that fail to exemplify one or more of the parameters. There are, for example, simple organisms, such as bacteria, or simple systems, such as heat seeking missiles, which reach their goals by fixed functional routes, thus failing to instantiate the plasticity and versatility parameters. Having thus clarified the nature of our analysis, I now take a quick look at the key teleological parameters needed by my project, acknowledge a few notions and distinctions that will be useful later, and then allow the parameters to define implicitly our notion of goal-directed system. The biological illustrations remain prominent, although the resulting definition transcends the biological domain.

Systemic Function

It is important to distinguish *two* concepts of function (Nagel, 1961, pp. 522–526; Lycan, 1981; Enç, 1982; Papineau, 1984; Sober, 1985). There is the formal concept according to which a function can be understood as a mapping or transformation of some input into some output by virtue of its intrinsic structural properties. Such is a function that takes an expression into another in virtue of the form of the expressions. Addition is an example. The formal function redescribes a local input–output correlation irrespective of a larger environment and an instantiating hardware. This is not the notion my argument needs.

There is also a systemic or system sensitive concept of function. This is the notion we want. Biological processes are systemic because so are the gene expressions responsible for them. A systemic function redescribes a causal relation in light of the role of its effects in a larger system of parts and processes. Such a function is executed when the implementing causal processes have dedicated effects in the system. For example, the light impacting the retina affects causally its cellular membranes, blood circulation, and other physical and physiological conditions of the retina. Yet none of these are visually dedicated effects, for they do not feed into the subsequent processes that produce visual images. There is no cognitively systematic relation between, say, blood pressure and visual representation. As a result, the latter is not a systemic function of the former, and the former does not have a function with respect to the latter, although there could be various causal interactions between the two in both directions (for instance, the blood pressure may affect the chemistry of the visual process, and what one sees may affect one's blood pressure).

Historically, a dedicated effect of the systemic function of a structure can be construed as the sort of effect for which the structure was selected. Once goal-directedness is fully characterized in the next section, the notion of systemic function will also be called *teleofunction.*[12]

Dedicated, Cumulative, and Orthogonal Patterns of Functional Contribution

We know that the effect of the execution of a systemic function is dedicated when we know how and why it fits into a larger sequence of effects that display some pattern of cooperation and cumulative contribution in a system relative to the execution of a task. Various functional events in the visual cortex have cognitive significance only to the extent that their contribution converges on the formation of an image. Systemic functions are organized in well patterned sequences. Cells differentiate at specific points as a result of the execution (causal process) of genetic instructions. As a cumulative result of many cells doing their thing, specific organs (dedicated effects) are built. One can draw a path that picks up these effects only in the dedicated pattern suggested and ignores all the other numerous and concomitant or subsequent but undedicated effects produced along the way.

The patterns of functional contribution are not only dedicated relative to the effects to be attained but also *orthogonal.* This means that the different causal paths that implement a particular function are independent of each other in that, within limits, the values of one path do not systematically covary with those of another (Nagel, 1977, p. 273). An example, to be discussed in more detail in later sections, is that of temperature stability. Several mechanisms could achieve it. Their job is not temperature stability as such, but something more specific (perspiration, vessel dilation and contraction, etc.), and to that extent the mechanisms work independently of each other. At any particular point one of them is in charge, and the others are back-ups. Temperature stability is the dedicated effect that matters; the means to get it are many and independent.[13]

---

[12]A function can be systemic without being a teleofunction if it works in a system that is not goal-directed. The general distinction between function, including systemic function, and goal-directedness is essential. Many teleologists fail to make it and take goal-directedness to apply wherever functionality applies. This failure weakens considerably the case for goal-directedness, as is evident from Woodfield's effective criticisms of Somerhoff and Nagel (1976, pp. 60–63).

[13]As Nagel (1977) noted, orthogonality may be the most critical mark of goal-directedness. If we ask why a pendulum is not goal-directed, given that it always seeks to reach a stable state of equilibrium, the answer is that "the controlling variables of the ball's motion are *not* independent of each other, since the restoring force is proportional to the magnitude of the displacement force, though oppositely directed" (p. 274). Orthogonality and its systemic effects (plasticity and persistence of implementation) explain why goal-directedness as such is not exhausted by physical or chemical laws, which are nonorthogonal, although its specific imple-

Terminality

The execution of developmental and behavioral functions often terminates in a final dedicated effect that may take the form of either a structure (a tissue, an organ); a state (having the right temperature); or a behavior or event (food grabbed, enemy avoided). A causal sequence of processes, viewed as the execution of a systemic function, is said to have a terminal outcome whenever the process persists as long as it takes to maintain or attain a state or structure as dedicated effect and upon bringing about that effect, the process is called off by a control or feedback program.

A terminal effect is not terminal absolutely—nothing in nature is—but only in the context of interactive systemic functions. Among the many, often uninstructed and distant, effects of genetic instructions, the terminal types stand out as those which, when produced, turn off the instructions or deactivate interim functional links, thus making evident the systematic correlation between instructions and causal termini. Grown wings terminate genetically initiated and controlled developmental processes; further effects of having and using the wings no longer concern the "growing-wings genes," although they concern other sorts of behavior instructing genes. Not only development but behaviors also have outcomes (i.e., getting to see something, grabbing some food to eat, or running away from predator), which are terminal with respect to some internal pattern of systemic functions.

Plasticity and Versatility of Means

Biological dispositions often show plasticity or versatility in how (i.e., by means of which causal–functional processes) they deliver their outcomes. A cell in movement to some destination (say, to build an organ) finds alternative ways to get there if confronted with obstacles. Likewise, animals often try various and sometimes novel behavioral maneuvers to avoid a predator, protect their offspring, or find food. Understanding what the cell's or the animal's movements signify would not be possible unless those movements are related to an invariant terminal effect. The more complex an organism, the more plastic and versatile its behavior relative to some target of interest. There is another, equally familiar and widespread manifestation of the invariance of dedicated effects. Many developmental and behavioral dispositions show persistence in deploying (often with versatility) processes needed to obtain assigned effects, often for as long as it takes. Not only are organisms persistent in some behavior in the same way hungry predators persist in chasing their prey, and the prey persists in running away, but so are, on a smaller scale, the soldiers of the immune system or the developmental cells.

---

mentations are. As Nagel noted, orthogonality is relative to a frame of goal-directedness: What is orthogonal in one may fail to be so in another.

Other things being equal, the processes involved tend to persist until an appropriate outcome state is reached, after which they are called off.

Control and Guidance

In both development and behavior, cellular formations, from the simplest to the most complex, display functions of control and guidance, which provide registration, tracking, feedback, and evaluation, and thus steer dedicated processes to their anticipated outcomes: signaling when such an outcome has been produced; ascertaining how good it is; checking with control or some other internal standard; making adjustments; and calling off the functional processes involved, if everything is right. Why would such control, guidance, and feedback mechanisms be selected for or installed in some other manner unless they govern processes that must reach recognizable outcomes? How would such control and guidance mechanisms know the identity of those outcomes and distinguish them from other undedicated concomitant or subsequent effects, unless the mechanisms are programmed to match and measure such outcomes against some internal standard or reference? The presence of the latter is perhaps the clearest indication that the system has specific functions whose performances in the outside world must be tracked and adjusted internally; if, moreover, the system is naturally programmed, as organisms are, to have such internal standards, that fact in turn indicates that its functions are likely to converge on definite classes of effects, its goals.

Functionally speaking, the simpler biological versions of internal control and feedback standards, variously called Sollwert, efference copies, or set points in the ethological literature, can be viewed as precursors of internal representations of goals—intentions, desires—in advanced species (McFarland, 1983). Those simpler versions find their mechanical echoes in the control and feedback mechanisms whose design has been the main practical preoccupation of the form of engineering that culminated in cybernetics. For the philosophically minded cyberneticists, like Wiener, Ashby or Somerhoff, those mechanisms provide the evidence that in principle both organisms and servomechanims could be goal-directed in the same internal sense, by being appropriately configured architecturally and programmed functionally[14]—other things (i.e., other teleological parameters and additional conditions) being equal. But other things are not always equal, which

[14]See Wiener (1948), Somerhoff (1974), Woodfield (1976, ch. 11), and Nagel (1977), for surveys. As Bennett (1976, p. 61) points out, control by feedback is not necessary for goal-directedness. In real life, control by feedback, like plasticity of behaviors, results from increased complexity of design, yet simpler organisms lacking such capabilities are nevertheless goal-directed. I take the importance of control and guidance to reside not in their constitutive relation to goal-directedness but rather in their manifesting, clearer than other teleological parameters, the identity of the goals of the system or organism.

is why teleological parameters must be weaved into a conceptual framework that approximates goal-directedness in realistic terms.

The Hard Frame

Putting things together, we can say that goal-directed are those systems that (a) autonomously maintain and replicate their internal organization, or that of their components, by (b) implementation means that (c) jointly instantiate most (though not necessarily all) the teleological parameters. This characterization, which I call "the hard frame," is admittedly strong because it rules out most of the usual suspects (i.e., thermostats, missiles, computers, robots, bodily organs by themselves) and some unusual suspects (occasionally entire organisms whose goal-directedness, either in a context or in general, is social, as is the case of ants or bees) while allowing in systems larger than we usually think of (societies). (a) and (b) are the hard (explanatory) conditions of the frame, whereas (c) is the soft (explicative) condition.

There are certain features of the hard frame worth emphasizing. As anticipated by my earlier discussion, the hard frame does not entail that goal-directedness must be biological. The hardware does not have to be made of amino acids or crystals or chips or any other particular form of matter, although evidently it must be made of some matter with appropriate capabilities. This posture is compatible with the fact that in our universe only amino acids might physically implement genetic instructions and that a different form of matter might conceivably maintain and replicate its structure in ways other than genetic.

To be goal-directed, aggregations of matter must do things functionally to maintain and replicate an internal organization in some ecological niche in ways characterized by the teleological parameters. It is worth stipulating that they do so autonomously, by internal programming, for otherwise one might have to assume that there are larger goal-directed systems that designed and/or run them—an implication which, from religion to philosophy of mind, has a way of obscuring the intrinsic properties of life and cognition. In order to get a consistently autonomous operation by internal programming, I stipulate further that the systems under consideration enjoy some form, not necesarily biological, of life and evolution. This is the point of the hard conditions and of the frame: to ensure that goal-directedness is a natural phenomenon in the world. Most teleologists are happy just with the soft condition, which allows goal-directedness without life and evolution. This leaves goal-directedness ungrounded naturally and invites a behaviorist and exclusively analytic reading of teleology, which I find neither realistic nor explanatory.[15]

---

[15]The soft condition had provided the standard frame of analysis in the most exuberant

The hard frame does not go into the specifics of history or natural selection and does not entail an adaptive (or indeed, any particular) implementation of goal-directedness. All of these factors, crucial particularly for the biological forms of goal-directedness, are needed to settle two critical questions about goal-directed systems, which the hard frame does not address. One is the origin of the system. The other question is the identity of the goals of the system, and by implication, the identity of the targets of the system's behavior and cognition. These identities cannot be determined without information about the history of the system and the specific ecology in which it operates. That is not the concern of the hard frame. The hard frame simply characterizes goal-directedness, without saying how and when it works or what it works on. History and natural selection characterize the biochemical implementation of goal-directedness, and to that extent, they specify how an organism's design was shaped in and by a given ecology, hence what its goals are, and what teleofunctions, including cognitive, service the goals.

5. GOAL AS OUTCOME PROGRAMMED

The notion of goal is commonsensical, not scientific. Commonsense talk individuates goals either in terms of an end or outcome condition (i.e., action, its object, a state of the environment, or a state of the body) generated by some internal and/or behavioral processes, or in terms of some internal indicators of goals, such as urges, desires, or emotions. I say more about commonsense teleology in chapter 8. Now I need its form of individuation to approximate the teleogenetic notion of goal implicit in the hard frame characterization of goal-directedness.

The suggestion is to count as goals those types of conditions that are the terminal effects of functional processes, which are configured, though not necessarily initiated, by internal programs and jointly satisfy most if not all of

---

behaviorist period in recent teleology, the 1940s to 1970s, in the works of Braithwaite, Somerhoff, Nagel, Taylor, Dennett, Bennett, and others. The quest for necessary and sufficient conditions favored a symptomatic (soft) rather than explanatory (hard) analysis. Examples and counterexamples of isolated teleological parameters were thought to settle the matter. Not surprisingly for conceptual teleobehaviorism, the central issue was the evidence for goal-directedness, the reasons for attributing it, on the basis of observation and analytic imagination. In spite of having bravely promoted the cause of teleology, identifying most of the relevant parameters, and working out the methodological constraints on the attribution of teleological properties, the analytic teleobehaviorists failed to make the strongest case for teleology. This failure in turn opened their enterprise to needless, often obscure, and eventually detrimental conceptual skirmishes (see Woodfield (1976, chaps. 3–6) meticulous diagnoses of the failures of analytic teleobehaviorism). The enterprise was ultimately ungrounded because of genetic (or internal programming) neglect.

the teleological parameters. Goals are the sorts of conditions that place a system or a part of it in a position to do something, undergo some process, exercise some function, or operate some program. An organism undergoes some internal process (perspires) or does something (runs) in order to be in a position to undergo (lower its temperature) or do (eat) something else which it is internally programmed to seek and bring about.[16]

Goals, so understood, explain the interface of various programs: The operation of one program (say, cognitive) places another (behavioral) in an operating position, and so forth. As long as the programs are chained in a rigid functional sequence and directly express genetic instructions, as in the simplest organisms, we can talk of *basic* goals. In the biological world, these are outcome conditions with immediate metabolic or reproductive import. For example, unicellular organisms have cognitive and behavioral programs exclusively dedicated to the identification, tracking, and appropriation of substances for metabolism. The operation of these programs relies on functionally specialized proteins that directly execute genetic instructions.[17]

A basic goal is a type of outcome state internally programmed (genetically instructed in biolife)—that is, a state at the receiving end of dedicated functional processes, internal and behavioral, and at the initiating end of informational transactions that eventuate in feedback, cessation of effort or adjustment. This is not a commonsense notion by any stretch of the imagination, although its formulation exploits a commonsense gambit. Concepts or actions are individuated in a relational sense by indicating their referents or results, respectively. We do the same with the notion of basic goal: Instead of referents of concepts or results of actions, goals are understood as outcomes that individuate the basic and intermediate programs, genetic or otherwise, responsible for them. This is, for example, how genetic instructions are redescribed in teleological terms as "being for wings, legs, or other organs and behaviors." We can schematize the notion of goal as outcome programmed as follows:

(2.2) input $\rightarrow$ programs $\Rightarrow$ internal processes $\Rightarrow$ behavior $\Rightarrow$ (basic) goal

Complex organisms reach their basic goals by first reaching intermediate or *instrumental* goals. The latter feat requires the interaction of various

---

[16]'In order to' is an explanatory locution indicating that this is how we explain the organism's design: that it is so configured that it can position itself in a behavioral–ecological condition to undergo or do something. Causally, of course, it is always some input that activates some program that discharges its function and steers behavior.

[17]What I mean here by direct execution of genetic instructions is that the proteins (the key functional executors in all organisms, and the only ones in the simplest of them) are fabricated as soon as the RNA reads the appropriate DNA instructions, given the stimuli.

programs. To be in a position to eat, an organism must first find food, say, by identifying and pursuing a prey, which in turn requires its own cognitive and behavioral programs. Most organisms execute the programs for prey identification and prey pursuit with teleological brio: functional dedication, persistence, versatility of means, control, guidance and feedback, terminality of effort when success is achieved or when failure is inevitable. This is evidence that the prey programs have their own instrumental goals. Once the instrumental goals are reached, other basic or instrumental goals and their programs take center stage, playing their own teleological scripts. Instrumental goals are defined by specialized programs that implement specific cognitive or behavioral policies, only ultimately conducive to maintenance and replication. Instrumental goals indicate a higher functional complexity. Their individuation scheme looks as follows:

(2.3) input $\rightarrow$ specialized (cognitive, conative, behavioral) programs $\Rightarrow$ behavior $\Rightarrow$ instrumental goal

6. THE RELATIVE UNIMPORTANCE OF CAUSAL AND FUNCTIONAL REALIZATIONS

Several of its parameters suggest that goal-directedness is causally and functionally underdetermined, essentially and often on a massive scale. I have in mind the orthogonality, plasticity, and versatility of goal-directedness, the relativity of what counts as a goal-directed system, and, consequently, the higher explanatory importance of the dedicated effect (goal) over how it came about (by what causal–functional means). As a result, causes and functions, and their laws and patterns, lose their eminent explanatory power in the domain of goal-directedness, even at the proximate level. (That is clarified in the case of mental cognition in chap. 7). Teleology, notoriously, downgrades the role of functional causation. Being underdetermined by triggering and implementing causes and functions, a goal-directed system can be best individuated and explained in terms of the dedicated effects (goals) it is configured and programmed to produce. The partisan implication is that goal-directedness cannot be reduced to or eliminated by nonteleological facts and laws. This implication motivates my opposition to the reductive policies of psychological Newtonianism and psychosemanticism.

I consider first the orthogonality, plasticity, and versatility of implementation, the resulting explanatory importance of the outcome, and finally the relativity of framing goal-directedness.

Think of an animal fleeing a predator. Within its capabilities, the animal does a number of things (i.e., runs, hides, pretends to be dead) to bring about the goal state. Each of the behaviors is a causal sequence of functional processes triggered by appropriate stimuli. Each sequence is ultimately made of atoms and molecules pushed around causally. So are its external stimuli. The behaviors can be individually framed and causally explained in a proximate fashion as motions-triggered-by-stimuli. Functional redescriptions are, of course, much better but not totally revealing unless a common denominator is found in the form of escape behaviors. Escape is the goal that explains these behaviors in an uniform manner. The ultimate explanation in terms of goals grounds the proximate and local explanations in terms of specific causal–functional processes and portrays the latter as implementations of goal-directedness.

Another example, much discussed in the teleological literature (e.g., Braithwaite, 1953, chap. 10; Collins, 1984; Nagel, 1961, pp. 409; Somerhoff, 1974), is that of homeostasis in general, temperature stability in particular. An increase in the temperature around the body triggers an increase in perspiration, which in turn causes a decrease in the bodily temperature. The proximate causation at work can be superficially schematized as follows:

(2.4) external heat increase → increased bodily perspiration → decreased bodily temperature

Two facts are critical for the relation between causation and goal-directedness. One is that the environmental changes in temperature can and very often are so drastic that, on a purely physical and proximate account of causation, they ought to cause equally drastic changes in the bodily temperature, yet they don't. The temperature compensation moves within narrow limits. The other fact is that there are several independent ways of maintaining temperature stability, indicating orthogonality and plasticity again. The rate of perspiration is one way, the dilation and contraction of blood vessels is another; so are the secretion of various glands, the adrenaline stimulation in the blood, and the muscular contractions. This is temperature compensation within pre-established limits and by various means, which characterize the range and the variety of internal bodily reactions to outside heat increase, relative to preset internal parameters. So (2.4) should read:

(2.5) external heat increase → internal compensation mechanisms activated ⇒ decrease in bodily temperature to preassigned limits ⇒ internal equilibrium maintained

Although it is the causal chain described in (2.5) that brings about the outcome (maintenance of a preset internal temperature), the proximate causation involved in the operation of one particular mechanism (say, perspiration) explains neither the existence nor the nature nor the rationale of the outcome. Other causal chains, involving other inputs and internal mechanisms, could have had the same outcome. This means that the sameness of outcome cannot be retrieved from and explained exclusively by the analysis of the interactions and mechanisms that instantiate the causal production of the outcome.

The explanatory demise of functional causation in teleological contexts affects every form of implementation along the hierarchy of levels of complexity considered. I stress this point because of a widespread propensity to confine the notion of implementing causation to a territory ranging from physical to neural states, which is the territory of hardware, and show that the hardware states par excellence fail, in their diversity of instantiations, to reveal the unity of teleological phenomena. I want to push this failure further up in the functional territory of software. All biofunctions redescribe causal processes and interactions of some sort or another, in the light of their dedicated contributions and effects in a larger system. Because they have a limited role and range and locally carry out larger biological tasks (metabolic, homeostatic, cognitive) under a narrow and proximate analysis, these biofunctions may also fail to reveal the nature of the tasks they execute.

The explanatory demise of causation extends to functionalized causation, whence the 'causal–functional' combination in my terminology. In particular, as I argue in chapter 7, although the symbolic and syntactic (or connectionist) redescriptions of brain causation define functions that drive our mental mechanisms, the redescriptions fail to reveal the unity and character of the cognitive activities these mechanisms implement, which is mental guidance to goal, to the same extent to which, deeper down, descriptions of electrical synapses or calcium transfers among cells fail to reveal the unity and character of the symbolic (activation) structures being syntactically (vectorially) processed.

The implementations that underdetermine goal-directedness are not only vertical (inside organisms) but also horizontal (among organisms). This is the *frame relativity* of goal-directedness. The contours of goal-directedness are not fixed forever, either geographically or temporally. Consider a mundane example: I want to go to the market. That is my goal. I know where it is and how to get there, by walking. I am a self-contained and self-sufficient, goal-directed system. If I don't know where it is and have to ask somebody for instructions, or if I have to drive, or if I am driven to the market by somebody who knows where it is, then I am much less self-contained and self-sufficient *as* a specific goal (market)-directed system. For, in these latter cases, either the knowledge of the goal, the means to satisfy it, or both transcend my resources. I cast around for other (eco-social) resources that can help. My goal-directedness is framed (expanded) relative to a context of behavior and what it takes to have it bring about the goal state. We navigate from one frame of goal-directedness to another. No single frame is absolute. This is true of many species and has to do with how the genes implement their policies. For many species, the frame of goal-directedness need not always be fixed in advance; for complex species, the frame can change from one context of behavior to another.

There is no standard way of being goal-directed. Whatever ensures the maintenance and replication of genes will do, and the space of opportunities and the manner of exploiting them are wide open. Bacteria are the simplest organisms with autonomous goal-directedness. Bacteria also commune, qua cells, in larger organisms, often only temporarily. In this alternation of sociality and individualism, no posture is definitive; it depends on goals and means. There are good reasons for bacteria to live communally in colonies, more like cells in an organism, and specialize functionally. In many ecologies, small means vulnerability—being eaten, crushed, not able to ingest or digest the only stuff available because of size or hardness. Some microbiologists think that most bacteria are social most of the time, and that their social organization, development, metabolism, communication, and movement are genetically regulated (Shapiro, 1988). Social goal-directedness may be more adaptive than the individual self-directedness.[18]

Many species are goal-directed only socially (mole rats, bees, ants); others are socially goal-directed from time to time in specific contexts, such as in hunting or migration. What about us? Is our social goal-directedness temporary, as my earlier market example suggests, or intrinsic and permanent? Are we in fact sophisticated teleofunctional cogs in larger goal-directed ensembles (families, societies, cultures)? When we behave independently, aren't we also implementing the work of larger teleounits (like cells in larger bodies, or insects in colonies)? Doesn't our own development and learning enable larger social teleounits to operate in ways that preserve and replicate their own structures? Don't we mature intellectually to preserve and replicate the cultural heritage of the tribe, society, species? And, like social insects, don't we divide our competence and labor along functional specialities such as professional cognizers (the scientists, physicians), professional food growers (the farmers), professional regulators (the politicians, judges) or professional memorizers (story tellers, historians)?

No matter how we answer these questions and draw the boundaries of goal-directedness, it seems clear that the answers would not be intelligible in causal or functional terms. Wherever evolution has rewarded a flexible and

[18]"By becoming multicellular, an organism can preserve all the advantages offered by cells for efficient metabolism and proper gene distribution and at the same time become very large" (Bonner, 1988, p. 62).

context-sensitive framing of goal-directedness with constantly changing boundaries, no causal explanation in terms of natural selection would capture how one goes about implementing the social forms of goal-directedness. Natural selection ultimately explains the social forms themselves, in terms of their adaptive virtues, but cannot explain proximately the ways in which the social forms are managed by the individual goal-directed organisms.

7. THE MERITS AND HANDICAPS OF TELEOLOGY

It is time to wrap up the case for goal-directedness by confirming the naturalist credentials of my teleological argument and exposing some of the misconceptions that obscure its truth and explanatory relevance. My conception of goal-directedness meets the adequacy conditions on mind naturalization presented in the first paragraph of section 3, chapter 1. I divide the conditions into metaphysical, having to do with the natural ingredients of goal-directedness; scientific, having to do with how goal-directedness fits into the scientific picture; and logical, having to do with thinking straight about these matters.

The *metaphysical* condition requires that teleology be about facts, properties, and processes, which (a) have material composition, (b) are caused by other material items in the lawful flow of causation, and (c) have a natural history. The metaphysical condition, as an expression of materialism, prejudges neither the type of material items, nor their form of organization, nor the causal form of their internal processes and behaviors, nor finally the particulars of their evolutionary history. These matters are for science to fathom.

All the variables of my account pass the metaphysical test: The genetic program, itself encoded in chemical structures, is responsible for a form of systemic causation, which embodies the teleological parameters; the causation flows in the right direction from material structures and processes, and results in other such structures and processes; the genes have a respectable, though still mysterious, material pedigree in the ur properties of mineral formations; through their physical impact on organisms, the evolutionary mechanisms regulate the symbiosis between genes and their ecologies. This entire process, blind and opportunistic, has no goals of its own, nor is it ruled by any design intent. Materialism, causation, and natural history are respected by our teleology.

The *logical* condition stipulates that a teleological account must be coherent and noncircular. Its key notions and propositions should not appeal to those of goal or goal-directedness. Likewise, the notions of goal-directedness, needed to ground and explain guidance to goal, should not presuppose the latter, and the notions of information tasks and cognitive programs should not in turn presuppose what they must ground and explain (semanticity, representation, cogitation). I am happy to report that both the general logical condition and its specific implications have been scrupulously obeyed.

This teleology does not beg any historical question, for it does not assume that either the (possibly mineral) pedigree of the genetic program, or its various local mutations and variations under environmental pressures, or the evolutionary selection of the genetic expressions, are themselves goal-directed and hence in need of a teleological story of their own. This creates no circularity and no regress in my argument. My teleology does not beg any metaphysical question, for it does not assume that the chemical components of the genetic code and the various executive and regulative functions are themselves goal-directed and in need of a teleological account.

The *scientific* credentials of the teleological stance are quite another matter. Even with good metaphysical and logical credentials, teleology cannot easily find a scientific home these days. Given the way the condominium of science is currently organized, and the restrictions on who can live there and how and where, teleology faces a serious housing discrimination. This discrimination gives elbow room to biopsychological Newtonianism and reinforces many of its prejudices, which explains why I sweat a bit—not only with argument but also with some historical reflections on and complaints about the current enterprise of science—to get teleology the scientific respect it deserves. Time for deconstruction.

The question I ask is why teleology is invisible to science. The question is not about nature and telos, for nature is organized and does operate in a goal-directed fashion at the biological level. Organisms are teleosystems. It is an undeniable truth that the biofunctions executed by molecules and other causal–functional pushers have dedicated effects, cooperate, persist, and desist in an enormous variety of types of biosystems, in an enormous variety of ecologies, subject to an enormous variety of selective pressures. The teleological truth shines through all these diverse manifestations. Explicating this truth, however, is no easy matter. Goal-directedness can be objectively invisible. Evolution implements the goal-directedness of life opportunistically, in small, improvised, disjointed, and proximate steps (by way of mechanisms and programs), without displaying pervasive and homogeneous properties and regularities. So I cannot speak of a uniform and well structured domain of goal-directedness with its own properties and laws. Nor, as a result, can a distinct and homogeneous type of teleological explanation be expected, as a distinct form of scientific explanation. The problem, then, is how to translate the teleological truth and display its unity in current scientific discourse. It is a problem not about the facts but about their understanding.

Most philosophers and scientists either do not see the point of teleology at all or else when they see it, are uncomfortable about it.[19] Haldane is reported to have said that teleology is like a mistress to a biologist: He cannot live without her but is unwilling to be seen with her in public. His analogy aside, Haldane was right. The facts about means–ends structures and processes are there, solid, visible, and stubborn. It is their early conceptualizations that messed things up. The traditional logos of goal-directedness, from Aristotle's to Lamarck's to Bergson's to some current views, construes goal-directedness in a wrong and often ridiculous way, in terms of such notions as the goal of evolution (or of the genes), final causes, nonexistent futures, preformationist blueprints, backward causation, élan vital, dualism, emergence, optimality, rationality, progress, and so on. Such notions have given teleology a deservedly bad reputation. Yet it is a fallacy to infer from this conceptual nonsense to the nonexistence of goal-directedness in the world.

I take Haldane's insight to signify that whereas teleology is the right stance for the biologist to take, there is no clear way to translate and legitimize its wisdom and explanatory power in the current conceptual framework of science. Goal-directedness is too global a phenomenon to be visible to and digested by contemporary science in general, biology and cognitive science, in particular. The means–ends structures and processes operating in an environment range over very diverse properties and regularities across extended and complex patterns of causal and functional chains. To explain fully the development of an organ, for example, one has to proceed from consideration about environment and evolution to genetics to cell biology to developmental biology, thus crossing several well established and often tightly compartimentalized disciplines. If the organ is cognitive, psychology must be brought into the picture. The disciplinary differences would prevent such an overview.[20] One can do molecular genetics without worrying much or even having to know much about cell behavior or organ development, and

---

[19]With a bit of terminological prestidigitation, I could have avoided, as many theorists do, any teleological talk. Instead of goals and goal-directed processes, I could have talked of structure and function and still get all my conclusions. After all, looked at from below, implementationally, a goal is nothing but the effect of the causal execution of a number of functions by specialized structures. But that is precisely the angle I urge not taking: From below, the more global properties that characterize goal-directedness are not visible, yet those properties are essential to and explanatory of life and cognition. The reduction of teleology is a loss of explanation.

[20]Think, for example, of vision or language. Their architecture has genetic roots, a developmental stem, of the embryonic sort, and the baroque variety of branches representing the mature specialized programs. Each level (roots, stems, branches) contains different forms of organization, of different complexities, governed by different functional regularities. One would not adequately and ultimately understand the biology of the visual and linguistic programs without crossing the various disciplinary domains. Yet we have no current scientific paradigm with which to attain and regiment such an interlevel and crossdisciplinary understanding, some valiant efforts notwithstanding.

one can work in any of these areas of biology without having to know much if anything about psychology.

Yet the fact is that not all of nature's compartments fit neatly into the disciplinary confines of current science. Nature is not that obliging. This is particularly true of those of its fragments, such as the biological ones, which not only build on and exploit a variety of lower level and widely distributed physical and chemical properties and regularities, but also systematically engage the environment in an unlimited variety of ways. There are biological properties that are not visible if we examine only their implementing structures, and do not track their overall functional interlocking across several forms of organization and levels of complexity, within and outside the organism.

Embryonic development, for one, is beyond the disciplinary grasp of molecular biology because many embryological properties range not only over intergenetic interactions but also over complex subsystems, such as cell formations, organ structures, and even organisms. Embryonic development is a topic the molecular biologist is trained not to think and worry about. Yet embryonic development, sandwiched between genetic instructions at one end, and organs at the other end, instantiates an important segment of the teleological descriptions. How could a molecular biologist decide whether such descriptions are legitimate? And why should he be an authority on these matters, when he was trained not to see them? Often specialized scientists do not care even about the truths of neighboring disciplines. Talk to a geneticist about organ development, and he will soon begin to yawn; talk to an organ development theorist about behavior, and yawning again. Put all their yawns together, and you have yawned not only goal-directedness but many other trans-domain properties out of existence. With all due but irreverent respect, if current science does not talk and think about it, and does not even know how to think about it, it doesn't mean that it doesn't exist.[21]

Given the current organization of science, I have no other choice but to

---

[21]Here is Weinberg (1985), in an otherwise upbeat review of successes in molecular biology:

> It is still far from clear that attempts to reduce complex systems to small and simple components, pushed to an extreme, can provide adequate insights for coming to grips with the great problem biologists confront today: describing the overall functioning of a complex organism. Can the biology of a mammal be understood as simply the sum of a large number of systems, each controlled by a different, well-defined gene? Probably not. A more realistic assessment would be that the interactions of complex networks of genes, gene products and specialized cells underlie many aspects of organismic function. Each gene in an organism has evolved not in isolation but in the context of other genes with which it has interacted continuously over a long period of evolutionary development. Most molecular biologists would concede that they do not yet possess the conceptual tools for understanding entire complex biological systems or processes having multiple interacting components. (pp. 55–56)

regard teleology as a meta- and mega-theoretical stance, which reflects the joint but implicit wisdom of a coalition of scientific theories. The teleological stance is megatheoretical since it extends beyond disciplinary boundaries, from genetics to cell biology to developmental, behavioral, and evolutionary biology, and then on to neuroscience and psychology. The teleological stance is metatheoretical because its concepts and axioms do not belong to the principled vocabulary of any one single scientific discipline. The teleologist is left to engage in a sort of metascientific hermeneutics in order to locate, deconstruct, and assemble teleological truths out of the intradisciplinary fragments and proximate models found in the domain-specialized literature. The result is not a neat picture, but then the goal-directedness of life is not neat either.

This diagnosis of teleology affects my project in several ways. Teleology was said to make both an ultimate and proximate difference to an understanding of the cognitive mind. In the area of ultimate difference, the mega–meta stance of teleology is reasonable and fruitful. About the goal-directedness of life, as a means–ends strategy evolved by the genes, there is not yet an established science (witness the recent debates about artificial life); a teleological account offers as good an insight into the organizational and functional properties of living systems as anything on the current scientific market. The scientific resolution might emerge from a future science of self-organizing and self-replicating systems, which enter into dynamic arrangements with their environments. I expect this resolution to be teleology-friendly.

The same is true of our teleoevolutionary taxonomy of forms of guidance to goal. A comparative evolutionary biology of forms of cognition does not exist yet, evolutionary psychology is still in its infancy, and the top–down style of analysis has barely begun to make its impact in these domains. My teleoevolutionary profiles of forms of guidance are meant to contribute to this emerging enterprise. How a teleological account makes a proximate explanatory difference in understanding mental cognition is a matter for the reader to decide after seeing the argument of chapter 7 and its implications in chapters 9 and 10.

One last defensive word about teleology before I put it to work: I want to stress that the explanatory value of the genetically based teleology used here is in the same methodological boat with the special sciences (e.g., chemistry and particularly the functional sciences). The reason special sciences exist, in addition to physics, is that there are emerging patterns of complexity and nonbasic or regional laws (of molecules, weather patterns, organisms, societies, and minds) which are simply missed, and cannot be conceptualized properly if looked at from below, with the theoretical eyes of elementary particle physics. This is a familiar point. It also applies to teleology precisely because it applies to biology and psychology. The latter two comply with causal explanation but deviate from physics by being generally functional (biology) or functional with respect to information (psychology). Goal-directedness redescribes complex types of functional patterns. That is all. So there is no point in trying to replace teleological talk with a mere physicalist talk about particles and causes because that would hurt biology and psychology first. The real Trojan horse in the Troy of physicalism is the phenomenon of function. Once there are functions, there will be some patterns of them (explainable under, but not eliminated by, natural selection) that exhibit goal-directedness. As noted previously, I could have talked about such patterns nonteleologically yet functionally and still have reached all my conclusions, but what's the point of not calling a spade a spade? Political correctness in science? For those still scared by teleology, this advice: Any time you see the word goal and cognates, remember it's just a pattern of functions satisfying the teleological parameters. A quick mental translation, and you are with me.

3 The Guidance Equation

The next step in my project is to see how a genetically grounded goal-directedness shapes cognition. The shaping force is that of guidance to goal. Whereas goal-directedness captures the general pattern of all organism–environment interactions, guidance to goal captures, more specifically, the systematic pattern displayed by all the informational transactions between organisms and environments. This chapter provides a framework of analysis that illuminates and motivates the top–down transition from goal-directedness to guidance to goal to cognition. The rationale for the transition is this. To pursue their goals, organisms evolve ways to identify and track those goals. Guidance to goal defines the sort of knowledge needed for such identification and tracking. To obtain such knowledge, organisms come to exploit systematically pervasive and recurrent patterns of information relations available to them. The exploitable information patterns define the information tasks that the organism's cognition must execute to accomplish the required guidance. The information tasks in turn select for appropriate cognitive programs and functional mechanisms. The grounding and explanatory order thus goes, top–down, from goal-directedness to guidance to goal to information tasks to cognitive programs and ecological opportunities to functional mechanisms. This chapter aims to sketch this general analysis, which connects goal-directedness and cognition by means of guidance to goal, and to focus on the critical link provided by the notions of information and information task.

1. UNFINISHED AGENDA

Suppose we discover an ancient tool. We want to establish what it is, so we examine its appearance and hardware. Although both have properties that may inform on its identity, they fail to tell the whole story. We also need to speculate on what the tool might have been used for, what function it could have had. To make out the tool's design and operation, we need to figure out how its function was performed, by whom, and in what conditions of utilization. All these factors, we reckon, must have confronted the designer with problems whose solutions were expressed in the design of the tool. The latter becomes intelligible when we frame and reconstruct it in terms of its task and the problems encountered in carrying it out in a given environment by a certain sort of agent.

The cognitive mind is a tool shaped by evolution to use information. What is true of any tool is true of the cognitive tool. An information processing system cannot be understood unless one knows what programs it runs; one cannot identify the programs unless one found the information tasks carried out by the programs, and the problems encountered in doing so. So, to do things right, analytically and explanatorily, one must start from the information tasks faced by the system, and the problems encountered in executing them, moving to the programs handling the tasks, and then to the mechanisms that run the programs. This top–down style of analysis has had a long and distinguished philosophical career and is very much at work in contemporary cognitive science (Dennett, 1978; Newell, 1982; Pylyshyn, 1984, 1989).

Developing an important methodological theme from Chomsky's work on language, Marr (1982) clarified this analysis and turned it into a precise and influential method, initially applied to vision but generalizable to other cognitive domains. Marr's method proposed that one begins by asking, at the topmost level of analysis, about the goal of visual computation, its appropriateness, and the "the logic of the strategy" by which computational problems are solved. The topmost level defines the nature of visual knowledge. At the next, cognitive level one asks about the program implementation of the answers provided at the first level, specifically, about the form in which data are encoded (symbols, representations) and about the operations on these encodings (computations under algorithms). Finally, the third level concerns the physical realization of the cognitive programs.

The appeal of the Chomsky–Marr methodology resides not only in the style of analysis, and its success, but also in the neat formal characterization of the information tasks handled by the computational programs of language and vision. These tasks are eminently psychosemantic, in that they map representations of meanings or scenes into appropriate causal–functional patterns under computational descriptions. It is tempting for cognitive science to assume that overall knowledge is as psychosemantic as the specialized information tasks carried out by the vision and language programs.

The psychosemanticism of knowledge is unmotivated and implausible. From the fact that many, though not all, information tasks performed by cognitive programs are semantic or involve some other sort of hook-up relation to the world, it does not follow (not without a further argument) that all information tasks are semantic or that the overall knowledge they contribute to is semantic. Nor does it follow that the theoretical resources needed to understand knowledge must be the same as those needed in the analysis of particular semantic information tasks. The information tasks of cognition, assumed to be semantic, are left ungrounded and unexplained. What works for a specific task analysis is not good enough for a foundational project. The latter must ask why the cognition of an organism systematically links with aspects of its ecology in the first place, and why semantically, when semantically, and why otherwise, when otherwise.

My criticism is more than logical. The semantic view of knowledge does not make much biological sense as the starting point of a top–down analysis. Genes have a propensity for casting around for patterns of information relations that guide to goal, just as—and often with the same resources—they cast around for patterns of energy and substance exchange that provide metabolic sustenance. These patterns range over ecologically and cognitively instantiated information relations and thus form so many local and distinct opportunities to guide behavior to goal. How the information relations that guide to goal end up being configured, in what combinations, and with what effects, is an open-ended problem with no predetermined solution, least of all a semantic solution. Imagine the guidance territory as an open information space between an organism and its goals, which must be filled one way or another. As far as evolution goes, there are no fixed rules for filling that space. Whatever works, works, whence so many guidance policies. Which patterns of guidance (or of metabolism or reproduction, for that matter) make behaviors possible—and when adaptive, spread a particular genetic formula—is the editing job of natural selection. The casting around for patterns is a prior genetic, authorship, initiative.

In spite of the open-ended character of the information space and the variability of forms of guidance, two overall constraints are at work in shaping guidance. One is the pull of the goal: The information space inside and around an organism is going to be stretched and organized in whatever manner guides to goal with systematic success. Any causal interaction inside and around an organism will do, as long as it contributes to guidance. Any such interaction is ultimately intelligible relative to its role in guidance.

This constraint is critical to our project. Goal-directedness is a shaper of the informational space around and inside an organism and of the causal–functional patterns of relations that occupy that space. The pull of the goal reveals how and why the informational vectors linking cognitive programs to behaviors and surrounding ecologies end up structured and linked as they do. The teleological stance reveals a sense of the systematic configurations of the informational transactions between organisms and their ecologies. How each particular set of goals interacts with particular cognitive and behavioral resources and thus articulates the informational vectors and the entire configuration is an empirical narrative that does not concern me here.

The other constraint, more local, is the push of the cause: The causal and functional interactions that provide guidance, do so by placing the organism in specific information relations to its environment. The systematically recurrent patterns of information relations that end up selected are those that constitute ecological–cognitive adaptations. Whereas the pull of the goal reveals what game is being played and by what rules, the push of the cause shows us how the game is being played, how the rules are obeyed, by what means, and what counts as a win. The challenge for the teleoevolutionary analysis is to convert the pull of the goal into the proximate push of the cause by mapping the teleology of knowledge into patterns of information relations that provide guidance.

We meet this challenge by raising the standard top–down analysis to a new level, that of guidance to goal, which defines knowledge (K) in the biological world. Guidance to goal in turn is secured by systematically recurrent patterns of information relations that must be in place among an organism, its goals, and its ecology, creating a second information (I) level of analysis. These information patterns fall into several categories that identify possible forms of guidance to goal. Finding the right, adaptive patterns of information relations constitutes the information tasks facing an organism's cognition. The ecological opportunities systematically exploited by the organism and the cognitive programs that do the exploiting can be regarded as the executors of the information tasks, the instantiators of the right informational patterns. This is the third level of analysis, that of ecological–cognitive execution or instantiation. Because the focus is on the organism, I label it the cognition (C) level, with the ecological counterpart always assumed as complementary in execution. This is to say that the cognitive programs, evolved to accomplish specific information tasks, represent adaptations that meshed with the right ecological opportunities and affordances. The cognitive programs are run by appropriate functional mechanisms. Thus our fourth (M) level. So the grounding and explanatory direction of our analysis is from *Knowledge to Information to Cognition to Mechanism (KICM).*

My discussion will focus on the first two levels. Their parameters constitute the guidance equation in the sense that they provide a formula for mapping the pull of the goal into the proximate push of the cause and function—that is, knowledge into cognition, by means of an intermediate layer of variables, namely, the information tasks that characterize the systematically general and recurrent patterns of causal/functional relations that guide to goal. The possible combinations of values of these intermediate information-defining variables will suggest the teleoveolutionary profiles of distinct forms of guidance to goal.[1]

2. KNOWLEDGE

An organism has *knowledge* if it has access to the information that guides it to goal. This notion of knowledge is goal-relative, information-based, contextual, descriptive, weak, and externalist. It is the only definition biologically realistic and capable

[1]From this anticipation of my analytic project, it should be evident that teleology is not meant here to explain and ground in any direct and immediate manner the semanticity (or intentionality) or representationality of cognition. Nor should the notion of goal be treated as an individuator of the objects of cognition. These proximate objectives are fashionable in philosophy of mind, but they are not mine. I take a wider and more ultimate view of the matter.

of grounding a top–down analysis of cognition and mind. The core idea behind this notion is that it takes a network of information relations inside and outside an organism to place it in a knowledge position relative to a class of behavior-to-goal routines. Having knowledge is having the information that systematically brings such routines to a successful conclusion.[2] To illustrate, the frog's knowledge of a bug to be eaten consists in having information with the effect that if the frog zaps its tongue (behavioral routine), it catches the bug (goal). The frog is programmed to get into such types of knowledge positions by situating itself in the pattern of information relations needed to trigger its zap-to-catch routine.

Two convictions inhabit this notion of knowledge. One is that cognition is insufficient for knowledge. This is not the insufficiency of the traditional notion of knowledge, where the outputs of cognition (representations) must be true and justified. The insufficiency I have in mind concerns the ability of cognition to secure by itself all the information needed for guidance. Cognition always needs the assistance of an informational ecology. That assistance can be best understood in terms of a guidance equation. The other conviction is that cognition is structured and operates as it does because of how it fits into and works with a larger guidance arrangement.

Given the variety of goal situations and informational contexts in which organisms operate, a good strategy for individuating instances of knowledge is to determine first the goals and what counts as a goal-directed system in a context; then to establish that both the basic and instrumental goals belong to the system in that context (not to its parts, thus excluding the dedicated effects of local functions from being goals); and finally to define the knowledge condition for that system, in that context, relative to a goal, as an instance of the systematically recurrent network of information relations required for guidance to goal.

3. INFORMATION

The notion of information has work to do here. It is not my aim to provide a definitive analysis of information. I do not think such an analysis is feasible, nor does my argument need one. All it needs are some general conditions on information, which, in making the notion of knowledge operational, suggest the *information tasks*

[2]The notion of behavior-to-goal routine is reminiscent of the notion of instrumental property introduced in the teleological literature by Taylor (1964, pp. 9–10) and applied to cognitive matters by Bennett (1976, p. 38). I would paraphrase Bennett's definition as follows: The state (S) of an organism (O) and of its instrumental ecology (E) are such (at time t_0) that a behavior (B) of (O) (at time t_1) is causally required and sufficient to bring about a goal (G) (at time t_2). It is, by the way, in terms of instrumental properties that teleologists like Braithwaite, Taylor and Bennett defined teleological laws (correlating such properties) and teleological explanations (qua arguments from teleological laws).

involved in guidance and the constraints on the ecological–cognitive solutions evolved to handle the tasks.

My skepticism about a definitive analysis of information acknowledges the infamous versatility of information. The notion of information has been taken to characterize a measure of physical organization (or decrease in entropy), a pattern of communication between source and receiver, a form of control and feedback, the probability of a message being transmitted over a communication channel, the content of a cognitive state, the meaning of a linguistic form, or the reduction of an uncertainty. These concepts of information are defined in various theories such as physics, thermodynamics, communication theory, cybernetics, statistical information theory, psychology, inductive logic, and so on. There seems to be no unique idea of information upon which these various concepts converge and hence no proprietary theory of information.[3]

Yet most of these concepts share three, necessary conditions that jointly define the physical possibility of information: One is the systematic interaction between two or more states whereby a change of properties in one state effects a change of properties in the other. The latter change is captured by the next reorganization condition: Assuming that changes of properties result from the reorganization of underlying structures, the interactions produce reorganizations of internal structures in the interactors. These reorganizations in turn have further effects upon other physical states down the line, whence the third uptake condition. Assuming one knows how to frame an information relation, we can say that:

> (3.1) [relative to a frame *F*, a system of states construed as source *S*, and another as receiver *R*]: *an information relation is instantiated* whenever (a) *S* interacts with *R* in *F*, (b) a state of *S* produces in *R* a state whose properties reflect the impact of the interaction with *S*, and (c), as a result of the interaction, *R*'s state in turn produces reorganizations or changes of properties in other states, internal as well as external to *R*.

For convenient reference, I call the state in *R*, which is reorganized or undergoes changes in properties through interaction and has further effects as a result, the *fulcrum* state or structure. The latter is the structure that converts an interaction into an effect. The notion of fulcrum structure is the key to the mapping of knowledge into cognition by way of information because fulcrum structures configure or organize causal interactions into the information patterns that guide to goal. Looked at from the standpoint of a fulcrum structure, information is doubly relational, as it

[3]The interested reader may look at Dretske (1981), still the most comprehensive philosophical explication of the notion (read: version) of information needed in the study of cognition; also Barwise & Perry (1983); Fodor (1986b); Cummins (1986); Bogdan (1988a); Israel (1988).

refers both to the source of interaction and to the effects generated as a result. It takes trilateral patterns of sources, fulcrum structures, and effects, to instantiate the information that guides a system. Whenever such trilateral patterns materialize in succession, the information flows.[4]

Information relations are instantiated everywhere, all the time. Any state of a physical thing at any time reflects physical forces, such as gravitation, at work in the universe plus the more immediate interactions with states of other nearby as well as distant things. As a result, the reflecting state causes the thing to occupy some further state, and so on. This is *material information*, the most pervasive form of information, brought into existence whenever bits of physical matter interact under physical laws (see Dretske, 1981, chaps. 1–2; Bogdan, 1988a). For this discussion, two properties of material information need mentioning. One is that its uptake condition is satisfied universally and promiscuously, to borrow Israel's apt word: The effects of an interaction between two bits of matter can reverberate in all directions, with no effect standing out as special, and no particular one, as opposed to another, being special in any sense.[5] The other property (or other side of the same coin, really) is that although material information is transmitted whenever an interaction between *S* and *R* modifies *R*'s properties, that modification carries no significance as far as its further effects are concerned. Imagine that *R* is a fulcrum structure in some frame of reference. Just as its uptake condition is satisfied promiscuously, so the sorts of modifications first occurring in *R* are inconsequential; none stands out because none of its effects do. That is not so when information relations are exploited functionally.

To exploit material information relations for particular effects is to "functionalize"

---

[4]The notion of information I am suggesting overlaps considerably with, what I take to be, the original core sense proposed more than a century ago in thermodynamics. It is the sense in which information reflects organization as a result of causal or correlational impact. The core sense was aptly captured by Brillouin's definition (1962) of bound information: "Bound information includes structure held together by forces extrinsic to the system as well as structure held together by inherent forces" (p. 112). This is part (the first, backward-looking part) of how I propose to think of information, to wit, as organization either generated or held together by extrinsic forces (causal interactions) and by inherent forces (organizational design). What Brillouin's notion lacked, relative to my scheme of individuation, is the forward-looking condition, the effects caused by virtue of the structure's organization. But, the absence of the forward-looking condition is totally harmless, for in the physical world the effects of informational interactions are inherently pervasive, isotropic, and undedicated. More on this point when I discuss the functional form of information.

[5]It is probably the promiscuity of the uptake condition that makes the notion of material information counterintuitive to many people. The counterintuition is wrong, for whatever counts intuitively as information, say, that of a gesture or sentence, must have its basis in material information. But the counterintuition is not groundless, for the promiscuity of the uptake condition in the case of material information almost nullifies the originality of the notion of information and appears to reduce it to lawful correlation. That is almost true but not quite. Many writers tend to underspecify, if not ignore, the internal reorganization condition on material information, which is why the reduction appears possible. With internal organization and its causal potency in the picture, the notion of material information begins to differ from mere lawful correlation.

those relations by singling out some distinct causal chains for their ulterior role in a larger system. That can happen only if systematic correlations obtain between changes in fulcrum structures, as a result of interactions with source structures, and their dedicated effects. This is what life does: It uses dedicated effects, goals included, for homeostasis and replication by functionally exploiting a variety of interlocking interactions and fulcrum structures, which cause those effects. Proteins breaking down ingested substances, cells generating antibodies, or concepts applied to organize data, all instantiate material information relations that have fulcrum structures, generated by internal programs, which produce dedicated effects with functional consequences for the rest of the system.

This change in the uptake condition by the exploitation of the fulcrum structures indicates that another form of information is at work. I call it *functional information.* If the world were only physical, in the sense that its structures, interactions, and laws were as physics or any prebiological science of nature portrays them to be, then the information in the world would be exclusively material. But the world also contains systems whose internal structures and causal interactions reflect functional constraints that are not governed by physical laws alone. In particular, biological systems are functional, and so are many of the information relations they live on.

Suppose that a system (*R*) is internally organized in such a way that any interaction with a source (*S*) instantiates in *R* sequences of fulcrum structures that configure dedicated outputs, which are functionally significant to other parts of *R* and its behavior. Although all the interactions and the states of *R* instantiate material information relations and thus obey the laws of physics, their internal sequences and effects are underdetermined and cannot be explained by any set of such laws. Functional information is a pattern of material information relations instantiated whenever the design of a receiver *R* forms fulcrum states that transform the interaction with source states *S* into specific and dedicated effects that can be regarded at the functional level of analysis as the execution of internal programs whose rules and constraints reflect a job to be done.[6]

The problem of knowledge for teleosystems is to convert material information into the functional information that guides to goals. The trilateral nature of information suggests the form of the solution. It consists in: (a) having sequences of dedicated effects of successive reorganizations of internal fulcrum structures, triggered by input interactions, correlate systematically with properties that identify the system's goals; and (b) utilizing these systematic correlations and their internal functional routes for behavioral guidance. The problem of knowledge can be managed or operationalized by reduction to a number of subordinate information tasks that meet conditions (a) and (b) in various combinations. Given how the world is, and how organisms develop and behave, the networks of information relations,

---

[6]Dennett (1969) may have been the first mind naturalizer to emphasize the uptake condition and suggest that the informational significance of an internal state is forward-looking and must be analyzed in terms of its subsequent functional work.

which place an organism in a knowledge position, are articulated in distinct temporal and spatial regions as well as functional stages. Separate information networks exist, whose specific, causal–functional instantiations can be construed as so many distinct information tasks to be executed externally by the organism's ecology and internally by its cognition.

Figuring out which configurations of information relations would provide guidance to goal is figuring out the tasks whose execution solves the problem of knowledge. It is important to note, and get accustomed to, the idea that at this second level of analysis one examines the configuration of the informational space in which guidance to goal is possible. This is different from the third level of the evolutionary or artificial design of the programs that manage the tasks by instantiating specific sequences of information relations.[7]

The parsing of the informational space of guidance to goal is as follows: First, we need a network of information relations between distal goal revealing properties and the more accessible ecological properties picked up by the inputs. I call it the connection network, for it connects an organism with its goals by means of an informational ecology. The *connection task* for a system consists in finding and hooking up to such a network of information relations. Guidance to goal also requires aligning the information handled in cognition and behavior to the connection network. The *alignment task* requires that the input data be internally organized and processed in forms that provide discriminations, which the organism employs to steer its behavior. There are three types of internal networks that manage such an alignment and hence three major tasks to be executed to instantiate the networks: One is the *production* of the right structures of data; another is the *categorization* of the data into useful discriminations; and the last is the *utilization* of the discriminations for guidance schematically:

(3.2) Knowledge = connection + alignment [information tasks to be executed by ecological and cognitive means]
Alignment = production + categorization + utilization [information tasks to be executed by cognitive means only]

---

[7]The same line of analysis works for metabolic, reproductive, and behavioral tasks. They can be modelled abstractly in terms of task demands and constraints before attending to the resources and conditions of their execution. For example, we can define metabolism in terms of a number of general tasks (i.e., energy exchange, breaking down into elements, etc.) before considering the executing resources installed by evolution. Such a task-to-execution reasoning allows speculations about the programs and conditions of execution. But only speculations. Any stronger inference from task to executors is in danger of committing the fallacy of affirming the consequent (Fodor, 1990a, p. 207), and is bound to be scientifically unproductive because there are too many mechanisms that can run a given program, and too many programs that can and in fact do execute a given task. This is precisely the point of my focus on tasks: to find a common denominator among the possible varieties of program executions and mechanisms implementations. This also explains my benign neglect of executing programs and mechanisms and of the natural selection that installs them as specific adaptations in specific environments.

(3.2.) is the conceptual core of the guidance equation. It sketches a general formula for mapping knowledge into cognition in terms of the information tasks that describe the key types of systematically recurrent networks of causal and functional relations, which are operative in guidance. For cognition the alignment task is the most critical. The task is that of generating the sequences of fulcrum structures capable of converting input and internal causal interactions (material information) into cognitive and behavioral effects (functional information). Cognition handles the alignment task by evolving programs able to configure the right fulcrum structures that accomplish the conversion in question. What is the right fulcrum structure depends on what specific conversion duties that structure has, given the dedicated effects it must generate. A pigmental structure that transduces a light wavelength into a chemical message is a functionally defined fulcrum structure that does its conversion job under genetic instructions, and so is, at a further remove from the genes and at a higher level of cognitive complexity, a conceptual structure that converts a visual input into a belief.

As in the pyramidal architectonics of psychological functionalism—where higher level functions are executed by lower level functions and more intelligent processes by less intelligent and automatized processes, eventually reducing to the simplest of interactions in which physical elements push each other causally—so it is in the pyramidal architectonics of information: Higher level fulcrum structures convert causal interactions into functional effects by having simpler fulcrum structures do their own conversion job, until it is, again, all balls pushing balls. The downward direction is that of implementation; the upward direction is that of the programs run by the implementers, and higher up, the information tasks carried out by the programs.

As an inhabitant of the world, the information that guides to goal works at the implementation level by realizing, through balls pushing balls, causal sequences of trilateral relations. The guidance equation looks at the process from high up, where it discerns more global patterns in the guise of the cognitive architectures responsible for shaping up the right sequences of trilateral relations, and still higher, the information tasks by which such architectures were designed or had evolved to channel the causal flow of information. My analysis is mostly task talk with some illustrations couched in program talk.

4. IMPLICATIONS OF INFORMATION

Our notion of information has some unorthodox implications which show up at critical junctures in later chapters. One such implication goes against the idea that information is encoded in a single and isolated state or structure (i.e., excitation pattern, image, sentence, thought, etc.); another implication goes against the idea that information is encoded durably in some such state or structure (in the form of a long lasting belief or memory or the like). The joint effect of these implications is to deny the coherence of the notion of content state or structure (thought, belief, etc.) as a durable and self-sufficient encoding of information that is capable, when attitudinized or placed in a functional mode, of psychosemantic duties (mappings of hook-up relations into causal–functional consequences). Or, to phrase the point more provocatively, there are no beliefs or thoughts or other such presumed occurrent or durable states that comply with psychosemanticism and are realistic executors of the information tasks involved in guidance. Because the notion of content state challenged here is the bedrock of psychosemanticism, on which I say more in chapter 9, it is important to see that its unrealism begins in the informational ur. A third implication concerns our ordinary notion of information and is taken up at the end of this section.

The first two implications flow from our trilateral notion of information. The idea that information can be individuated in terms of a particular state alone, in the sense that the information is exhaustively encoded in or by that state, presupposes that the individuation is made exclusively in terms of the intrinsic properties of the state in question. That won't do, if information is trilateral. Trilaterality means that information can be individuated only extrinsically and relationally, in terms of backward- and forward-looking relations. The second implication follows immediately, for the trilateral patterns of relational individuation are always occurrent and short lived. This is because so are the physical interactions that implement the "laterals."

The fact that information relations persist over time (for example, light keeps conveying the same distal information if the conditions are right, and one continues looking in that direction; the retrieval of the same thought or image from memory after some interruption) indicates not that the numerically same individual information relations persist over time but rather that the temporal succession of information relations is treated in the same way by the cognitive programs involved. This is because the programs convert the variability and physical uniqueness of the information relations instantiated at each moment into cognitively stable correlations. The programs achieve this stabilization by generating fulcrum structures responsible for cognitive effects that are similar relative to the information task executed.

What about DNA structures, books, or documents on a computer disk? Don't they store information even in a passive state, uninteracted with? The question is indeterminate. If one means material information, then any of these forms of storing data, like anything else in the world, is part of some, indeed many, material information relations at any time. If one means functional information, as I suggest, then one must acknowledge already its relationality because we presuppose that the storage structure in question has a function, which, by definition, is a relation to something else. So what remains to be done is to establish the conditions in which that relation obtains, and we have our trilateral relationality. This is just about right, although perhaps too fast. So here is a bit more detail.

We were asking about functional information stored somewhere in some form. Let me first defuse the question before making a mild concession. What about the computer disk in its virgin state? Or the molecular structure of a blank piece of paper at any particular moment? They have an internal structure, of some physical complexity, which constantly undergoes changes and thus instantiates material information relations. We do not care about these relations. Why would one say that as a result of a rearrangement of structure, by copying a document on the disk or writing something on the paper, suddenly there is functional information? It is because we care about the internal structure and a specific uptake (e.g., a visual display), given some appropriate interaction (our seeing the display). This is to admit that, for individuative purposes, we care about a trilateral arrangement of input interaction–internal structure–functional uptake.

Unlike the structures implicated in material information relations, the document on the disk, or the text on paper, or the DNA, even when passive and not accessed, potentially constitute fulcrum structures of a functional sort about which we reason, conditionally, as follows: If they were subjected to appropriate input interactions (i.e., accessing the document on the disk, reading the text, RNA opening up and reading the DNA structures), then certain dedicated effects (i.e., document processing, text understanding, proteins synthesis) would follow. This is to say that if (with the help of the right programs) the fulcrum structures were placed in the right relational networks, an information pattern of the functional sort would be occurrently instantiated. Outside such an embedding into an array of relations, the structures under analysis are not of the right fulcrum sort, and therefore do not materialize functional information.

Now the mild concession. The types of structures considered (disk document, text, DNA) are major classes of fulcrum structures durably installed by evolution or by individuals to do a certain job when accessed. Programs, too, may take the form of such structures. Yet all these are fulcrum structures only potentially. Their functional effects are implicit in the structures, ready to flow, once the structures are activated through interactions. This, I think, is what is behind the ordinary intuition that the text or the DNA structures contain information. I concede (in chap. 7) that organisms endowed with memory may retain durable datal structures that fit this intuition. But even in their case, as in the cases discussed here, I deny that the durable structures literally encode information, as opposed to being potentially able to yield the right effects as a result of interactions. In all organisms, the real work in instantiating task-similar information relations is done by programs, not by individual states. Such programs evolved or were designed to bring about sequences of fulcrum structures capable of mapping causal interactions into dedicated effects that have a systematic bearing on how the organism registers conditions of the world and adjusts its behavior to them.

The information that accomplishes a certain task (e.g., the information of a visual image about a scene) through the application of a program is not normally the information trilaterally instantiated when a particular fulcrum structure is caused to have some effects (e.g., the information transmitted by a nerve impulse). The latter is only a minute part of the former. Relative to an information task, a program generates numerous sequences of fulcrum structures and dedicated effects, through which the information flows, that fit into other arrangements such as ecological regularities or design assumptions, to become the information that accomplishes the task. This is why no single content state or program application can by itself cause behavior or have some other functional effect by virtue of covarying with features of the world. Such an accomplishment would require the cooperation of factors other than particular programs and their outputs.

This fact puts considerable pressure on the ordinary sense of information that exercises philosophers and cognitive scientists alike. This is the sense, for example, in which one wants to know the information that a moving dark spot conveys to the frog. The determination depends on how the information tasks involved are construed, and therefore on the range assigned to the programs, their assumptions, and to the role of surrounding ecological regularities. Yet again, it would be unreasonable to think that the information in question could be encoded in an isolated sensory structure. We need to tell a longer story.

That story becomes even more complicated when one makes comparisons among species. For a frog, a moving dark spot may be evidence only of food in the form of flies, given the frog's world and what it needs to know to survive in it, for human beings, a moving dark spot is evidence of so much more because we live in worlds in which there are many more connections between moving dark spots and various sorts of objects other than flies, and also because we have the resources to read much more into the evidence of moving dark spots and to react in many more ways (see chap. 5, particularly section 6) than the frogs do. As a result, the moving dark spot is much more informative to us than to a frog because it is compatible with many more alternative states of the world and many more categorizations of and inferences from data about such states. This difference might not be and typically is not reflected in the structures that register dark spots either in frogs or in us. The difference concerns the scope of the individuation of information: A particular registration (e.g., that of a change in intensity values at the retina), handled by a local program responding to a very specific task, is so much less than the information resulting from categorization (lo, a fly!) or utilization (let's zap it). Psychosemanticism is in the bad habit of asking questions about the latter sort of information while expecting the answer to individuate the former (typically, production) sort. This is a sure recipe for confusion.

My inquiry is interested in the general conditions in which information adds up to knowledge; that is, the conditions in which myriads of functionally linked sequences and hierarchically organized input–fulcrum structure–output sequences manage to carry out the various information tasks that provide guidance to goal. Occasional lapses notwithstanding, my analysis does not intend and does not develop the resources to extract from this complex flow of information qualitative determinations of precise semantic "aboutness," either narrowly from the properties of particular cognitive states or more widely from a story of the alternative states of the world accessible to a system, given its assumptions, background knowledge, and expected behaviors. The narrow or content gambit is one in which I do not believe, as chapter 9 attests, while the wider gambit is still in need of clarification. This chapter aims to contribute something to that clarification.

5. CONSTRAINTS ON GUIDANCE

Think of the simplest and most local information task as something that a single trilateral input–fulcrum–output sequence must do in and for a more complex task; think of the latter as what a hierarchy of simpler trilateral sequences must do in and for the rest of a system that runs on information. At its simplest or its most complex, an information task must reflect objective constraints. I am not thinking of the constraints on its execution; those constraints, pertinent to the third, cognition–ecology level of analysis, concern the adaptations that evolved to handle the tasks in concrete conditions. No, I am thinking, antecedently, at the second level of analysis, of the constraints and limitations on how the information flow must in principle—prior to its instantiation in real systems confronting a concrete world—be organized or configured and sequenced if it is to do a certain job at all, and, if need be, do it competitively.

So I am distinguishing two sorts of constraints, constitutive and regulative. If a system has to do a job, simply do it, it must meet certain conditions of design. (If a knife is to cut anything, it must have a thin blade. Having a thin blade is constitutive of the knife's cutting function.) Meeting design conditions necessary to a function is a constitutive constraint. If, for some reason, a system has to do its job in challenging or competitive circumstances in which some ways of doing the job are better than others and the better ones are selected, then to do its job and be selected for doing it, the system must also satisfy regulative constraints. (If a choice must be made among several knives with respect to which does the job better, then, if cutting fast and clean is the value defining the better knife, the sharpest wins.) A regulative constraint provides a measure of comparison and choice among distinct ways of satisfying the constitutive constraints on the task under analysis.

Just as anything that happens physically, whatever its real world instantiation, is lawfully subject to such constitutive constraints as the passage of time or the dissipation of energy, likewise, anything that conveys information to an organism, prior to the concrete forms in which it does so, must respect a number of similar constraints and be subject to their limitations. For example, the configuration of the connection task places restrictions on how the alignment tasks are themselves organized and sequenced. Suppose that the organism's basic goals are ubiquitous and signalled directly and unfailingly by lawful goal-input correlations, as is often the case in teleonomic guidance (see next chapter). In such a case, as a matter of principle, a production task needs to involve no more than registration of input and activation of control. The presence of a computational production subtask (i.e., one in which, roughly, datal structures are encoded by first encoding their simpler substructures in order to read the input for more distal features it indicates) is not a reasonable constitutive option in the design of the alignment task, because there is nothing to reconstruct from the input; the input just covaries with the goal under a natural law. And such an unnecessarily complicated design of the production task is not a reasonable regulative option either, because a computational task is more error- and breakdown-prone than a lawful registration of goal revealing input.

The most salient constitutive constraints on information tasks, which matter to the argument, are all relational and concern the interplay of the information patterns that guide to goal, how this interplay is reflected in the internal organization of the patterns, and how both the interplay and the internal organization exploit surrounding natural opportunities and laws. So I distinguish: (a) the division of labor between the tasks executed—or, equivalently, the information patterns instantiated—ecologically and cognitively; (b) the resulting allocations of role and complexity among and inside the tasks—or patterns; and, finally, (c) the assumptions that make the division of labor possible and the allocations effective. For the time being, I merely identify the constraints, and let the next few chapters provide concrete analyses and illustrations.

The division of labor is built into the very definition (3.2) of the guidance equation. Different information tasks (types of patterns) do different things, having guidance to goal as cumulative effect. If the goal is distal, as it most often is, information relations must be exploited if the organism is to have its inputs and other cognitions identify and track the goal. Some of the exploitable relations are ecological. The work of the informational ecology that instantiates such relations comes for free, and, given how the laws of nature work, is reliable. The genes know a good bargain when they see one. Given the competitive pressures on organisms, letting the ecology do as much work as possible in handling the connection task is a wise policy. Neither the genes nor the natural selection care much which participant to guidance, the connection or the alignment tasks, does most of the informational work, as long as the work gets done. As a result, the allocation of role and complexity among the information tasks (patterns), and their component substasks (subpatterns), may vary considerably. If the connection task is primary in securing guidance, as it is in the simplest cognizers, then the alignment task remains relatively simple; quite the opposite in the case of sophisticated cognizers. The same is true of the intra-task division of labor and allocation of complexity. Within the alignment task, for example, the production task does most of the work in sensory–motor reflexes and the fixation of perceptual belief, while the utilization task does most of the work in problem solving and decision making.

Because the information tasks (patterns) involved in guidance are so different, some executed (instantiated) ecologically, others cognitively, the question arises as to how they get linked with one another so as to divide and integrate their work and ensure an information flow that guides to goal. The answer is *assumptions*.

This is our third major constitutive constraint. The notion of assumption is familiar in cognitive science and was carefully analyzed by Marr (1982), and in more general biological terms by Vogel (1988). Marr's seminal idea, in particular, was that the design of the visual system evolved to compute information under assumptions about proximal–distal correlations in the informationally relevant ecology. The fact that light bounces off surfaces and carries information from some properties of the surfaces is assumed by vision in its information task of registering the proximal light patterns. Further assumptions are also at work. The visual system registers intensity changes in the raw image on the assumption that, computed further in the system, such changes correlate with and thus yield information about visually significant features of the environment such as shapes and surfaces. On this inferential model of computation, assumptions are construed as major but implicit premises of computations.

From an executive or instantiation standpoint, the assumptions can be seen as implicit because the information they make available is nowhere explicitly encoded as data. The assumptions are built into and reflected by how the programs work. Because they shape the information that guides to goal, the assumptions explain what and how an organism cognizes without any occurrent causal–functional involvement; this goes to show that the cognitive–theoretical explanation need not be causal–functional, certainly not about everything that is important in cognition, and, furthermore and crucially, that the information that actually guides to goal need not be encoded (have psychological tokening), as internal data, to do its job.

All of this is true because, antecedently, at the informational level of analysis, the internal complexity and the sequencing of the tasks (patterns) can be regarded as reflecting via assumptions what other tasks are doing, given how the world is and how the system's behavior engages that world. Consider, again, Marr's analysis of vision. Distal objects and the light that carries information from them constitute the informational ecology of vision. This ecology defines the possible information patterns in the scope of the connection task for vision. Any objects on earth have surfaces and boundaries that reflect light. These two facts, among others, specify what information is in principle available to vision. As a result, the internal tasks of alignment, particularly the production of visual images, must be so organized, at the level of the sequences of (trilateral) information structures, as to take advantage of those facts in the domain of the connection task in that ecology. This is done under assumptions. Nothing is yet said about cognitive execution. In fact, one would not know what sort of programs could bring off the tasks, and how, unless one were antecedently clear about the tasks (patterns) themselves, how they are organized, and how they fit each other. That organization and the fitting are revealed by taking account of the relevant assumptions.

6. THE JOB OF THE EQUATION

Having identified the key parameters of the guidance equation, I conclude by previewing how the equation is supposed to work. Recall that the formula (3.2) contains two global information tasks, connection and alignment. The latter in turn divides into production, categorization and utilization. My survey of forms of guidance follows this three stage branching, identifies, and labels a form of guidance in terms of the information task(s) that does (or do) most of the work or equivalently, in terms of the types of information patterns most instrumental in guidance. Thus, a first division is between, on the one hand, the form of guidance where the connection task is mostly in charge, relying essentially on ecological laws and accidents, and only minimally but cleverly on an internal (cognitive) exploitation of these laws and accidents, whence its label of teleonomic guidance; on the other hand, there is the form of guidance where the alignment task does most of the work by means of internal signs of distal goals and goal revealing properties, whence its label of teleosemantic guidance.

A second and subordinate branching focuses on the alignment task itself and tracks two major versions of teleosemantic guidance: one in which all the semantic information tasks are primitive, in the sense that their execution does not presuppose the execution of other semantic tasks, but rather reduces to teleonomic tasks; and another version in which some semantic tasks are not primitive because their execution does presuppose that of other and simpler semantic tasks. In either version, the semantic tasks are mostly of the production and categorization kind. I

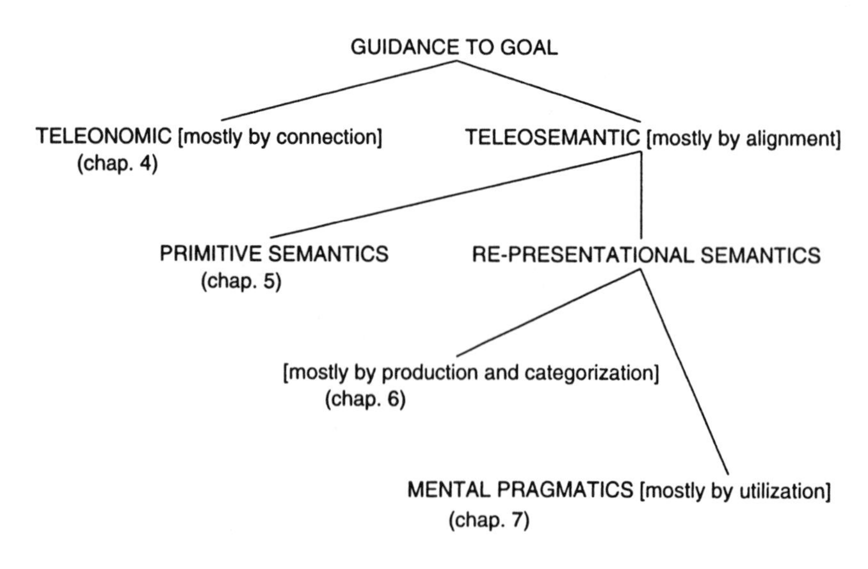

FIG. 3.1. Outline of topics.

label these two forms of teleosemantic guidance primitive, and re-presentational, respectively.

Finally, a third and still more local branching occurs within the re-presentational form of semantic guidance. The branching is caused by the nature of the utilization tasks. Both primitive and re-presentational guidance, as well as teleonomic guidance, are characterized by simple and rather rigid utilization tasks, typically executed by simple categorization and control functions issuing in behavioral reflexes. In chapter 6 on vision, I contemplate the possibility of a re-presentational semantics whose outputs feed directly and reflexly into behavioral routines. This would be a re-presentational but unthinking form of guidance. In contrast, as seen in chapter 7, a re-presentational semantics, not necessarily linguistic, can enjoy mental utilization as thinking before issuing in physical or verbal behavior. The utilization is eminently pragmatic, through the constant creation of goals and of plans to satisfy them, and bears most of the burden of guidance. The result is mental guidance.

So, schematically, the picture to be drawn and examined in the next four chapters parses guidance as shown in Fig. 3.1.

PART 2

FORMS OF GUIDANCE

4 Teleonomic Guidance

This chapter is about the simplest form of guidance, those biologically closest to other vital tasks. For any organism, guidance to goal is as basic a challenge as metabolism. The two challenges begin in the same bioevolutionary boat, and their solutions tend to float or sink together. The first section of this chapter, on the metabolic parallel, explores the similarity between the information and metabolic tasks in the simplest organisms, which is followed by an analysis of teleonomic guidance, illustrated mostly by bacterial cognition. An organism's pattern of information relations to its goals is *teleonomic* when the pattern is jointly instantiated by lawful or nomic ecological correlations and by alignment tasks whose range is input-bound or proximal. These information patterns are teleonomic because they track a distal telos by means of a (mostly ecological) nomos. The guidance formula is to telos (mostly) by nomos.[1]

1. THE METABOLIC PARALLEL

To manage their metabolism, the primeval cells must chance upon and harness appropriate sources of energy. This is their goal problem. It can be solved only by external interactions. No cell is a metabolic island. Their problem is to chance upon the right ways to do the job. This is an inextricable

[1]The notion of "teleonomy" was first proposed by Pittendrigh, in 1958, and popularized by Ernst Mayr (1976, chap. 26). I am hijacking the name teleonomy for the notion of guidance to goal that neither author discusses.

problem of both internal and ecological tasks. The solution must reflect the fit between the two.

To stay alive, organisms must maintain their structural integrity. Think of maintenance as a global task, the way guidance to goal is a global task. Both tasks divide into further subordinate tasks. To maintain their integrity, the simplest cellular organisms must separate themselves from the environment to avoid being flattened and dissolved out of existence. Think of it as the separation task. Its solution must be compatible with the solution to another task, that of engaging in energy and substance exchanges with the ecology so as to fuel the cellular metabolism. Think of it as the exchange task. All are understood at the second task level of analysis. But instead of talking of information tasks, I am talking of metabolic (or maintenance) tasks. Anything that must preserve its integrity goal-directedly faces these two tasks and must find design solutions to them (to be analyzed at the third level). Given regulative constraints, one can anticipate that a joint architectural solution to both tasks is the most likely to be naturally selected. Indeed, the postmineral entities, lucky to have chanced upon a membrane that isolates the inside from the outside and at the same time lets in the chemical stuff needed for internal combustion, survived, and we are here to thank them and write about why and how they did it.

One can fancy other metabolic tasks in the same methodological spirit in which their informational colleagues are understood. To echo the alignment task, consider that the (substance and energy) exchange task can be carried out only if other subordinate tasks are also activated. There is, for example, a transport task: get substances inside the organism. There is also a substance dissolution task: to get the energy out of substances by dissolution. The metabolic tasks can be accomplished only if the metabolic goals are recognized and tracked (information tasks), and in case the goals are distal, only if some transportation is available (locomotion task), and so on.

Thinking of goal-directedness in terms of tasks is intellectually illuminating and explanatorily useful. The tasks display the common denominators of what organisms do so differently, and given the pressures of the real world in which they live, also the reasons why they had to do it one way or another. To handle their various tasks, organisms must evolve functional architectures (metabolic, cognitive, behavioral, and so forth). The notion of *architecture* describes, at the third level of analysis, the ensemble of functional resources that are immediately and systematically sensitive to, responsible for, and explanatory of the structures and processes that execute specialized tasks. These resources include functionally identified mechanisms, from proteins to organs, and their task-oriented programs (for substance transport, locomotion, vision, etc.). The relations of immediacy and systematicity cited in the characterization of architecture are needed to exclude an implementational or hardware reading. There are plenty of chemical and physical processes that implement, say, metabolic programs, but their laws are physical or chemical, not functionally metabolic. The notion of *cognitive* architecture should be treated in the same spirit. It includes the functional resources that are immediately and systematically responsible for, sensitive to, and explanatory of programs ranging over the datal structure and processes that execute information tasks. (The same observation about immediacy and systematicity applies.)

The simplest unicellular organisms, bacteria, have certain properties that are relevant to our argument. Their architectural solutions reflect very visibly their various maintenance and guidance tasks. The bacterial architectures take the form of task-specialized proteins: sensor proteins to identify the food; receptor proteins to bind to the food; transportation proteins to take the food inside the membrane; metabolic proteins to break it down into simpler molecules; who knows, perhaps pleasure proteins to motivate and reinforce the whole process; and so on. The direct hand of the genes could not be more visible; the proteins are fabricated and operate through RNA transcriptions of the DNA instructions. That is all that happens in a bacterium. From a functional point of view, the sophisticated organs and capabilities of complex organisms (eyes, stomachs, legs, brains) are architectural extensions of these simplest task-specialized proteins. Moreover, the design cleverness found in bacteria, whereby the same functional means are used for different tasks, is a reminder of how closely linked are some classes of tasks, such as the metabolic and informational, and how similar their execution. Some of the proteins do both a metabolic and cognitive job. This is a connection that is much less visible in complex organisms.

2. TELEONOMIC TASKS: BACTERIAL SCRIPTS

An intuitively as well as analytically satisfying way to understand guidance is to begin with the a designer's top–down view of the matter. This view illuminates first the information tasks that the designer has in mind before she imagines what programs can accomplish them, and whether evolution has chanced upon them. Envisage, therefore, a designer of cognitive artifacts considering possible guidance equations as simulations of key stages in the evolution of cognition. The methodology is familiar (Bogdan, 1988a; Braitenberg, 1984; Dennett, 1978, 1987; Dretske, 1986, 1988; Lloyd, 1989). The suggestion is to begin with the information tasks of the simplest cognizer and gradually to increase their complexity to approximate evolutionary plausible forms of knowledge. These forms are then compared with empirical data on the relevant architectures and ecologies of real organisms.

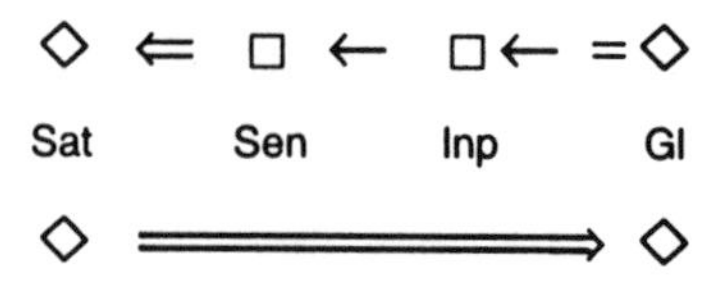

FIG. 4.1. Very proximal guidance.

Script 1: Very Proximal and Lazy Guidance

I begin with what may be the most degenerate case of guidance. Imagine a system whose metabolic goal (Gl) is as proximal and simple as possible. The system's only information task is to register the presence of the goal. The goal is registered, or not, but is not tracked in any way. There is no need for tracking. All that is expected by way of execution of this simple information task is an on–off sensor program telling the system when the goal is on is not present. The sensor (Sen) reacts to the state of the input (Inp) and in turn activates a goal-satisfying program (Sat) or doesn't. The discrimination needed for behavior is built into the sensory reaction. The input happens to be the goal state. Figure 4.1 outlines the teleonomic task and its execution. The single arrows mark the ecological execution; the double arrows mark the cognitive and behavioral execution.

The first and simplest natural valuations of the equation of teleonomic guidance have emerged at the cellular level. Cells, after all, are the roots and atoms of life: by themselves, as bacteria, they are the simplest organisms around; in functional combinations, they build and animate multicellular bodies. In either posture, cells operate on the basis of the same functional design.

For a cellular example of our teleonomic script, think of very early bacteria feeding on sugar. With sugar in abundance around the membrane, ready to stimulate the sensor protein, input and goal coincide; the bacterium does not have to move, and all is well. As in other bacteria, its chemosensor also does transportation duties, carrying the sugar inside for metabolic treatment. As long as the sugary soup existed in the right concentration, life posed no problems. When the concentration changed, for some reason, so did the chances that the lazy bacteria would survive, which is why the bacteria are not around anymore, if they ever were.

Script 2: Less Proximal and More Active Guidance

Life is bound to be more demanding and complicated than the first script suggests. Goals are not usually so proximal, which is why locomotion is needed. A different form of guidance must now connect locomotion with

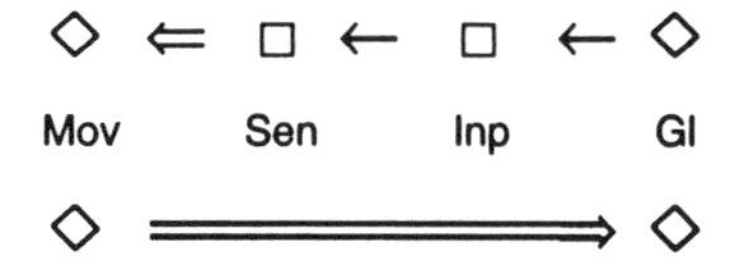

FIG. 4.2. Less proximal, more active guidance.

distal goals. The teleonomic equation changes. Think intuitively of an information task as ranging over a network of nodes connected by interactions. The nodes represent major classes of fulcrum structures whose activation produces cognitively significant effects. In Script 1, with the goal as input, the connection task involved only two nodes, instantiated by input and the sensor–discriminator, respectively, and one interaction between them, instantiated chemically. The new connection task needs more nodes and interactions to provide guidance. The registration of the goal is going to be less direct. Because the goal is distal, it can only be signalled by some covariation with the nearby events that the organism registers.

Imagine that the connection task is rigid and simple, as it relies on a fixed causal interaction between goal and input. The alignment task links with the locomotion task as follows: Whenever the input is positive, the motor moves the system, as Fig. 4.2 shows.

In real life the lazy sugar loving bacteria did not do too well when they ended up in one place of the primeval soup with the sugar in another place. An evolutionary improvement occurred when some lucky bacteria mutated a locomotion capability, the flagellum, accompanied by a sensor, which registers and discriminates a chemical sign of the distal presence of sugar in the form of traces of sugar or something else. When the sensor is on, the bacterium either moves randomly or tries one single direction or meets an uninterrupted chain of the chemical signals leading to sugar.[2]

Script 3: Same Stuff, More or Less

A still more realistic teleonomic script would be that in which the input–goal relation is one of degree of sameness of composition—for example, degrees of concentration of the some substance. The degree of sameness relation becomes evidence of the goal. With behavioral mobility in place, this poses

[2]Perhaps a more realistic counterpart of this latter version is that of developmental cells, which follow certain physical or chemical paths to get to their destinations (some react to the positional information implicitly provided by adjacent cells; others follow fibrils of collagen, whereas axons growing on clotted blood track specific structural discontinuities in the clot). The difference is that the bacteria imagined in my example are autonomous goal-directed systems whereas the developmental cells are not.

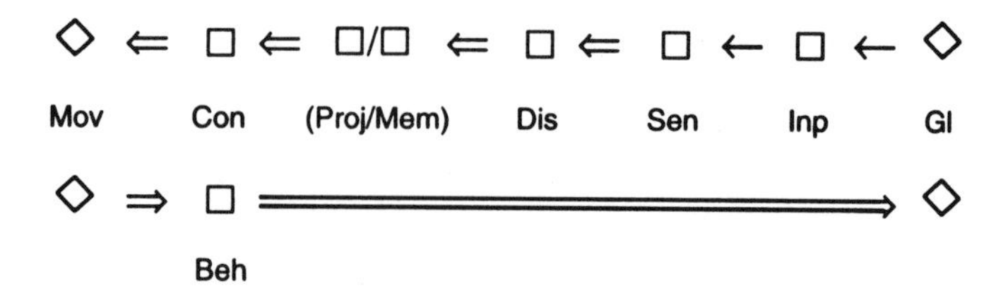

FIG. 4.3. Mobile and distal guidance.

a new informational challenge as well as an opportunity. As both the system and possibly the goal are mobile, the former can identify and track the latter by way of input discriminations only if certain connection and alignment conditions are met. On the connection side, the variations of the input states correlate with variations in the spatial and possibly other properties of the goal states. On the alignment side, the production–categorization phase, the sensory registrations are discriminated and compared by a discriminator (Dis) looking for indices of the location or the movement of the goal; the discriminator does its job either with the help of some sort of memory (Mem) that briefly stores past values of sensory discriminations to be compared with current ones, or with the help of some sort of projection function (Proj) that triangulates the position of the goal or of an intermediate landmark from the patterns of activation of the sensors matched against what is memorized. At the utilization phase, the output of the production–categorization phase must be fed to a control program (Con) that takes account of the overall state of the system and activates (or not) the motor program (Mov). This script complicates the teleonomic guidance as shown in Fig. 4.3.

Let's turn again to the real life valuation of this teleonomic equation. We said that when the concentration of the surrounding sugar varies, the variation itself, in the form of chemical gradients, becomes evidence for where the real stuff is. The bacteria evolving a sense (that is, registration, discrimination, and memory programs) for the degrees of sugar concentration will do well. With the gradient as evidence of food, what is directly sensed (the input) is not necessarily the goal itself (sugar), although it is is pretty close; so no major change in the chemosensing is needed. The executive burden in these conditions is more than before on the internal programs, which discriminate and measure the gradient, remember earlier values, and match them against current ones.

Recent studies (Adler, 1976; Koshland, 1975) of the *Escherichia Coli* or (informally) *E. Coli* support this information script and its cognitive execution. *E. Coli*'s guidance is chemical and goes by the name of chemotaxis, which is movement by chemical sensing. The internal information nodes speculated about in Fig. 4.3 turn out to be instantiated by specialized proteins (sensor, integrator, regulator, and motor proteins) whose program execution establishes the right internodal connections and as a result guides behavior to goal. The cognitive execution unfolds as follows: The sensor protein recognizes a sugar attractant as stimulant; the combination of the stimulant with the sensor protein interacts with the discriminator protein that centralizes the available data; the result is transmitted to the tumble regulator unit that releases a regulator protein, which in turn activates the motor protein and causes the rotation of the flagellum in the direction of the goal. The bacterium moves on busily toward food.

Script 4: When What You Sense Is Not What You Eat

What about situations, more frequent in life, in which the input and other intermediate evidential states have nothing in common, substance-wise, with the goal? A new formula for teleonomic guidance is in order. The system must rely on more numerous and different information tasks being "executed" ecologically to provide the right input–goal connection. The alignment task must be responsive to this new set up: The discrimination and categorization tasks must pick up features of the input that connect through a succession of correlations with the goal. The latter connection must be assumed in the design of the alignment task.

This script is fairly typical in the animal world. At its simplest, it is well illustrated by the magnetotactic bacteria (Waterman, 1989, chap. 7). Their case was recently brought to philosophical attention by Dretske (1986, 1988). His example is of marine bacteria whose internal magnets or magnetosomes guide to goal (oxygen-free water) by sensing and tracking the earth's magnetic fields. These bacteria do not like oxygen and hence must avoid the ocean surface. The northern bacteria, in particular, sense and move toward the geomagnetic north (i.e., downwards) and thus avoid the surface oxygen. They do so by virtue of their cognitive programs that assume (a) a lawful correlation between the proximal values of the surrounding magnetic field and the distal position of the geomagnetic pole; and (b) the fact that in northern waters the magnetic lines are inclined downwards. This assumption allows a lot of guidance to be done by the ecological correlations.

3. ARTIFICIAL TELEONOMY

To further train our intuitions and back up my methodology from a different but converging direction, I want to run the analysis of teleonomic guidance in an even more straightforwardly top–down, engineering fashion, by considering the deliberate design of artifacts endowed with guidance capabilities. Consider a heat guided missile. It is designed with a teleonomic equation of guidance in mind, subdivided into a number of suitable information tasks.

Given the goal of the missile and the resources at its disposal, it is not surprising that its guidance equation is teleonomic, and that the component information tasks are not that different from those of the simple organisms considered previously. The missile scripts are very much like the bacterial scripts because the information problems faced by their guidance equations are pretty much the same.

Imagine that the basic goal of the missile is blowing up planes. The basic goal is achieved by hitting and destroying a plane's engine, an instrumental goal. A property of the engine, heat, becomes the key information source. From this point on, the designer's aim is to imagine a sequence of connection and alignment tasks that connect heat differences with what is registered and acted on by the missile. As in the bacterial case, what is needed is to have the input and internal information nodes (qua major fulcrum structures) track heat differences (sugar differences, in the bacterial case) on the assumption that a proximal sensory experience links systematically with certain heat (sugar) levels; this link, in turn, connects systematically with the instrumental goal of hitting the engine (sugar ingestion) on the further assumption that the engine is in contact with the basic goal of plane destruction (metabolic prosperity).

The next stage is conceiving of the execution of these information tasks by causal and functional relations that flow along the network of information nodes and correlations configured by the tasks. An informational ecology enters in the designer's model of the situation to join hands in execution with the cognitive architecture of the missile. The temperature replaces the bacterium's sugar diffusion as an indicator of the goal (the source of heat). The cognitive architecture of the missile has a heat-sensitive sensor, a discriminator whose program is to register differences in temperature, and a control that tracks and adjusts motion to changes in temperature. The designer assumes that in the ecology of the missile increases in registered temperature generally lead to the basic goal (object to be destroyed). Another assumption is that the engine is the hottest part of the target and that its destruction achieves the basic goal.

The comparison between organism and artifact is useful in understanding teleonomic (and other forms of) guidance because the natural manner in which organisms evolve their cognitive architectures is something the artifact designer must explicitly think about. That forces a thorough explication of the nuts and bolts of the guidance equation. I am not saying that the designer necessarily simulates the workings of evolution, although he might. Nor am I implying that there is any convergence between the fruits of bioevolution and those of the designing mind. I am saying that the designer must make explicit in his linguistic brain and on his drawing board his thoughts about how to design the cognitive and motor architecture of the missile. These thoughts may approximate the information tasks of evolution itself in the sense that they individuate the information nodes and correlations that constitute the proximate arrangements that turned out to be cognitive and behavioral adaptations in real life. This is a parallel Dennett (1987, 1991a) and others have illuminated in recent years.

The guidance equation of the missile delivers the right epistemology. If some object other than the typical target, say, a hot asteroid or a hot mega-sausage just passing by, is identified, tracked, and hit by the heat seeking missile, one would not say the error originates in the cognitive architecture of the missile executing the wrong programs. One would not say that because the architecture has done all the right things it was designed to do. Nor was the missile's guidance equation misvalued, for all the values were fixed the right way. What accounts for error in this case is an assumption about the identity and frequency of goal like objects in that ecology; those objects happened not to be of the right sort. The goal assumption constrains the guidance equation but is really outside its scope. The missile was not designed to check on the distal identity of what it senses as hot. The missile could be redesigned to do the checking (if hot mega-sausages inexplicably proliferate), but that would be a different equation. As things stand, the guidance to the hot goal was all right.

The world can be different or different at times from that imagined by the designer. Indeed, the biological world often changes in ways that violate earlier evolutionary assumptions, which is why many species vanish. Or the ecological correlations assumed in teleonomic guidance may be only statistical, to begin with, in which case flukes and accidents are part of the deal. Hot asteroids are possible, even likely, in the missile's environment, but not as likely to require a modification of the cognitive design of the missile. Likewise, the evolutionary design of the frog's cognitive architecture assumes that every so often a dark spot is not a bug. Yet that does not happen often enough to imperil the frog's well being and reward cognitive recalibration.

Even at this primitive level of guidance, there are significant implications for the naturalist account of cognition and mind. So a reflective detour is in order to firm up the theses put forward so far and anticipate their critical import.

4. THE EXPLANATION OF SIMPLE COGNITION

Although simple organisms, such as bacteria, are closer to human beings' organic and mineral ancestors and thus to physical nature than we are, it does not follow that the explanation of their cognition is going to be Physical (i.e., categorized and explained in the vocabulary of physics), as is so often and mistakenly assumed. This critical point is worth stressing as a warning against both reductionism and the hope for a single and simple account of guidance to goal. As physics does not do bioevolution, an ultimate evolutionary explanation of simple guidance cannot be Physical. The other question is what sort of proximate explanation is appropriate for the cognition of simple organisms. There is a strong propensity to regard the architectural simplicity of cognition as inviting a Physical or Chemical proximate explanation. This propensity should be resisted. I want to motivate my position by comparing it with an apparently sympathetic yet eventually misleading reading of simple cognition. I quote at some length from Johnson-Laird (1983):

> [The *E.Coli*] . . . is able to detect a chemical gradient . . . and modify its behavior so as to migrate up a nutrient gradient and down a toxic gradient. This behavior might be thought to display perception, memory, and choice, but, as Koshland and others have shown, the reality is rather different. . . . [The bacterium's] path is a random walk that is biased by its ability to detect ambient chemical stimuli. [Likewise, the paramecium's] behavior seems as if it depends on an ability to make a decision based on a perceptual representation of the world, but once again there is an alternative explanation. Mechanical stimulation causes the membrane of the organism to depolarize. The sequence of ensuing electro-chemical events leads to the cilia's reversing the direction of their power strokes. . . . Bacteria and protozoa appear to move in their respective worlds in a thoughtful way, but in reality they are what I shall call *Cartesian* automata [in which] there is a direct, physically mediated, causal link from stimulus to response. Cartesian automata are a Behaviorist's dream: they respond to the world, yet their responses are based not on representations of the world but on direct causal interaction with it. . . . The simplest organisms have no mental life. Their behavior . . . in no way depends on internal representations of the external world. More advanced organisms, however, do not merely react physically to their immediate environment but seek to anticipate it [with the help of internal mental models] . . . Cartesian automata interact with the world but make no use of internal models. (pp. 399–403)

Taken literally, the remarks about bacteria displaying perception, memory, and choice must be rhetorical, for the latter notions belong either to commonsense or scientific psychology, and in both cases these notions assume powers of representation ("internal models") that the bacteria do not have. The question is not how the cognitive programs of bacteria are labelled but whether their explanation is Physical or not. In deciding that bacteria do not perceive or choose, Johnson-Laird is setting up the wrong alternative. That alternative, captured by the notion of a Cartesian automaton, is that if the organism does not perceive, decide, and represent, then it must simply respond *Physically* to stimuli, the way a physical effect follows physically its cause. If I am not mistaken, Fodor's (1986a) position on paramecia was not much different from Johnson-Laird's. Although a widely shared position, it is wrong as a matter of both ontology and proximate explanation.

It is wrong ontologically because bacteria, like all organisms, are functionally organized to cognize and behave the way they do. So it will not do to say of any organism, no matter how simple, that it merely responds physically to a stimulus. Physics is not a science of functions, nor is chemistry. Registrations of and responses to stimuli are functional events and cannot be conceptualized and explained by physics or chemistry.[3] Johnson-Laird gives us the major premise from which to mount a critical syllogism to contradict his own conclusion. He said, rightly, that "all biological processes finally depend on protein molecules" (1983, p. 403). This is all my argument needs. For the next premises are: Bacterial sensing, discriminating, and moving are executed by proteins; proteins are biomolecules with specialized functions; and, whatever is biologically functional is not (type-wise) physical. The conclusion is that the way bacteria and (a fortiori) more complex organisms respond to stimuli must be explained Biofunctionally, not just Physically. This conclusion holds no matter how the functional responses and treatments of the stimuli are labelled.

I admit that Johnson-Laird's and Fodor's readings of bacterial cognition are more deflationary than mine. Their readings are impressed by mechanical stimulation, depolarization, and other electrochemical events, while I am impressed by the cognitive functions executed by specialized proteins and see the electrochemical events only as implementers of the proteinic functions. These explanations occur at different levels, and I think I know why. But before turning to that, let me mention that I am not alone in my reading of bacterial cognition. One of the leading bacterial psychologists that Johnson-Laird and I have read, David Koshland, emphasizes, as I do, programs and functions, not only their electrochemical implementations. Koshland talks explicitly about "temporal sensory mechanisms that allow bacteria to remember the concentration of their immediate past" and about "devices for comparing their previous environments with the present one" in the form of a "primitive memory," and concludes that "the behavior patterns of the single cell bacterium will obviously be simpler than the more complex processes in higher species but the preliminary indications are that the similarities are significant" (Koshland, 1975, pp. 251, 257; Lin et al., 1984). Likewise, when Fodor (1986a, p. 6) magnanimously conceded only photosensitivity to paramecia, he is pointing to an implementing physical capability of the creature, not to the function of that capability in the paramecium's cognitive architecture.

I suggest that the widely shared intuition at work in Johnson-Laird's and Fodor's Physicalist thinking lies elsewhere. The intuition, as I see it, is that (a)

---

[3]With apologies to the knowledgeable reader, experience tells that these trivial truths must be repeated as often as possible.

the cognitive programs of the specialized proteins are implemented simply, under a few basic (i.e., physical) laws, and (b) the overall effect of the execution of these programs is itself simple mechanical reflex and close to the level of the physical and chemical laws exploited in the process. That is true and part of the bioevolutionary deal. An organism cannot be that simple in design without being, in terms of complexity of implementation, close to physical nature.

The contrast, drawn by Fodor's argument, is that in sophisticated cognition the implementation of both the cognitive programs (computing representations) and their overall effects (having mental representations about crumpled shirts which cause complex behaviors) cannot be subsumed under any set of physical or chemical laws. The contrast is still about implementation, not about the nature of the cognitive programs: In the bacterial case, a few basic laws account for the implementation of cognition; in the case of human cognition, none can, because the implementation of complex functions relies on the implementation of simpler functions, and by the time one turns to the basic laws, the explanation is so baroque as to elude any meaningful Physical subsumption.

Because, in the bacterial case, a few basic laws of implementation appear to tell the whole story, what else is needed? That, I surmise, is how one gets the notion of Cartesian automaton: from an implementation perspective, one can see that for the simplest organisms there is a consistent match between the functions performed and the basic laws that implement the performances; it can be concluded that the sciences of the implementing laws can handle the explanations of the functions. But the conclusion does not follow. The simplicity of program and of the resulting match with the implementing resources does not change the direction of explanation: we are still looking at implementation, not at the programs being implemented, and the explanation of the former does not help with the latter.

The distinction between what is implemented and its implementation might not be so visible in simple cognition for another reason. That reason, too, may be at work in the reductionist intuitions of Johnson-Laird, Fodor, and so many others. I noted (in chap. 2, section 5) that simple organisms like bacteria may fail to instantiate such teleological parameters as orthogonality and the versatility and plasticity of performance that go with it. This is why they are simple. Their programs are executed nonorthogonally by fixed and unique causal routes. Physical laws are also instantiated nonorthogonally. If the instantiation of a physical law happens to be the very fixed causal route by which a bioprogram is executed, it appears as though the bioprogram is merely a physical mechanism (Cartesian automaton) and the explanation of its work Physical, too.

This is a non sequitur. Even though the causal routes implementing the execution of a bioprogram are fixed and nonorthogonal, they are still functionally defined by the bioprograms, and the bioprograms in turn had been naturally selected for their functions (dedicated effects), not for the nonorthogonal causal routes they happen to chance upon in performing their functions. The coincidence between the causal route governed by a basic physical law and the program execution of a simple function is explained by the architectural poverty of the organism and the adaptive value of this form of parasitism, not by the laws of physics. The organism itself remains goal-directed, despite the fact that the functional executions of its programs are so simple and fully aligned to the basic laws they exploit. Among the teleological parameters, the presence of systemic functions and the terminality of their dedicated effects remain paramount; they suffice to configure and explain goal-directedness.

5. TRANSITION

The teleonomic equation reflects the give-and-take of complexity, role, and division of labor between the connection and alignment tasks, given the goals and behaviors of simple organisms. Their basic goals are geographically pervasive and unspecific (substances all over) or else more localized and specific but reliably linked with gross proximal properties (say, air vibrations that lead to prey). Their behaviors are simple and direct (i.e., move and ingest, grab and smash), and do not require handling intermediate goals. In this case, the connection task does most of the work, while the alignment task remains uncomplicated and generally proximal.

An important implication of this trade-off between the connection and alignment tasks is that what the latter accomplishes has little if anything in common with what guides to goal and therefore with what the behavior tracks. The teleonomic equation of guidance is set up in such a way that the information the organism has access to and encodes is only a small part of the information that guides it to goal; the remaining information is not handled by the organism, so there would not be any architectural trace of it in the form of cognitive programs. The information tasks executed cognitively are not designed to recover distal information on goals. In teleonomic knowledge there is no alignment of the production, categorization, and utilization tasks to the goals of the organism or to the distal properties specifying those goals. The business of the internal tasks, individually and collectively, does not reflect such an alignment, as will be the case with semantic knowledge. Translated at the cognitive level, this limitation tells us that what teleonomic cognizers sense and cognize has little in common with what they know, that which guides them to goals.

To check the alignment of the internal information tasks to the goals tracked behaviorally, one must descend to the level of cognitive execution and ask whether the programs in charge of the internal tasks reflect such an alignment. One intuitive test, to which I return from time to time, is to imagine discovering the operating system of an extinct organism and trying to reconstruct its goals and informational ecology from its cognitive programs. If the organism's cognition instantiated a version of teleonomic guidance, this reconstruction would be impossible. The only cognitively systematic relations, reflected in the design of the cognitive programs, would be proximal.

In the magnetic bacteria, for example, the cognitively systematic relations will be relations between the magnetosomic registrations and discriminations and the values of the surrounding magnetic fields. The rest of the cognitive architecture utilizes the sensory data to do its work, relative to assumptions with ecological range (relating magnetic fields to geomagnetic poles, the latter to the disposition of oxygen in northern waters, and so on). If one does not know independently about the goals and the ecology of the magnetic bacteria, there is little in their cognitive architecture that would reveal what, aside from magnetic fields, is being identified and tracked as data for behavioral utilization and goal satisfaction.[4] The ability to sense magnetic fields could have been compatible with many distinct ecologies and goals; one can imagine earthbound bacteria migrating from place to place using magnetosomes and eating metals. Even in the case of the more complicated architectures of Script 3, where several programs of registration, discrimination, and memory were at work, all the programs reveal is that values of a proximally available substance were systematically tracked; the goals of the organism could have been different or differently related to sugar or another substance.

And still, one could ask, isn't the human eye, in case we take it as a semantic information processor, working on the same principles? Doesn't it register light and exploit proximal-distal and other ecological correlations, under suitable assumptions, to form the visual image of a distal object? The answer is yes and no. Yes, ecological correlations are exploited and assumptions about them are made in more advanced forms of guidance such as those executed by vision; but no, the internal alignment tasks, production in particular, are no longer compatible with a possibly indefinite variety of informational ecologies, for their design configurations execute tasks that reflect to a much more considerable and systematic extent the goals tracked cognitively and behaviorally or the distal and specific properties that individuate the goals. This is what teleosemantic knowledge is all about.

---

[4]Consideration of the metabolic architecture would narrow down significantly the class of the organism's goals, and that is (Dennett, 1991b) the way to determine goals from such an archeological stance. But note that this more realistic method of identifying goals does not affect our point about the proximal and goal indifferent relation that the cognitive architecture bears systematically to its surroundings.

5 Primitive Semantics

Guidance can be finely tuned to pick up distal and specific properties that individuate the goals of a system. This can be done if most of the guidance work is done by internally executed information tasks, particularly those of production and categorization. The challenge, in setting up these tasks, is to have internal encodings systematically track the specific and distal properties of the goals. This is why teleosemantic guidance is guidance to telos (mostly) by internal sema (signs). There are two formulae for teleosemantic guidance. One is primitive in the sense that the semantic tasks range over simple and fixed patterns of signs or presentations of the external covariations with specific distal properties sufficient, in a given ecology, to pick up the goals of the system. This is why the tasks are not executed in terms of simpler semantic tasks. This is guidance by *primitive semantics.* A semantics that secures a flexible and combinatorially versatile triangulation of goal revealing properties from internal signs or presentations of other such signs or presentations, with the effect that complex semantic tasks are executed in terms of simpler such tasks, is *re-presentational.* At the executive level, the first formula works because the cognitive architecture is designed or has evolved to have its fixed functional paths automatically lock into properties that identify goals; the second formula works because the combinatorially generated and context sensitive re-presentations do the semantic triangulation on their own, by virtue of how the data are organized and processed. This chapter is about the first formula; chapters 6–7 are about the second.

1. THE VERY IDEA OF PRIMITIVE SEMANTICS

I begin conceptually. *A semantics* is *primitive* in that the execution of its information tasks does not presuppose, as those involved in re-presentational semantics do, the execution of simpler semantic information tasks. For a contrast, recall that a sentence is understood by understanding its words. The sentence understanding task is carried out by the execution of word understanding tasks. The former task is not semantically primitive because the latter task is also semantic. Nor, generally, is the word understanding task itself semantically primitive. Most words are understood by understanding other words and/or by executing other nonlinguistic but semantic tasks, such as perceptual recognition, concept identification, or inference. The formation of a visual image is semantically nonprimitive because, as seen in the next chapter, it involves further semantic tasks geared to tracking specific and distal properties, such as shapes, boundaries, or volumes. But the latter tasks are primitive because they do not depend on the semantic individuation of specific distal properties; instead, they rely on functional but nonsemantic and proximal information about intensity changes at the retina and other such phenomena.

What makes an internally executed information task semantically primitive are its sort of target and the manner of identifying it. The target must be specific and distal and unlike the input from which it is identified; its identification must not require the prior identification of other such targets. The semantically primitive identification is achieved by a functionally fixed pattern of internal markers or presentations of those features of the input that, in a specific ecology, manage to lock systematically into the distal and specific properties of the target. By contrast, a semantic task is nonprimitive or re-presentational whenever the identification in question is achieved by means of other internal markers or presentations, which are themselves semantic in a primitive or nonprimitive sense—whence the terminological concoction of re-presentation. Although in both teleonomic and teleosemantic guidance the production and categorization tasks engage the connection task and exploit informationally the surrounding ecology, only in teleosemantic guidance do these tasks manage to track distal and specific goals through ecological and input variations. The result is more guidance from within the system, hence more autonomy than in teleonomic guidance.

At the executive level, a primitive semantics is semantics by brute causal–functional force exercised by complex causal and functional arrangements, inside and outside the organism. Cognitively, the semantic triangulation of the target properties is the outcome of a vast functional conspiracy embodied not in the datal outputs of the program operations—otherwise those outputs would be semantic re-presentations—but rather in the way these nonsemantic outputs are formed, sequenced, and utilized. Examples follow in the next sections.

As a guidance formula, the primitive semantics of the alignment tasks is a viable option if the system has: (a) only basic goals that are simple and stable; (b) goals that are reliably specified by properties that the system detects easily and reliably; and (c) the discriminations and categorizations that follow the detection feed fairly directly into behaviors, which are themselves (d) simple and standardized. It is a reasonable assumption that either nature or a designer would select or opt for such a guidance formula if the system to be evolved or designed satisfied these conditions. A primitive semantics also makes evolutionary/design sense at the executive level. It is cheap, simple, and efficient to wire in programs whose rigid and mandatory execution yields quick, systematic, and invariant detections and categorizations of a relatively small number of distal items in the organism's ecology. As an intermediate step between teleonomic and re-presentational guidance, a primitive semantics would, if biologically realized, be consistent with the propensity of evolution to tinker with and improve on prior teleonomic capabilities.

2. SEMANTIC UPGRADINGS

Imagine that such an upgrading takes place. How would it work? There is a small literature on the matter (see Bogdan, 1988a; Braitenberg, 1984; Dennett, 1978, 1987; Dretske, 1986, 1988; Lloyd, 1989). Dennett (1987) captures well the spirit of the enterprise with the example of a thermostat upgraded to possess awesome semantic powers:

> [T]he more of this [cognitive architecture] we add, the less amenable our device becomes to serving as the control structure of anything other than a room-temperature maintenance system. . . . [T]he class of indistinguishably satisfactory models of the formal system embodied in its internal states gets smaller and smaller as we add such complexities; the more we add, the richer or more demanding or specific the semantics of the system, until eventually we reach systems for which a unique semantic interpretation is practically (but never in principle) dictated . . . At that point we say this device (or animal or person) has beliefs *about heat* and *about his very room*, and so forth, not only because we cannot imagine another niche in which it could be placed *where it would work* (pp. 30–31).

The basic strategy is to enrich and focus a system's guidance by inserting it in an information network containing several sensory routes to specific and distal properties *D*, which pick up its goal *G*. This can be done either in the same sense modality (say, visualizing distinct properties of the target, such as color, shape, motion) or in different modalities (say, vision and smell). Any time a sensory route is activated by an input *P*, correlated with a distinct distal property *D* of *G*, a categorization is made and fed into behavior. Suppose that in the system's ecology either the goal *G* alone has the distal properties $D_{1.....n}$, or else *G* has a probability higher than anything else in having those properties. The system is informationally positioned to systematically track $D_{1....n}$, and nothing else, or nothing else with a high risk of error.

This supposition offers a plausible historical explanation of why a system has been designed or has evolved to have a cognitive architecture that makes the information just described available to its behavioral routines in a specific ecology. This explanation excludes a proximal semantics, according to which the cognitive programs connect systematically only with the inputs *P*, and not with the distal properties *D*. The notion of a proximal semantics (evolutionarily nonsensical) cannot account for why the system registers only the inputs *P*, in the combinations suggested, with certain categorization and behavioral effects, and not other inputs, in other combinations, with other functional effects.

The story of such a semantic upgrade story gains plausibility when the design is complicated still further in response to more demanding semantic information tasks. Suppose the inputs in several modalities of sensory interaction are conjunctive, as opposed to disjunctive as before: Only when several highly specified inputs are jointly registered are the categorization and utilization tasks executed. For good measure, imagine that the combined input activation needs to reach a certain intensity level to initiate further functional connections, or, even better, that multiple inputs, variously positioned and mobile, and gates, feedback loops, compensation and constancy tasks, are also available. These are informational arrangements designed to triangulate specific distal properties, ignore within limits input perturbations and variations, and guard against false candidates. There is no other ultimate explanation for these information tasks and the patterns they describe, and no other proximate explanation for why the architecture designed or evolved to carry out these tasks operate as it does.

Further efforts to prevent error may require tasks that sharpen the semantic focus and range of the programs run by our system. Imagine that the tasks require dominant registration routes in some modality (say, visual), and also back-up and less dominant routes (say, auditory). The reason for this arrangement is that the dominant registration routes, when individually available, have only an average frequency of 60% of covariation with the distal properties of the goal. (The informational ecology is behaving statistically, for some reason.) So, as a back-up, the system is designed to appeal automatically to less dominant registration routes, when in doubt. It would not be plausible to explain this arrangement by saying that it provides the system with proximal information about the dominant 60% of the inputs, for such a relation fails to be systematic under any constraints (Dretske, 1986, p. 34). And when the dominant input fails, why transfer the information relation to the back-up inputs? Why several sorts of inputs and why such frequency relations between the dominant and less dominant inputs? A more cogent explanation is that the frequencies in question allow the system to relate to distal properties.

3. HOW IT WORKS

Is guidance by primitive semantics conceivable? And is it biologically possible? I think both questions have positive answers. The conceivability issue, first. Consider a familiar example of procedural, as opposed to descriptive, guidance to goal (Cummins, 1986; Bogdan, 1988b). I give you instructions how to reach my home from where you are: Straight on street X, left on Y, go three blocks, right on Z, stop at the third house on your left; that is your destination. A goal can be construed as a destination that can be reached by following instructions. The instructions to reach a goal need not relate semantically to the goal itself by covarying with, representing, or in some other way being about, its properties. My instructions tell you how to reach the destination without telling you anything explicit about the destination itself. Being sentences in English, my instructions have their semantic values, as they represent various conditions connected with the destination. Yet the sentences are not about the destination. So it is possible to get to a goal by following instructions that have no semantic relation to the goal.

The next step is to have the instructions themselves desemanticized, so that they do not describe anything (they are not sentences in English or, more generally, representations of anything) but are simply followed. The desemanticization of the instructions must bear not only on the goal (as in my example) but also on the interim pointers involved. Some of my instructions did name such pointers as street, block, and house, and so they were semantically valued. Other instructions were procedural (go right, then left). They could have had other descriptions to the same effect (such as, chase that smell or follow that light path). The procedural instructions are not semantic, for they merely link some behavior (effect) to some condition that must be satisfied in some fashion. Once this desemanticization process is completed, an overall semantic effect results, which is obtained by nonsemantic means. You get to my house without being told anything specific about anything in particular.

The foregoing is a conceivable scenario with real biological bite. The genes provide instructions in a geographic sense. These are instructions to do this and that, where 'this' and 'that' have nothing semantically to do with either target or target indicators or anything else for that matter, yet the process so instructed ends up in precise and distinct goal states. Consider development. Through appropriate transcription processes, the DNA instruct the developmental cells where to go, and when to differentiate into a tissue or organ, without "telling" them anything about the developmental goal itself or about the interim stages. This is how homeotic genes control the development of the spatial organization of an organism. When these genes are turned on, the cells they inhabit are directed down the route to becoming a particular organ; the cells are given 'positional information' on where they happen to be at a given time. The information comes in the form of material clues (shapes, chemical gradients) that the cell is primed to recognize and react to. With the position determined, the cells consult some map, presumably encoded in the DNA segment shared by homeotic genes, which tells them what to do in, or where to go from, their particular position. As a result, cells differentiate into bone, cartilage, wings, or whatever (Gehring, 1985; Wolpert, 1991).

All of this is pertinent to my argument because the genes do instruct a good deal of vegetal, animal, and human cognition, and do so in the spirit of my geographical and developmental examples. Instead of having cognitive neurons literally travel and then do something, the cognitive genes ensure that the neural transactions, responsible for mapping inputs into goal-directed behaviors, take place in functionally compiled patterns. These patterns engage the ecology in ways that give the flow of information a semantic uptake, although none of the neural nodes and networks have a semantic relation to anything.

The emphasis so far has been on the production task. I turn now to the categorization and utilizations tasks to see how they fare in primitive semantics.

4. BEHAVIORAL CATEGORIZATION

The alignment task requires that the outputs of the production tasks (sensory registrations, in cognitive terms) provide discriminations and categorizations, which guide behavior to goal. With simple and stable basic goals, few if any instrumental goals, reflex behaviors, and a flow of information along fixed causal and functional routes, the categorization tasks are themselves going to be simple, rigid, with direct behavioral utilization. To summarize these features I call the task *behavioral categorization*, and the programs executing it *behavioral categories.* In teleonomic guidance, the categorization took the form of behavioral discrimination. It had proximal range. Behavioral categorization has distal and specific range and yields discriminations considerably more indifferent to sensory and ecological variations.

Behavioral categorizations map production outputs into behavioral routines. The task is captured by the notion, imported from cognitive psychology and artificial intelligence (AI), of the input–utilization rule. The rule has the conditional form: IF [input], THEN [utilization]. To put it colloquially, an animal may have the following rule as its behavioral category: IF [small, dark, and smells good], THEN [chase it]. The categorization task relies on discrimination and matching subtasks. The discrimination is needed to recover the features of the input that the organism acts on, while the matching tracks the conditions in which the acting is appropriate. Neither task requires the executive programs to operate on explicit datal structures, nor do the discriminations result in structures that are compared with or matched against other structures stored in memory. The discrimination values are built into the sensory programs (via intensity thresholds, for instance), and the matching may rely on preassigned reaction levels for registered magnitudes (color, smell, temperature). In an animal's ecology, discriminations of smallness, darkness, and smelling good may suffice, statistically, to identify its edible goals. That sufficiency is expressed in the matching subprogram that activates behavior when all the right discriminations are in.

What defines a primitive semantics and is executively reflected in the composition of its behavioral categories is that the utilization condition is functionally inseparable from (and may be hardwired to) its input part. No information tasks other than discrimination and match need be executed before behavior is initiated. Once the input data are in and categorized (recognized and matched), no further tasks (inference, deliberation, memory search) are needed. Even when some habituation or learning takes place, the connection between new categories and behavioral routines is still automatized and direct. Imagine that the animal learns some new things that enable it to recategorize the same prey in terms of: IF [only head is visible and has this shape], THEN [chase it]. The new category cannot be added to the old (small, dark, smelly) and somehow detached into an independent and self-contained cognitive rule, free of behavioral utilization, something like: IF [only head is visible but has that shape], THEN [it must be small, dark and smelling good]. The latter would be a *concept*, about which I say more in chapter 7, section 1.

As programs, concepts are multitrack dispositions whose tracks integrate flexibly various datal structures. Behavioral categories, by contrast, are programs that automatically feed inputs into behavior by preassigned functional routes instantiating single-track dispositions. The animal blessed with a primitive semantics has neither the encoding resources (re-presentation programs) nor the utilization resources (inference, memory programs) nor the behavioral needs to form concepts. As a matter of program execution, a behavioral category can be primitive architecturally and yet encode lots of data about many properties. The category is primitive in that it is neither learned nor built out of other categories. Its outputs are preset to carry information about what observers, but not the animal analyzed, would regard as relatively simple and independent properties (e.g., small or dark). The animal registers and categorizes the whole package of properties. It does so because the entire aggregation of properties is needed for teleosemantic guidance. The programs resonate to sensory clues that nomically correlate with entire packages of distal properties.

Not all behavioral categories need be genetically preset, not even in simple minds. Semantic cognizers learn that alternative sensory clues and/or alternative distal properties pick up the same goal. As a result, if lucky, they may expand the input condition of the behavioral category by disjoining registrations, as in: IF [either small and dark] or IF [head is thusly shaped], THEN [do it]. Or by linking them in some order: IF [such and such sounds are heard, or such and such movements observed], THEN [gather some more data in the best positioned modality], and THEN [IF [indeed small and dark], THEN [you know what to do next]]. None of these are genuine inferences. They are compiled expansions of the input condition needed for behavioral utilization. The disjunctive expansion is likely to work as a back-up source of discriminations, whereas the conditional expansion is more common in trial-and-error learning.

Behavioral recategorization involves recompilation. This form of learning is a narrow variation on the same broad cognitive–behavioral themes. Whatever is learned is compiled the way skills are. The reason I mention this matter here is to preempt any association of learning to re-presentational semantics by showing that behavioral recategorization is not concept formation. There is associative learning in the form of new proximal–distal correlations and discriminations. As in the case of Pavlov's dog, this form of learning occurs when an innately recognized clue (smell) is replaced by a new clue (the bell ringing). One behavioral category replaces another. Associative learning is a form of acquiring new behavioral categories and hence new sensory–motor links. There is also trial-and-error learning in which organisms form new behavioral patterns in response to new challenges. What is missing in such behavioral recategorizations (for lack of re-presentational resources and intelligent use of them) is a utilization of the recategorized inputs for the cognitive rehearsal of the solutions to the problem encountered.[1] That would

[1]Gould & Gould (1986, p. 31) suggested that not only chimps but rats engage in trial and error by reasoning out a course of action before acting. The example is of a rat carried passively to each of two goal boxes at opposite ends of a runaway and shown that one box contains food and the other does not. Upon release, the rat runs unerringly to the food box. Much as I tried, I could not see why this example shows deductive reasoning and cognitive rehearsal on the rat's part, as opposed to memory plus some good sensory and navigational skills. But perhaps I do not understand rats.

be problem solving micromanaged by the individual organism on an improvisational and short-lived basis, and it requires concepts.

Many animal psychologists take behavioral recategorizations as evidence of concept formation. This can blur the distinction between primitive and representational semantics. A concept is worth attributing not only when the datal structures it ranges over pick up invariant properties, but also, essentially, when its utilization is cognitively significant irrespective of ecological context and behavioral consequences. To operate conceptually, a categorization program needs the production resources of re-presentation, as discussed in chapter 6, and the inferential resources of cogitation, which are discussed in chapter 7. Most animal species lack both.

Consider the much discussed case of pigeon concept formation. For the sake of the argument, let us assume that pigeons are semantic cognizers. We are told by animal psychologists that hungry pigeons can be trained to form the "abstract" concept of redness through exposure to various color slides, with only red being rewarded with food. Pigeons are said to learn many other concepts in such rewarding conditions, most of them (about photographed fish or women's dresses) being new and unnatural for the species. My philosophical naiveté recommends questioning that this is a case of concept formation. All it illustrates is that pigeons are capable of new systematic discriminations with immediate behavioral consequences. The evidence of a behavior invariantly activated by the discrimination of redness and not of other properties is not enough to settle the issue. The question to ask is how the discriminations made by the pigeons are produced and utilized (i.e., what information tasks are being executed). The answer would tell us whether the outcome of the experiment is a behavioral category or a concept, for the difference between the two is essentially one of form of production (in the input condition of the input–utilization rule) and utilization (in the utilization part of the rule).

As far as I can tell from the experiments, the upgraded pigeon may be forming one of two sorts of behavioral categories. One has the form: IF [. . . red, . . . , etc.], THEN [IF [peck], THEN [food]], where "redness" is packaged in the input condition slot with other contextual properties such as "shape on the wall screen of a box." The experiment varies the images projected on the screen, not the screen itself, the wall, the box, or other contextual properties. In this case, one may assume that more than redness is encoded and categorized to steer behavior. The other sort of behavioral category that the pigeon may be forming in the clever experimental setting or even in natural circumstances would be one in which the food-indicating categorization is contracted to the registration of redness. This is not reason enough to talk of the pigeon's concept of redness, or of anything else, for that matter. The simplest bacteria register and react to sugar and nothing else, yet that does not mean they have the concept of sugar. The fact that pigeons learn to react to a property, while the bacteria are wired to register one, shows a difference in how categorizations programs are formed, not in what they do.

The pigeon may learn to contract its input to redness within the specific behavioral category: IF [red], THEN [IF [peck], THEN [food]]. This is important. Outside that behavioral category, relative to behaviors other than pecking, the registration and discrimination of redness may amount to very little, if anything. I doubt that such a single-track and single-minded employment of a datal structure is worth treating as conceptualization. Concepts are expected to display sufficient invariance across contexts and forms of utilization.

Humans also employ behavioral categories. They may be wired (as are defensive bodily movements initiated by signs of danger) or learned individually, often explicitly in the beginning and then compiled as automatic sensory–motor routines. Driving is a well known example. It begins with explicit instructions, which are first conceptualized (in the strict sense intended here) and then deliberately and often problematically translated into appropriate behaviors. After some practice, the knowledge of driving is compiled as a largely unconscious routine. The driver has packaged the initially explicit concepts and the slow and precarious inferences they allow into smoothly and reliably operating behavioral categories and routines. The same is true of music playing, sports, or writing. The pigeon would agree.

Primitive semantics and behavioral recategorization bring part of the guidance game inside the organism, within its cognitive grasp, thus allowing it some further autonomy.[2] It is possible that advanced species, such as apes, have a large repertory of behavioral categories with sophisticated choice programs. That can be regarded as an anticipation of mental utilization. At some evolutionary point, re-presentational cognition could emerge as a miniaturized execution of the alignment task: Instead of so many behavioral categories and choice programs for various contingencies, let context- and goal-sensitive production outputs (datal structures) be computed and categorized conceptually to provide suitable internal simulations of a goal situation and of the behavior planned to handle it. This is the topic of the next two chapters, but first a further transitional upgrade on the way to re-presentation.

---

[2]I do not mean here and elsewhere in this book that such cognitive progress is evolutionary progress. Ants and roaches, cognitive idiots that they are, are likely to survive us. One does not live and survive by cognition alone. I construe cognitive progress as representing an advance in the internal control an organism has over how to track and pursue its goals. In this sense, primitive semantics is superior to teleonomic cognition.

5. TOPOMAPS

So far we have examined production and categorization upgradings, and speculated that they accomplish a smooth sensory–motor coordination. For many animal species or artifacts (such as the heat-seeking missile), the coordination may be short lived or continuous, along some input dimension; in either case, it is fairly simple and straightforward. Snapping the tongue out upon the detection of a moving dark spot or following the sunlight for directing one's movement might not require more than simple sensory–motor coordination. Following a ball or chasing a fly or grabbing the prey and bringing it to the mouth is a different matter, for each task requires a continuous, flexible, and adaptive sensory–motor coordination that a fixed and simple architecture cannot provide. Following and catching a moving object requires production and categorization programs whose task is to finely and continuously adjust behavior to the changing proximal clues of an object in motion, relative to the position of the body and of its moving components, themselves possibly in motion.

Biological nature has evolved a solution to this complex engineering problem, which is worth considering briefly, as it anticipates not only the next cognitive saltation—vision by re-presentation and re-presentational cognition—but also a central form of utilizing re-presentations, mental imagery. Although the notion of topomaps is useful to my project, nothing important depends on it.

Since the bacterial beginnings, the key information task for cognition has been adjusting motion to what is sensed. I have not so far attended to the fine print of such an adjustment, for there was not much need for it. Teleonomic guidance involves diffuse goals (sugar or oxygen all over). Primitive semantics goes for more specific goals by triangulating them from their proximal and internal signs. Following, adjusting continuously to, and grasping a moving object with a moving part of a body, however, is not the same as moving the whole body in the general direction of a goal or using a motion reflex any time a sensory sign is on. The design problem, in the former case, is to find a way to align the dynamics of the motion of the bodily part (e.g., an arm) in the motor space to the dynamics of the proximal signs of the distal object (e.g., flying ball) in the sensory space. It is a problem of encoding such sets of coordinates and connecting them in the right way.

The solution to the task of coordinating sensory and motor spaces takes the form of *topographic maps* or simply *topomaps*.[3] Qua maps, they are displays

[3]This story closely follows the Pellionisz–Llinas neuroscientific script as summarized, developed, and illustrated by Llinas (1986), P.M. Churchland (1986, 1989), and P.S. Churchland (1986, chap. 10).

of data organized in ways that can be accessed and utilized by various processes by virtue of the spatial organization of the maps. The data carried by the maps is neither distal nor focused on anything in particular, which means that the maps have no semantics at all. They are more refined tools within the primitive semantics of the organism, yet they contribute something novel and important to it. The maps are *topo*graphic in that they encode spatial data about position and motion (as change in position) in terms of the topological organization of the peripheral sensory space; and they are topo-*graphic* in that the form in which they encode the sensory and motor data is intrinsically sensitive to spatial organization and motion through space.

The solution to the task of coordinating sensory and motor spaces takes the computational form of a transform function, in a formal sense, which correlates the coordinates in the sensory space, indicating, say, the ball's position, with appropriate coordinates in the motor space; indicating the arm's position, with the effect that arm moves in whichever direction the senses are excited so as to track the ball's position. It turns out that an optimal computational solution for this sort of case is a tensor, which is a transform function coordinating different spaces by neglecting their metrical or real distance values while preserving their topological or neighborhood relations. The informed speculation is that in most organisms, sensory–motor coordination is likely to be some sort of tensor implementation (Llinas, 1986).

The topograhic maps contribute an important though local refinement to the overall semantic work of the organism's cognitive architecture. The maps coordinate what is sensed with what is grasped and when, or with the motion of the entire body. They do so by picking up what is distally identified by the rest of the architecture (various sensors and integrators), and tracking only the spatial position of the target as evidenced in the topograhic organization of the sensory space. In other words, once the distal presence and motion of an object is established by other means, it is the business of the maps to make the position of the object available to the motor programs. The tensorial computations performed on the mapped encodings exploit the fact that the sensory space is deformed, metrically, in order to preserve the information on the spatial evolution of the distal object in the motor space. As a result, the object can be reidentified through successive mappings (P.S. Churchland, 1986, pp. 426–427).

Needless to say, one sensory map and one motor map are not going to do the trick. It takes plenty of intermediate maps to encode the dynamic information and make it available to the motor programs. If sensory modalities other than visual are contemplated, then further types of mappings are to be expected. In many organisms, there are auditory maps as well as somatosensory maps (facial or whisker maps) that coordinate the eye toward the source of sound or bodily stimulations. These new sorts of maps are themselves organized so as to feed into one another and eventually into the motor maps.

6. CRITICAL RECAPITULATION

The case for primitive semantics is not foolproof. So this is as good an occasion as any to engage the critic and review the story so far. I begin with some of the questions that can be raised about the notion of primitive semantics, relate them to my position, and then answer them.

The fact that the notion of primitive semantics is tightly sandwiched between teleonomic guidance and the re-presentational version of teleosemantic guidance is not very helpful, at least polemically. The fragile newcomer could be squeezed out, leaving the notion that simple guidance is teleonomic only and distinct from teleosemantic guidance, which, in turn, is re-presentational only; or else, that all guidance, from the simplest to the most complex, is teleosemantic, and the teleonomic version is out of the picture.

The notion of semantics is a source of trouble. From one side, there has been the almost analytic equation in which semantic equals re-presentational, based on the assumption that only re-presentations (qua explicit datal structures formed and transformed under semantically sensitive rules) have the range and focus associated with semantic aboutness. From the other side lies the argument for the possibility of a presemantic guidance effected, internally, by compiled or primitive functional paths that exploit lawful proximal–distal correlations. The result is another, almost as analytic, equation to the effect that primitive equals presemantic.

I have never bought these equations but I did buy something else that favored primitive semantics at the expense of its teleonomic predecessor. In an earlier work (Bogdan, 1988a) I liberally treated bacteria and other simple minds as semantic cognizers of the primitive sort. Teleonomic guidance was not in the picture. Many teleosemanticists take this position. There is merit in it. Bacteria guide themselves to goals by means of ecological regularities exploited architecturally under a variety of assumptions; so do superior organisms. On this semantic continuum, the difference between simple and complex cognition seems to reside in the design and its manner of exploiting the ecology, rather than in the nature of the information tasks (all semantic). While it is easy to see why bacteria and other simple minds do not re-present anything (in the technical sense of explicit and semantically pregnant datal structures), it is harder not to grant their cognitive programs semantic tasks. After all, bacteria were shown to operate simpler versions (specialized proteins) of the programs that superior organisms have with pretty much the same functions. These programs pick up features of the input which exploit lawful ecological correlations. Isn't this the way humans do it? True, we are less dependent than bacteria on external contingencies of input and ecological laws, but that again seems to be a matter of task sophistication in how we and our simpler predecessors are guided to distal and specific goals, rather than a matter of being guided semantically at all. The difference, then, seems to concern the ecological and compiled execution of semantic information tasks rather than the nature of the tasks.

Furthermore, in both teleonomic and teleosemantic cognition, the knowledge task is to guide to distal goals, while implementationally the guidance is effected by sequences of causal and functional interactions that extend from goal-revealing properties to inputs to internal states governed by cognitive programs. So where is the difference? I have said that the pervasiveness and diffuseness of goals, or of the properties revealing the goals in the teleonomic case, as opposed to their specificity and distinctness in the teleosemantic case, partly explains the difference. But is that really so? What is wrong with saying that the bacterium's aggregate cognitive state is semantically about sugar or oxygen or some such diffuse substance, not unlike the way the aggregate cognitive state of an organism with primitive semantics, perhaps a cat, is about a mice, or the way my visual image is about that house on the corner? After all, the gross aboutness of the bacterial cognition reflects its simplicity. Can't we say (as I did in 1988a, p. 109) that the simpler the design and the behavior of a system, the coarser the semantic information it encodes and utilizes?

And, to return to a point about the alternative-based notion of information (chap. 3, section 4), shouldn't the idea of a neutral and universal measure of what counts as specific and distinct target of cognition (qua goal-revealing properties) be abandoned in favor of attending to the concrete ecological–cognitive frame of each species (as my doctoral student Tian Ping has suggested)? Couldn't one say (to take her example) that, whereas dark spots are not sufficient for us to identify insects—as our cognitive world is so much more diverse and complicated than the frog's, and dark spots indicate to us so many things other than insects—in the frog's much simpler world, dark spots are as insect revealing as anything can be because their evidential role is to reveal nothing but insects and statistically they do reveal insects most of the time? In which case, the frog's registrations and categorizations of moving dark spots ought to be as semantically about insects as my visual image is about the house on the corner, for the properties represented by my image pick up that house (almost) as uniquely as the frog's registrations pick up insects, mutatis mutandis.

And what about error? To fool an information system is to fool a semantic system (I opined in 1988a, p. 108; and so, I think, had Dretske 1986). If that is true, then either teleonomic cognition has no room for error, in which case it is not genuine cognition, thus reinforcing the reductionist views like

Johnson-Laird's or Fodor's, discussed in the previous chapter (section 3); or else, if teleonomic cognition is error prone, then it must be semantic.

Finally, what about the sensible distinction (suggested to me by Norton Nelkin) between what an organism tracks systematically and what makes the tracking successful? The answer to the first conjunct may be the input, always, while the answer to the second conjunct may be the distal goal, always, in which case it is all teleonomy; for, what explains the success of the tracking, namely, lucky ecological fit and natural selection is the same in both forms of guidance, and therefore the reach of the cognitive programs must be proximal, hence teleonomic, in both.

Given these sensible considerations, why the change of mind? In particular, why teleonomy in addition to teleosemantics? Or, if the other direction made sense, why teleosemantics at all, instead of an all embracing teleonomy of various sorts?[4] The change of mind had to do with the realization that cognition works in the larger framework of guidance to goal, and that many of the things said in the earlier work, and by other authors, about cognition are in fact things that should be said about guidance. From the standpoint of guidance, which is explanatorily ultimate, all teleosystems have distal goals, more or less specific, tracked by means of laws of nature and ecological accidents, which are assumed by the cognitive programs. So read, all forms of guidance seem either all teleosemantic or all teleonomic. Semanticity, however, is a property of the information tasks executed in cognition. Semanticity is not a property of guidance, of its ecological segment, in particular. This is why the success conditions of the ecological tracking of goals do not bear on the information tasks executed cognitively, and hence cannot distinguish the internal programs executing those tasks as semantic or not. From the global angle of guidance, the tracking of specific and distal goals appears as a unitary and far-reaching or long-armed information megatask executed by the organism's cognitive programs together with ecological correlations. From that angle, then, the megatask may seem semantic or nonsemantic for all organisms.

From the angle of the tasks executed cognitively, the view is different. In teleonomic guidance, a good deal of the information needed to identify and track goals is simply not available to the organism in a form that has any functional import; that information is simply not cognized. That is the case, for example, with the ecological correlation between the geomagnetic pole and the presence or absence of oxygen in the ocean; this is a correlation to which the magnetic bacterium has no cognitive access whatsoever. The

[4]In Bogdan (1988a, pp. 105–109) I considered some of these objections as directed against the primitive semantics of cognitive simpletons. Teleonomic cognition was not part of the picture at that time.

bacterium has cognitive access only to the input information from the alignment of the surrounding magnetic fields. The access is not semantic, for the magnetosomic programs do not systematically track a target (oxygen-free waters) in the distal ecology.

In vision, by contrast, the proximal features of light input are "read" for—that is, computed into re-presentations of—specific distal properties (shape, surface, volume) on the basis of ecological laws of optics. These laws are cognitive enablers, helping the vision pick up distal items from their traces in the light; they are not informational extensions that carry by themselves all the information the input makes available to the organism, as is the case in teleonomic guidance. The same is true of primitive semantics. Ecological laws enable a hardwired functional gadgetry to target definite distal properties. The semantic tasks executed by that gadgetry consist in recovering distal properties from the input and reidentifying these properties across many ecological variations. The design of the primitive semantic programs reflects to a considerable extent this systematic tracking of distal and specific properties.

Recall my paleocognitive reconstruction. I speculated before about recovering the goals and surrounding habitat of a long extinct bacterium whose cognitive architecture was discovered, say, in a mineral deposit. I reasoned that if the cognitive architecture alone was discovered, then the task of reconstructing its distal goals, the world in which it lived, and the ecological contingencies it exploited for guidance, was facing an objective indeterminacy. The reason is that the same programs could fit into indefinitely many guidance equations with different goals and different proximal–distal correlations. Given that in teleonomic knowledge there is a vast ecological area where a significant part of guidance depends exclusively on ecological facts, any changes in the latter that do not affect the organism's pursuit of its goals need not be reflected in its cognitive architecture. It is conceivable, then, that some magnetic bacteria had evolved a different metabolism, hence new goals, while retaining the same cognitive architecture. Their programs do not reflect the imagined change in goals and ecology. So, in my sense, they cannot be executing semantic tasks.

The paleocognitive angle also helps with the distinction between what the cognitive programs track systematically and what makes the tracking successful. The reconstruction of the semantic architecture of an extinct species would tell us what properties its programs could track systematically (i.e., smallness, redness, certain shapes and movements, etc.). The architecture would not reveal anything definite about the surrounding ecology or the goals of the species, that is, the items displaying the tracked properties. One would infer that the properties picked up by the programs are goal specifiers, but those properties could have specified many other items in the same ecology or other goals in different ecologies. If successful tracking requires goal identification, then this would not form a picture of successful tracking in that vanished ecology. In the teleonomic case, the reconstruction of the cognitive programs leads no further than the input, while in the teleosemantic case, the reconstruction can also individuate the distal goal specifiers without necessarily picking up the goals themselves or other items specified the same way.

What about the frog's registration of the moving dark spot? Is it semantically about insects in the sense in which my visual images may be about insects? I begin by noting that the attempt to read the semanticity of cognition from peripheral input states is a mistake, which I discuss at some length in chapter 9, section 2. With this correction in mind, let us consider the entire alignment task and its executive programs. Is, then, the frog as semantic as I am? Not if I can help it. The fact that in its world, the frog's registrations of dark spots are statistically sufficient to specify its basic goal (flies to be caught) explains the success conditions of its goal tracking (this is how the ecology is set up) and the assumptions under which its tracking programs work (reflecting the statistical sufficiency in question). Likewise, the fact that in my world, images of three dimensional flying objects with, say, such and such a shape, color, and volume are statistically sufficient to specify insects explains the success conditions of my insect cognition (that is, why those properties, outside the reach of my cognition, reliably connect with insects) and the assumptions under which my cognitive programs work. True, my world is so much more complicated than the frog's, and as a result of this difference in complexity, neither moving dark spots nor certain shapes, volumes, or colors may suffice to distinguish for me insects from so many other items of interest. This means that my internal signs are compatible with so many more distal referents, and I need *more* complex combinations (via computational programs) of such signs to pick up the insects that the frog identifies only with one or two internal signs.

Does it follow that the frog and I are both semantic but in different degrees? It doesn't. The explanation just surveyed does not yet tell which information tasks are accomplished by what sort of cognitive programs. It tells only the conditions in which and the assumptions under which the registrations and re-presentations, respectively, track properties sufficient, in the respective ecologies, to specify the items of interest, whatever tasks are accomplished by whatever programs. It is an explanation of successful tracking, not an explanation of the nature of the internal tracking.

Turning to the alternatives-based notion of information, it too helps with the determination of successful tracking. It is an external story. In contrast, the question whether the frog is semantic or not concerns its internal (alignment) tasks. With respect to the semantic character of the internal tasks, the difference between the froggish registration and my visual image is that the former has proximal range and individuates only a light pattern and nothing else (whatever its success condition in the *frog's* ecology), whereas my image goes beyond the light patterns it reconstructs, and systematically tracks shapes, surfaces, and volumes out there (whatever the success conditions of the tracking in *my* ecology). This is the semantic difference. The frog stays teleonomic.[5]

Finally, the matter of error. The question was whether error is a mark of semantic cognition. It isn't. But a determination must be made as to whether error is construed in the narrower frame of cognition or in the wider frame of guidance. My answer is the same for both cases. Consider cognition first. I take it that cognitive malfunction is the least interesting form of error. More revealing is the case in which cognition works normally, and yet the system is fooled. Any functional system that relies exclusively on the proximal information of the input, hence any teleonomic cognizer, can be fooled because it has no systematic access to what is beyond the input. Move a coin in front of a frog, and you will see its tongue reaching out. If that is error, then error does not require semantic cognition.

Another case of error for simple functional systems is possible when their nonsemantic cognition is programmed to operate inductively, by taking statistical risks. According to one reading (Matthen & Levi, 1984),[6] this is how the immune system works. It can mis-identify self for enemy and proceed to destroy it. It makes an error because it has a preassigned function (to defend self) with dedicated and terminal effects (dead enemies). Barring malfunction, when it errs, the immune system does the right thing (eliminates enemies) on the basis of misperception (confuses enemies with self). It makes evolutionary sense for the immune system to operate inductively by assessing the danger on each major occasion and reacting accordingly, even learning from such experiences. This policy leaves plenty of room for error yet the policy pays off; it would be counterproductive, if not impossible, to have the immune system programmed from the outset either against some specific invaders only (what if new ones show up?) or against all possible invaders (how can that be done?).

---

[5]In a more comprehensive analysis of the semantics of cognition than that attempted here, these remarks should be taken to support the externalism of reference determination, if by reference we mean the goals of the organism or any other types of targets in the form of real objects and situations that its behavior engages and its internal capabilities are geared to handle in some fashion. That reference determination relies on successful tracking of such targets, and that is as much a matter of ecology and assumptions as of cognitive adequacy. As organisms become more complex cognitively, they manage to track more specific properties, which specify their targets systematically and often uniquely, but even then, from inside the organism's cognition, we can get as far as its goal or target specifiers. There is no magic route to the targets or goals themselves; it still takes a consideration of an ecology, assumptions, real or possible alternative items compatible with the same specifiers, to nail down the targets or goals as referents of internal signs.

[6]But see Piattelli-Palmarini (1989) for a less inductive story.

Nor does error, taken in the wider frame of guidance, distinguish between semantic and nonsemantic cognition. Misleading changes in the ecological conditions that make information available to an organism count as error by messing up the success conditions of the cognitive tracking. Viewed from the standpoint of guidance, such ecological changes constitute error when the assumptions under which the cognitive design has evolved no longer adjust the inputs to the relevant distal ecology. This can happen in both teleonomic and teleosemantic guidance. In a frog's environment, coins may become much more frequent than flies; in Alvin's epistemological environment, Potemkin barns may become much more frequent than real barns. In either case, the error is not cognitive, strictly speaking, and it is the overall guidance formula that must be renegotiated. Both information and error, based on alternatives, pertain to the success conditions of the cognitive tracking and therefore must be relativized, not to cognition, but to the wider configuration of the guidance equation.

6 Intimations of Re-presentation: Vision

Vision occupies an intermediate position, probably in evolution and surely in my argument. Vision is perhaps the evolutionary transition and certainly the theoretical link between primitive and re-presentational semantics. Insofar as vision is primitively semantic, it shows task continuity with primitive semantics, and further vindicates that notion. Insofar as vision is re-presentational, yet primarily dedicated to behavioral guidance, there is re-presentation without perception (viewed as the supplier of re-presentations to thinking), re-presentation that is not yet mental. Although mentation, as construed in chapter 7, requires re-presentation, they are distinct. Re-presentation is a matter of production and categorization, mentation a matter of utilization. Vision helps draw these important distinctions, thus freeing my analysis of utilization to focus on what is essential and unique about mental cognition.

Vision is important in another respect. If vision is re-presentational, then it is so in a nonlinguistic sense. This matters if one wants to entertain seriously not only the idea of a "language of thought" as prior to and independent of a public natural language, but also, and relatedly, the idea that thinking itself could had evolved prior to and independently of a public natural language. (Chimps and robots may be thinking without speaking.) In that case, assuming that thinking operates with and on re-presentations, the latter must be produced and categorized relative to some sensory modality for reasons of behavioral guidance rather than of expression or communication of internal conations or cognitions. Vision, again, is a likely such producer and categorizer of re-presentations. Without going into many details or touching the awesome problem of the evolution of thinking, my aim is to explore the notion that vision is a springboard for a re-presentational semantics, and the latter a nonlinguistic prerequisite for mental guidance.

So this chapter has several objectives that are going to be pursued in a more exegetical fashion than readers may have become accustomed to so far. This exegetical policy has to do with the professional disagreements at the heart of the current research on vision, disagreements which turn out to be instructive for my project. One objective of the chapter is to examine the notion that vision is semantic, whatever the format (next section). Another is to consider the bifurcation of its semantic tasks into behavioral and mental utilization (section 2). That allow us to examine the case for a primitively semantic vision involved in behavioral guidance (section 3), which, retrospectively, further supports the argument made in the previous chapter for a primitive semantics. Finally, and most important, I conclude with a proposal for an analysis of visual re-presentation that is responsive both to behavioral and mental tasks. This is where my technical notion of re-presentation is defined explicitly. Nevertheless, because the discussion leading up to the section on re-presentation is largely exegetical and involves (computationalist or syntax-over-symbols) views on representation, which are compatible with my own analysis of re-presentation, I refrain from hyphenating the word as long as it means re-presentation in my sense. The hyphenation resumes briefly in section 4.

1. VISION IS SEMANTIC

A primitive semantics involves a finite and fixed repertory of mappings of data production patterns into behavioral categories and inflexible behavioral responses. A change to a very large and inherently variable repertory of mappings from production outputs to categorizations and utilizations would require different programs. As Pylyshyn (1984) put it:

> . . . [T]o be instantiated directly by functional architecture, a function must not be inherently combinatorial. That is, certain inherently combinatorial functions (perhaps, parsing) with an infinite domain or range do not qualify as being instantiated by the functional architecture. Such functions must be realized by computations in which intermediate expressions or representations are computed in the course of arriving at the output. On the other hand, if both the domain and the range are finite, the function can be realized by primitive table lookup . . . as an instantiated function. . . . [I]t is not the overall complexity of the instantiation (that is, the amount of "wiring") that matters but whether the system must go through intermediate *representational* states. If the subfunction is rigid (for example, if it is input bound the way transducers were defined to be stimulus bound), then, . . . , we have prima facie reason to take that function as instantiated rather than computed by a process operating over representations. . . .

So far I agree, because the talk is of the nature of the information tasks involved, and of the correlated complexity, power, and versatility of the cognitive programs executing them. Pylyshyn went on to say:

> Based on such considerations, it is far from clear to me that the complex computations involved in deriving representations in "low-level" vision systems (such as those discussed by Marr, 1982) are to be viewed as cognitive, representation-governed processes. . . . The reason I feel they are probably not cognitive is that capturing the regularities of these processes seems not to require appeal to semantic properties. Even such general constraints on the process as the rigidity constraint or the continuity constraint, which are stated in terms of the properties of the visual world, are not semantic properties that are encoded in any representations. Rather, they are descriptions of characteristics of the mapping from proximal stimulations to representation, worded so as to make clear why the process is veridical. . . . Now it may turn out that there is reason to view what is going on in these low-level vision systems as representational processes, as performing genuine inferences; but my inclination is to take their extreme inflexibility over cognitive variations (that is, their cognitive impenetrability) as evidence that their behavior may be explainable without reference to semantics. In other words, they may be merely complex neural processes that instantiate pieces of functional architecture—in this case, transducers. (pp. 214–215)[1]

The quoted text displays a notorious Pylyshyan equation, which says that to be semantic is to be a representation computed (syntactically) AND to be mentally and penetrably utilized as belief or thought.[2] For expository purposes, I separate the equation into two halves, one that says that to be semantic is to be a representation computed, and another that says that to be semantic is to be a representation mentally and penetrably utilized as belief or thought. I discuss the latter half and show it to be wrong in chapter 7. I reject the entire Pylyshyan equation and find semantic cognition in organisms and artifacts that do not re-present anything and do not have resources for mental guidance either. Right now I want to explore the possibility of vision being semantic and nonrepresentational, a possibility the first Pylyshyan subequation would have precluded because it rejects primitive semantics.

---

[1]In the next paragraph Pylyshyn went on to say that the same reasoning works for connectionism: The cognitive functions the latter posits are architectural, not representational, because they do not involve symbols combinatorially, and hence do not require an explanation in terms of semantic properties. My criticism of Pylyshyn's position, which follows in the text, also applies to this diagnosis of connectionism.

[2]Fodor's (1983) notion of module would not have qualified as a semantic engine because modular computation of representations is not cognitively penetrable. Fodor's notion of module pretty much covers what Marr's notion of computational vision does.

It is rather surprising of Pylyshyn to hold that vision need not be explained in terms of semantic information tasks. If vision is not so explained, I don't know what is. My guess, supported by his other equation, is that Pylyshyn thought that only mental cognition (beliefs, thoughts, plans) allows for explanation in semantic terms. This is probably why he has maintained that the various assumptions involved in vision—for instance, that objects in the world have surfaces, that surfaces reflect light, that objects are rigid in motion—have no semantic import and describe only mappings from proximal stimuli to re-presentations so as to make them veridical. The disagreement is essential as it bears not only on my argument for primitive semantics but, more generally, on the idea that cognition operates in a division of informational labor with its ecology within a guidance equation.

The design assumptions involved in vision, or in simpler but still semantic forms of cognition, do describe veridical mappings of proximal stimuli into datal structures. It is part of their job to do this. The assumptions are not explicit encodings of data about what makes the mappings veridical. Nevertheless, the informational work of the assumptions has semantic import because it contributes to producing datal structures and categorizations that are semantic. To explain the assumptions is to explain them in terms of the semantic task they help execute. Cognitive programs of all sorts execute information tasks that are semantic, so the explanation of the programs must be in semantic terms; yet most often the programs themselves are not explicitly encoded. Assumptions are no different in this respect. Carrying out a semantic information task does not requires that the work be done by explicit datal structures.

Marr and other theorists take the visual design assumptions as the premises about the distal environment, which the visual processor incorporates implicitly in order to transform proximal stimulations into veridical representations, thereby inferring the distal properties that have caused the proximal input. If the assumptions allow the visual system to produce datal structures that are veridical of distal properties, then the assumptions have semantic force.

Why would Pylyshyn deny this point? Didn't he write that the way to "get from detected properties of the light to perceived properties of the layout is by inferring the latter from the former on the basis of (usually implicit) knowledge of the correlations that connect them" (Fodor & Pylyshyn, 1981, p.165)? Assumptions are part of that implicit knowledge of correlations, which forms the basis of computational vision. The problem, again, is that Pylyshyn thought that only explicit representations are semantic, and those assumptions are not explicitly encoded, hence are not representations, so they cannot have semantic value. In Pylyshyn's view, only mental cognition is semantic.

As recent debates have shown,[3] the view of cognition as computation of representations need be committed only to the notion that representations are (symbol) datal structures computed by combinatorial executions of functions under certain rules and assumptions; the view need not be committed to the further notion of an explicit encoding of (a) the program that executes the computations, or (b) the assumptions the program relies on. The unrepresented rules of computation and the unrepresented knowledge of assumptions may still need an explanation in terms of their *semantic* task, which is to secure specific distal aboutness. In a word, there are plenty of compiled programs in vision whose information tasks are semantic. The fact that the program execution is rigid, cognitively impenetrable, and informationally encapsulated has nothing to do with vision or anything being semantic or not. It has to do with how the semantic tasks of vision are executed cognitively.

In humans, vision does more than one thing. That complicates matters further.

2. WHAT IS VISUAL PERCEPTION UP TO?

What is the business of visual perception? Here is the choice. I quote at some length from Fodor (1990a):

> What is perception supposed to do? Psychologists have tended to disagree about this in ways that have deep consequences for the rest of what they say about cognition. There are, for example, those who take it for granted that the primary function of perception is to guide action. (Illustrious psychologists who have held this view include Piaget, Gibson, Dewey, Vygotsky . . .) It is no accident that such psychologists invariably take the reflex to be the primitive mode of psychological organization, to which cognitive functions must somehow be reduced. . . . In reflexes, specific perceptual events are lawfully connected to correspondingly specific behavioral outcomes. To take the reflex as the paradigm psychological process is thus to see perceptual mechanisms as detectors that function to monitor an organism's environment, looking for occasions on which the associated behavior is appropriately released.
>
> I am going to assume that this picture is profoundly misled. In my view, behavior is normally determined decision-theoretically, viz. by the interaction of belief with utilities; in the interesting cases, perception is linked to behavior only via such interactions . . . I was once told (by a Gibsonian) that this decision-theoretic understanding of the relation between perception and behavior won't do for flies, since it is plausible that their behaviors really are all reflexive. If this is true, it is another contribution to the accumulating evidence that flies aren't people.

[3]See, for example, Searle (1972); Stabler (1983); and Fodor (1990a).

> Perhaps minds started out as stimulus–response machines. If so, then according to the present view the course of evolution was to interpose a computer—programmed, as it might be, with the axioms of your favorite decision theory—between the identification of a stimulus and the selection of a response. (p. 208)

And now, a quote from Goodale (1987), offering a similar choice from the standpoint of animal vision:

> In sharp contrast with this [Ewert's] visuomotor approach, most workers in the field of mammalian vision treat the visual system as a piece of perceptual machinery in which the different visual channels are seen as contributing to a rich and complex but largely monolithic representation of the external world. Thus, great emphasis is put on the way in which different features of the visual world are extracted and analyzed but almost no attention is paid to the way in which visual information is used to produce different kinds of visual behavior. Indeed, it is this theoretical commitment to vision *qua* perception that has shaped the methodology used in most laboratories that study the functional architecture of the visual system in mammals. . . . Thus, the argument appears to go, the organization of the visual system can be studied quite independently of the motor output. . . . What matters is that the animal discriminates (or does not). It is the *decision*, not the motor act, that interests most of these investigators. (p. 379)

These views identify two different yet essential information tasks of visual perception. One is to guide behavior to its goals by tracking objects and events in space relative to our body and its position at any particular moment, and by allowing the body to navigate through the environment. The other task is to encode the visual input so as to provide recognition and categorization of objects and situations as a basis for forming judgments and beliefs about the environment, other matters, and the actions contemplated. I call the first task *topographic* (which is a version of the sensory–motor coordination task), the second *perceptual*. The programs that execute the first task come under the notion of vision, and those that execute the second under the notion of perception. Representations utilized topographically are visual representations or images, and those utilized in perception are perceptual representations or percepts. So it is vision versus perception.

As currently understood, visual perception appears to have three stages: transduction, modular computation of visual representations, and the mental utilization of those representations as percepts. The latter stage is that of perception proper or "integration of current inputs with background information," as Fodor & Pylyshyn characterized it (1981, p. 183). The first two stages constitute vision. This view may suggest that vision is basically for perception and thought, at least in the human case (Fodor's earlier point). The suggestion is neither obvious nor very plausible. Forming percepts, fixing beliefs, and entertaining thoughts is not necessarily what vision was originally for and may not be what vision is exclusively for.

3. THE AMBIVALENCE OF VISION

Most animal vision is topographic. It is a form of compiled vision, possibly involving topomaps but no representations. Perception relies on representations that are utilized not only to guide behavior but also to model goal situations by fixing beliefs, drawing consequences from them, imagining alternatives, and deciding which one. The human visual system appears fractured by this bifurcation of information tasks. The topographic or sensory–motor coordination task, of course, has evolutionary primacy. Because evolution is opportunistic and tinkers with available structures, mixing their functions, pirating old structures for new functions, and old functions for new utilizations, it is possible that the representational capabilities for perception have evolved out of capabilities for topographic vision. Once available, the perceptual programs acquire new nonbehavioral utilizations that are only indirectly and not always involved in behavioral guidance. But perceptual programs may end up being often more efficient than those for topographic vision even for a good deal of behavioral guidance. In many contexts, fixing beliefs perceptually, as a guide to action, may be more prudent and advantageous than feeding visual images directly into some behavioral program.

There is also a possibility that conceptual utilizations are activated in a regimented and automatic fashion by representations of inputs, not unlike the way in which, in simple cognizers, the transduced input data run behavioral categories and behavioral routines inflexibly. In that case, vision would be representational yet utilized only navigationally or for other simple tasks. The computational production of representations does not by itself determine the utilization of the representations.[4] The modularity of vision, which is a mode of production, does not prejudge how visual representations are

[4]In an interesting debate about teleological rationality with Bruner's nonmodular approach to perception, Fodor considered an argument about the game–theoretic costs of misperception (Fodor, 1990a, pp. 219–222). I will not go into the details of the argument except to note that when it comes to situations of survival and biological competition, where fast and reliable sensory–motor coordinations are needed, topographic vision wins hands down. But whereas Fodor emphasized the modularity of topographic vision, which has to do with how representations are produced, I emphasize its task, which has to do with how modular representations are utilized, namely for sensory–motor coordination. The modularly produced representations can be used either behaviorally or cogitatively. What the modular production ensures is semantic triangulation of distal properties; it makes representation possible (in the sense of section 4). Both navigational behavior and cogitation about the world can benefit from such semantic accomplishments.

employed. No biological expectations are violated by this claim, because there is no necessity that the modular programs for computing visual or linguistic representations and the mental programs that utilize the representations, as percepts and thoughts, evolve at the same time. The concept of visual or linguistic morons (representational production, stupid utilization) is not incoherent.

One could invoke animal vision or the incrementality of evolution, or exploit whatever is valid about theories of ecological vision, to substantiate the idea that topographic vision is continuous with the simpler forms of sensory–motor coordination. Because the preceding chapter has covered that territory, I switch to the theoretical domain of computational vision where some interesting clues await. A first set of clues points to a promising overlap of information tasks and programs between transducers and computational modules. For easy reference, I call it the transmodular overlap. A second set of clues indicates that the transmodular overlap may share some information tasks with the more primitive animal architectures involved in sensory–motor coordination. This chain of overlaps suggests some significant (though by no means total) continuity of information tasks between primitive semantics and vision, at least in the early functional stages of vision.

So here is my exegetical reconstruction. First, some reminders. Vision begins with the transformation of the proximal energy (light) into those internal energy forms (electrical, biochemical) in which the brain conducts its business. This is the transduction stage. The information task of the transducers is to encode the input in a format appropriate for further production and utilization. If vision is of the human sort, then the format in question must allow for the datal and computational treatment of the input by the visual module. This means that the transduction function associates classes of physical events (light intensities) with semantically relevant classes of computational events (datal structures). The visual module analyzes the transduced data in a series of steps during which it computes successive intermediate encodings of the input until the full three dimensional representations are produced and fed to appropriate categorizations (recognition patterns, templates, prototypes) and then to the mental utilization resources (Fodor, 1983; Marr, 1982; Pylyshyn, 1984).

The major difference between transducers and visual modules, reflected in their division of informational labor and functional complexity, is that the transducers, unlike the modules, carry out their information task in a functionally primitive fashion, in the sense that they do not carry out other semantic information subtasks and thus do not execute further cognitive subfunctions, in order to produce their outputs. The transducers make datal structures available to the organism by simply tokening functional link ups that by themselves have no semantic significance. This is why the transducers do not produce representations, for that would require executing complex semantic information tasks in terms of executing more elementary semantic information tasks, and so on. Unlike the transducers, the modules analyze and compute the transduced data in a format capable of combining semantic simples (points, lines, curves) into semantic complexes (shape, volume), and the latter into further complexes (objects, scenes).

This enormous difference notwithstanding, transducers and visual modules seem to share important properties. Both operate exclusively bottom–up and are stimulus-bound, data-driven, and immune to top–down influences from other cognitive programs and sources of data. Both are domain specific because they are sensitive only to data provided by the light input. Once activated, they both operate in a mandatory, tightly sequenced manner, and fast. Both are architecturally localized and hardwired and seem genetically programmed (Fodor, 1983).

Why would transducers and visual modules share such properties, if indeed they do? Why would the modules compute visual representations under such conditions? Why, to put it Fodor's way, is vision smart like cognition, in that it is "inferential," but dumb like reflexes, in that it is encapsulated? Being inferential makes vision more apt than transducers or topomaps to construct semantic complexes out of semantic simplicities and therefore finely triangulate the objects and situations of interest. But why dumb, reflex-like, encapsulated? Here is Fodor's (1990a) answer:

> Perception [vision, in my terminology] is above all concerned with keeping track of the state of the organism's local spatiotemporal environment. Not the distant past, nor the distant future, and not . . . what is very far away. Perception [vision] is built to detect what is right here, right now—what is available, for example, for eating or being eaten by. If this is indeed its teleology, then it is understandable that perception [vision] should be performed by fast, mandatory, encapsulated, etc. systems that—considered, as it were, detection-theoretically—are prepared to trade false positives for high gain. (pp. 202–203)

This is an argument that uses considerations of teleological rationality to define the information task of a system and then uses that task to constrain the resources that are evolutionarily likely to execute it. I like this sort of argument. It begins to suggest that transducers and modules, and more generally semantically primitive and representational vision, share some information tasks and may have endured similar evolutionary pressures on their execution. Even if teleology and evolution are put aside, it is still true that transducers and visual modules have a lot in common with respect to both tasks and programs, and this is a fact that must be explained.

It could be that visual modules share properties with transducers because modules are transducers. This is a point made in Pylyshyn's important analysis of transduction (1984, pp. 148, 162–165, 213–215). We noted that in the standard account (Marr, 1982; Fodor, 1983) the transducers are said to translate physical properties into symbolic encodings, which the modules then compute into visual representations. These are two distinct information tasks, which are executed differently, in a primitive versus computational manner. The transducers can also execute the information task of organizing and preserving metrical or configurational information, which is basically topographic, if: (a) their range is large enough; (b) they are arranged the right way; and (c) the identity of the transducers, including their topological positions, are part of the output code. The same is true of sets of transducers encoding data about several dimensions in the stimulus space by way of similarity metrics. One may speculate that in earlier evolutionary versions the transducers might have provided topographic data directly to the control and motor centers by appropriate mappings, including topomaps and that the modular innovation follows this path.

Pylyshyn noted that the topological arrangement of the transducers and their ability to signal their location and identity by various neural connections in their outputs may succeed in maintaining a high semantic quality of the transduced information, an information task, despite the noncomputational character of transduction as a matter of program execution. The lack of computation is compensated by a reallocation of the complexity of the information tasks to be executed noncomputationally. No limit is placed on how complex a transductive mapping can be, as long as its execution is compiled and noncombinatorial, hence semantically primitive.

I read this as suggesting that to a significant extent what visual modules execute by computational suppleness, sets of transducers can execute by the brute yet clever force of compilation. That significant extent is defined by the same information task, which is sensory guidance of behavior, *not* perception or thinking, by means of topographic data. If transducers could do what visual modules do, namely execute simple semantic information tasks, by compiled, not computational means, then the notion of guidance by primitive semantics, defended in the previous chapter, is not only descriptive but also explanatory. This is an important retrospective implication of my current discussion.

The notion that with enough functional complexity and topological fine tuning, the transducers could do the topographic work usually attributed to visual modules helps also establishing the converse notion that, with respect to sensory–motor coordination, the modules may have refined what the transducers once did or could do by themselves, which was executing topographic tasks. This line of thought is further fortified by the difficulty of drawing a sharp demarcation between where the work of the transducers ends and that of the visual modules begins. This is how I read Pylyshyn's suggestion (1984) that "the kind of process that produces what Marr calls the 'raw primal sketch' is a likely candidate for a primitive transducer function, even though it appears to be quite a complex many–one mapping from the proximal retinal stimulation to a (arguably noncombinatorial) data structure" (p. 164, pp. 214–215).

Even if vision were only computation of representations, one and perhaps the first of its tasks may still be topographic. This means that visual representations are symbolically encoded and computed for detection, recognition, and action, not primarily for thinking. Recall that the information tasks executed in primitive semantics and even in teleonomic cognition follow similar detection-theoretic principles, for the same reasons. The difference is in the complexity and scope of the information tasks involved, not in the trade offs between false positives and mortal error. This, to resume my dialogue with Fodor (1990a), is the answer to his next question:

> Why, then, isn't perception even stupider, even less inferential than it appears to be? Why doesn't it consist of literally reflexive responses to proximal stimulations? Presumably because there is so much more variability in the proximal projections that an organism's environment offers to its sensory mechanisms than there is in the distal environment itself. This kind of variability is by definition irrelevant if it is the distal environment that you care about—which of course it almost always is. So the function of perception [vision?] . . . is to propose to thought a representation of the world from which such irrelevant variability has been effectively filtered. What perceptual systems typically 'know about' is how to infer current distal layouts from proximal stimulations. (pp. 202–203)[5]

That's it! The key information task is semantic, and that is good not only for thought but also for action. Action, too, not only thought, can benefit from "a representation of the world from which such irrelevant variability has been effectively filtered." And action comes evolutionarily first. The order in which we have considered several forms of guidance to goal marks a progress in distal triangulation, including semantic triangulation. So far in our story, the organisms benefitting from these forms of guidance utilize the fruits of triangulation only for behavior. Most animals (sugar-loving bacteria and other what-you-sense-is-what-you-eat organisms excepted) are vitally interested in their distal ecology, not in the variability of proximal projections, and for the same reasons humans are; it is just that most of them have not got the

[5]The reader may have guessed that Fodor's notion of inference (and inferential) is my notion of computation (and computational). I reserve the notion of inference for the central utilization of representations involved in mental guidance. It is worth pointing out that modular computations of data have been portrayed by computational theorists (Chomsky, Fodor, Marr, and many others) as being inductive and involving the formation and confirmation of hypotheses, as they generalize and go beyond the input. Again, although quite legitimate and warranted by the facts, this is a sense of induction involved in production (computational induction), not the utilization of representations, and thus different from the one (cogitative induction) I use in the next chapter.

resources to do it our way. This goes to show, as Fodor's reasoning has suggested, that the representations computed by the visual modules first enhance the semantic ability of an organism to register and engage its distal ecology, primarily for behavioral purposes, *whatever else* the modules do on the side, as a result of later variations elsewhere on the cognitive chromosomes.

There appears to be a consensus among the theorists of computational vision that the information tasks of early vision (picking up and encoding the components and preliminary stages of representations) are determined by the demands of higher level visual tasks (computing the low-level outputs into visual images), which in turn may be determined by categorization tasks (object and event recognition). The categorization outputs could be mapped directly into behavior-to-goal routines involved in spatial navigation, locomotion, and manipulation of objects (Hildreth & Ullman, 1989, p. 610; Jackendoff, 1987, pp. 194–200; Marr, 1982, p. 326). Suppose that a part of animal and human behavior is controlled by high level visual representations directly fed into behavioral categories that are preset to convert patterns of visual representations into predetermined classes of behavioral routines. This is a case of visual images guiding behavior by virtue of how they make the world representationally available to behavior. This would be the closest that a representational semantics comes to running behavior.

The marriage between representational semantics and behavior is subject to detection-theoretic principles. The right reading of Fodor's earlier claim could go as follows. The major information task for vision is to propose to behavior—and not only, and not primarily, to thought—a representation of the world from which the irrelevant variability of the input has been effectively filtered. (Behavior would be thankful for that, and natural selection would approve.) Mapping proximal effects into distal causes is vital for any organism and concerns primarily its behavioral guidance. How the mapping is done varies a lot. One sort of mapping is computational and results in representations. If the representations issued by the computational mapping also help thought, as they do in perception, thus opening new categorization and utilization possibilities, so much the better. But this is a different matter. One should first acknowledge that there is plenty of unthinking semantic cognition in humans as in the rest of the living kingdom.

4. RE-PRESENTATION

Following the hints planted so far, particularly in my discussion of vision, let us flesh out our notion of *re-presentation*. The point is not to produce a definition of re-presentation but to illuminate the respects in which re-presentational semantics differs from primitive semantics. Crucial about representation is the fact that a complex datal structure has semantic value because its component structures have such values and are computed into the complex one for (or because of, in an evolutionary sense) the cumulative semantic effects of the computation. (For example, individual re-presentations that pick up objects and actions are combined in complex re-presentations that pick up events.) This means that in re-presentation, complex semantic tasks reduce to simpler semantic tasks. The execution of the latter helps in the execution of a large variety of complex tasks, if what is semantically specified in the simple tasks shows up in different combinations in the targets of the complex tasks. As this section begins with an official notion of re-presentation, here on I resume the normal unhyphenated use, as it will always mean re-presentation.

It helps to think of the visual representation task as a joint solution to several information problems or tasks. I first identify them and then say a few words about each. One problem is ontological, specifically ecological, and consists in finding a supply of simple distal properties and relations that can be efficiently encoded and flexibly combined so as to specify, sufficiently, most of the complex properties and relations typical of the objects (things, facts, events) of cognition and behavior. The other problems are cognitive. Two are production problems. One of them consists in reliably separating and recovering the invariant identity of the simple distal properties and relations from the proximally variable and fragmentary clues registered by the senses; this is the recovery problem. The other consists in assembling the recovered simple distal properties into complexes that are objects of cognition and behavior; we can call this the assembly problem. The representation task is a joint solution to the ecological, recovery, and assembly problems.

The outputs of the assembly processes are then fed into the categorization programs. The task of the latter is to classify the representations for use in action or thinking. If the organism is action bound and works solely with behavioral categories, its representations must be matched against a fixed set of recognition patterns. This is the matching problem. If the organism has access to concepts, then a third informational problem arises. This is the conceptualization problem, which consists in activating and connecting representations of clusters of simple properties, or of complex objects and events, for utilization in internal models of goal situations.

The first ecological problem is which distal properties, at what level of detail and in what combinations, can efficiently and reliably specify the targets of an organism's behavior. Unlike simple organisms, which care about relatively few items tracked through gross and pervasive ecological correlations, superior animals care about a large variety of types of food, enemies, and opportunities for play, cooperation, or education. It may be difficult, if not impossible, to have enough fixed and ready-made ecological pointers to all these items of interest. And even if, miraculously, such a supply of goal pointers were available, it must be so enormous and cumbersome that no preset cognitive architecture with rudimentary semantic triangulation and behavioral categorization could handle it efficiently.

What about evolving a formula (task) whereby a small number of simple and ubiquitous distal properties and relations can be consistently identified and combined to specify the ecological objects and situations of interest to the organism? It would help, for example, to isolate a few simplest geometrical properties—such as line, curve, edge, margin, contour, surface, and so on, which in various combinations form complex properties, such as volume, configuration, posture, or parts of objects—on the assumption that most visible things in the world accessible to the visual organism are made this way (Hildreth & Ullman, 1989, pp. 616–619). I call the simplest such properties, with the most widespread manifestation among the organism's goals, ecological primitives. The primitives must be relativized to the guidance equation of a given species; different species may stumble upon quite different ecological primitives.

Suppose there is a solution to the ecological problem of finding such primitives. How is cognition going to take advantage of the solution? What information problems must it solve, what tasks must it execute, in order to make the ecological solution work for the organism? This is where the other two problems of recovery and assembly show up. Because the proportions and combinations of the ecological primitives vary a lot from object to object and event to event across countless contexts of observation and behavior, programs are needed for the tasks of identifying and combining the registrations of the primitives to fit a particular object or event and guide behavior to or away from it. Distal targets then could be flexibly and constructively recalculated in terms of ecological primitives and their relations, as the context and the conditions of cognition and behavior dictate, instead of being detected wholesale by a chain of rigid patterns of distal–proximal and sensory–motor correlations. This is the assembly solution. But it cannot work without a solution to the recovery problem.

To be recalculated, the ecological primitives and their relations must first be properly registered and identified. Notoriously, the proximal stimuli are not going to deliver the ecological primitives in the most objective of forms. The visual input is light, whereas the ecological primitives are properties of what the light reveals. The ecological primitives must be read off the appropriate light patterns. This is one information subtask involved in the recovery problem. Another emerges from the fact that the light patterns themselves reveal, often poorly and variably, only fragments of the ecological primitives with which they are correlated. So another information subtask is to eliminate the variability of the sensory input, compensate for the vicissitudes of perspective, motion or illumination, and recover the ecological primitives as invariants that can be fed to the assembly programs.

As we saw earlier in this chapter, there is debate as to whether vision solves these subproblems of recovery computationally or by sophisticated compilations (complex transducers). At some point one must assume that the simplest recovery tasks are executed in a compiled fashion, with resources like those surveyed in the previous chapter. The notion of representation considered here concerns the output of the work of the recovery and assembly programs. These are production programs that assemble datal structures about ecological primitives, which are picked up by registration programs, into complex structures about objects and events.

If, then, the representation task solves the ecological, recovery, and assembly problems, it follows that a datal structure itself is a *representation* whenever it is semantically related to specific and distal objects and situations, as a result of being assembled from simpler datal structures about invariant ecological primitives, which are recovered out of sensory inputs, in order to be further categorized and utilized in some form, behavioral or cogitative. A production program is representational only if it produces representations as outputs. This characterization applies to various forms of representations, typical of various species of natural and artificial systems; in our case, they apply to depictive representations, typical of vision and possibly mental imagery, and, with further qualifications, to linguistic representations.

The representation programs are only half, the production half, of the cognitive solution to a semantic information task. The other half is the solution to the categorization task. The rationale for the representation programs is semantic in that both the recovery of ecological primitives and their assembly into behavioral or conceptual categories can be best explained as ensuring the triangulation of specific and distal targets of cognitive and behavioral significance. The mainstream view in cognitive science is that the recovery task is executed mostly by low level programs, whereby generalizing hypotheses are inductively projected from the input clues, relative to assumptions. The assembly task is executed by high level constructive programs, which recombine the registrations of the same ecological primitives (say, lines, edges, corners, and surfaces) into classes of invariant components (cylinders, simple volumes or other features) whose combinations identify various types of objects such as sticks, cats, and houses (Biederman, 1990). By analogy with language, though in a considerably weaker sense, the visual representation programs can be said to be not only productive (complexes out of simples) but also systematic or nonpunctate (Fodor, 1987, pp. 147–153). The latter feature indicates that the ability to form the representation of a locomotive is correlated intrinsically with the ability to form the representation of a table or of anything else that can be visualized. Not only are the two representations built out of a common supply of ecological primitives and assembled components under similar rules and constraints, but even some of the categorizations they rely on (solidity, density, and so on) and the utilizations they prompt (move around, don't bump into) share some of the same principles. One would not perceive a table as solid or heavy or dense unless one perceived a locomotive the same way, and conversely; if, for perceptual reasons only, one is consistently prone to bump into tables or judge them to be immaterial, one is likely to do the same with locomotives, or with God knows what else.

5. UPTAKE

Suppose that, task wise, my notion of visual representation is a plausible instance of a natural representational semantics, as opposed to the mostly conventional semantics of linguistic representation. How does it fit into the other major information tasks involved in guidance? On paper, a representational semantics of the visual sort could service behavioral categories that contain simple object and event recognition patterns and schemas, which pick up the frequent targets of the system's behavior. The behavioral categories are employed in behavioral navigation and manipulation. Such a representational vision requires neither concepts nor thinking to do its guidance job. The change from primitive semantics affects the production tasks alone. Whether evolution had shaped representers of this sort, fairly smart semantically, but dumb mentally, is a question I cannot answer.

What I can say, however, is that the notion of visual representation entails no epistemic progress or epistemic discrimination. Being a natural representer does not bring an organism closer to the way things are (whatever that means). If there were any progress of this epistemic sort, assuming one could explain it coherently, it must come from how representations are utilized in various cognitive practices culminating with science. It is a matter of goals—science has its goals—not just of means, and semantics is a matter of means, in particular of means of production. Like its primitive predecessors, the representation programs embody cognitive answers to the semantic tasks of guidance. The execution of these tasks secures a coordination between the targets of behavior and their ecological contexts, on the one hand, and the cognitive tracking of both targets and contexts, on the other hand.

If representation marks an advance, it has to do not with a truer grasp of the world, but rather with how goals, behaviors, and ecologies are coordinated. This coordination claim is about the semantic tasks involved in behavioral navigation and manipulation. It is a fact about human ecology that midsized physical objects are made of lines, edges, corners, surfaces, and volumes; it is a cognitive fact that human visual programs pick up such features of midsized objects and generate representations of them; but what brings these facts together and coordinates them is the further fact that human actions handle mostly midsized objects as the visual representations portray them.

My notion of natural representation in the service of behavior allows for other species or artifacts having representation programs different from humans'. Given different goals, differently targeted behaviors, and different ecologies, other species may have their semantic cognition pick up different ecological primitives, no less objective than ours; out of these ecological primitives representations of complex and distal states of affairs are generated that have little in common with the ones humans represent. If humans were to fly, our visual programs would have evolved ways of picking up new ecological primitives in terms that enable us to represent visually those aspects of objects and situations that display our new goals and facilitate our new behaviors. The newly represented aspects would have been no more and no less objective, no farther or closer to the truth, than the ones we actually represent as land based animals. The objects of representation are simply different. We might not be able to fancy what other forms of representations portray and what experiences they afford (the limitation made infamous by Thomas Nagel); but to the extent that they are generated by programs that execute ecological, recovery, and assembly tasks, they are representations, all right, and can be studied by a cognitive–scientific theory and perhaps even simulated on computers.

There is, finally, another reason for insisting on the possibility of natural representation, such as vision, in the service of behavior. It allows one to contemplate another guidance possibility, that of conceptualization and thinking by means of natural representations such as visual, primarily for behavioral purposes. Many are accustomed to the notion that these novel categorization and utilization tasks could be executed only with the help of the representational resources of a spoken language and for purposes that are not behavioral, such as communication, persuasion, play, science, art, pleasure. I do not think that follows. In light of recent research on ape thinking (Byrne & Whiten, 1988), it is fairly likely that evolution may have stumbled on natural representers who conceptualize and reason nonlinguistically in managing their social behavior. This evolutionary likelihood squares with my drawing board speculations about guidance; at its simplest, the mental form of guidance can accommodate this evolutionary scenario. The next chapter outlines an account of conceptualization and thinking tasks that are executable by both natural yet nonlinguistic representation architectures and by more powerful language based architectures, in both behavioral and nonbehavioral contexts.

7 Mental Guidance

In the forms of guidance surveyed so far the advances in knowledge had taken place at the production and categorization stages. Vision, in particular, brought a dramatic change in the production stage by allowing a small but versatile cognitive vocabulary to reconfigure computationally a large variety of goal relevant properties of distal objects, thus allowing new categorizations and possibly new forms of behavior. The next revolution in guidance, however, lies elsewhere. It concerns the utilization of the production and categorization outputs. This is the mental revolution.

Imagine a system that reaches its basic goals by first positing or identifying intermediate instrumental goals and reaches the latter by positing or identifying still other, more intermediate goals, and so on. Each of these exploits poses new challenges for cognition. I am not talking merely about representing the complexity of goal situations but also about framing and tracking these situations so as to extract the right information that guides to goal. These latter tasks involve mental scripting of and reasoning about goal situations. This is the job of a new form of guidance that requires the execution of radically new and vastly more complex categorization and utilization tasks, which I label conceptualization and cogitation, respectively. This is *mental guidance*; and the programs that handle it constitute *mental cognition*.

A good deal of guidance to goal now becomes mentalized.[1] To understand

---

[1]In the larger scheme of evolution, the revolution brought about by mental cognition is often portrayed as the brain having taken over some of genome's duties. Here is how a biologist, Bonner (1980), put it: "The only way some primitive animals can adapt to extreme low temperatures is by the slow appearance of genetic variants that develop more fur or more blubber; but in man

mental guidance we need to bring teleology back into our story, this time in a proximate explanatory position. This reinsertion of teleology is needed because the execution of the tasks of mental guidance requires the programs, whose operation is goal-directed, occurrently driven, and shaped by the constantly changing goals of the system, to align the system's guidance to the results of the programs' operation. In simpler forms of guidance or in the representational execution of the production tasks, the cognitive programs do not operate goal-directedly and do not have to align the organism's guidance to the results of such operation; these programs are mere functional cogs that execute limited, often psychosemantic tasks whose cumulative effect causes guidance to goal. The difference is crucial. What matters in mental guidance is how representations are categorized and utilized to individuate the information that guides to goal.

On its constructive side, the duty of this chapter in the framework of my project is to identify and argue for the proximately teleological and pragmatic properties of mental utilization. The chapter is not meant to offer an account of thinking or of the architecture of the thinking mind, although inevitably, in pursuing its objectives, it anticipates consequences for both. Its key objectives are to show that concepts are deployed in a teleopragmatic manner (section 1); that the main forms of thinking are goal scripting and reasoning with goal scripts (section 2); that the principal forms of thinking or cogitation

---

the problem is solved in a flash by donning heavy clothing. In this instance the brain has bypassed the genome. . . . The genome has produced a [device] that can now respond to selective forces with lightening speed. . . . The slow genome has, over millions of years, given birth to the rapid brain. Because they both process information, the evolved brain can now provide some of the processing that had been the sole province of the genome (pp. 30–31)." A number of philosophers have construed the same development as evolution mentalized—a spontaneous anticipation in the mental time and space of how evolution would have worked in real biological time. Popper said that to think is to let beliefs die in our stead. Instead of having natural selection treating humans as walking hypotheses ready for its brutal test, we mentally rehearse natural selection tests anytime we must. There are variations on this Popperian theme. Dennett talked of "intra-cerebral evolution" as an analogue of natural selection that allows a plastic brain to sort the functional structures appropriate to specific forms of behavior (1969, pp. 49, 52; 1991a, chap. 7). P.M. & P.S. Churchland (1983, p. 14) wrote that an organism capable of such internalized natural selection "has become so well-tuned that it seems to have an evolving world picture, rather as though the organism has tricked up an analogue of the evolutionary process itself."

Attractive as a metaphor, the notion of evolution mentalized is misleading if taken literally. Evolution starts with random genetic variations, mental cognition doesn't. Evolution neither has its own goals nor is driven by goal-directed mechanisms and processes, whereas mental cognition does represent goals, and is driven by its goal-directed programs. Evolution maximizes inclusive fitness; the mindful brain does nothing of the sort; the brain is a tool evolved in the pursuit of specific instrumental goals. Finally, the mindful brain can be neither an agent of evolution nor its psychological counterpart in the organism, because what the brain accomplishes by way of actual cognition has no genetic repercussions.

are teleopragmatic (sections 3 and 5) and involve goal scripts (section 4); and that the same is true of the mental attitudes to the information handled in thinking (section 5). There is also a speculative section (6) on the teleopragmatic dimensions of mental imagery.

On its critical side, the chapter argues that the nature of the utilization tasks in mental guidance requires abandoning the popular psychosemantic views of propositional attitudes. The pragmatic dynamics of scripting and reasoning about rapidly unfolding goal situations leaves little room for the sedate and durable relations to datal structures that psychosemanticism taxonomizes as beliefs or desires. The moral of the chapter is that it is the mental pragmatics of utilization, not the semantics of representation, which functionally runs the human psyche, and does so in a goal-directed rather than causal way (section 7). Psychosemantically construed, the notions of mental causation and of semantically pregnant structures that handle thinking by mental causation are both incoherent.

1. CONCEPTUALIZATION

Categorization is the information task that mediates between the production and utilization. I showed that animal categorization is accomplished by aligning behavioral reflexes to sensory stimulations fed into preset control values. By contrast, conceptual categorization, or *conceptualization*, allows more freedom of utilization, of thought and speech, in particular. One task that conceptualization shares with behavioral categorization is the spontaneous semantic identification of types of objects and situations. This is done at the program level by templates, prototypes, concepts, or other recognition and classification devices. Another key task of conceptualization, responsible for the flexibility of mental guidance, is to allow the access and utilization of data by various information routes, which cognitively translates into various encoding paths. The possibility of thinking depends on these two categorization tasks.

Here is an example. I can see a particular house, read or be told about it, think or image or remember it. In all these instances I may access and utilize the same cluster of house properties by different encoding and computational routes. Unlike behavioral categorization, there is no umbilical chord between conceptual categorization, the data production programs, and the representations they generate. The result is not only versatility and flexibility of data utilization but also systematic underdetermination of utilization by how the data are represented and how they cause what they do. So, no bottom–up explanation of encoding and computational rules would illuminate what is conceptualized in a particular situation and how.

Representations service concepts. A concept is activated when particular semantic distinctions are made available by appropriate representations. I recognize a particular cat as belonging to the category cat only after I have represented it as a physical object that is, say, three-dimensional, of a certain shape, size, volume, way of moving, and so forth. It is pre-conceptual (say, visual) processes that generate such representations. My notion of concept is modest. Regarded as an input or data–utilization rule (chap. 5, section 4), a concept picks up specific yet fairly invariant or prototypical properties of objects and events and links them with other such properties. My concept of cat allows me to form linkages of the form: IF [object is furry, shapely, four-legged, and simulates indifference], THEN [expect "meowing" and mild irritation if approached too vigorously]. Unlike behavioral categories, concepts have access to representations as inputs and outputs and hence to specific properties recovered invariantly and articulated combinatorially. The resulting flexibility in encoding explains how the other major task of conceptualization is effected.

That other task is to support cogitation by selecting and linking the right properties in forms apt to handle a particular goal situation. I call this task goal-adjusted categorization. When I think of a house in a concrete goal situation, I think of it in terms suited to that situation. I do not have to activate all the properties connected with my concept of house, which can literally run into hundreds. I activate only those that matter in that situation, at the right level of abstraction and detail. Likewise, if I have to make a decision on how to handle the bunch of dogs looking rather quizzically at me, all that I need is (very quickly) to access and connect the property of dog-barking with that of dog-being-friendly-because-wagging-the-tail. The resulting network aggregates only those properties that articulate an appropriate plan for action, even though each of the properties represented (being a dog, barking, tail) connects with many other properties across other conceptual networks. Conceptual categorization allows for local and economic networking while remaining open to other redeployments if the goals change. Cogitative walks through conceptual networks are determined by where we want to go (goal) and the route that gets us there. Concepts are designed to be accessed and activated as locally or extensively, concretely or abstractly, as required by the data, the tasks, and the variables of the goal situation. There are various accounts of how concepts do all these things.[2] My aim is merely to note that and how their work services the teleology of thinking in the form of goal scripting.

---

[2]See Smith and Medin (1981); Holland, Holyoak, Nisbett, and Thagard (1986); Sperber and Wilson (1986); Jackendoff (1987); and Smith (1989).

2. GOAL SCRIPTING

The information tasks of cogitation must be sequenced and executed expeditiously to keep pace with the succession of goal situations systems like ourselves face constantly. A particular cycle of cogitation, whether spontaneously or deliberately concerned with a goal situation, does not generally take much time, unless there is a sustained and extended effort of attention to deploy, maintain, and manipulate the conceptual representations needed for the tasks involved. At the cognitive level, cogitation must be serviced by some form of short-term memory where the data relevant to a goal situation are briefly held and manipulated. Given that, as a result, there is a constant competition for cogitation space and time from various input sources, what typically settles the competition depends on what is relevant to the agent's goals in a given situation at a given time (Sperber & Wilson, 1986).

The competition for cogitation resources and relevance is due not only to the fact that we monitor and handle many goal situations in rapid succession. We also create many such situations ourselves. We are goal-authors and goal-directors. This is a novel ability, absent in simpler organisms. All organisms have needs, as fixed and enduring measures of metabolic, reproductive, and other basic goals. The information tasks of their cognition consist in aligning the, typically behavioral, satisfaction of the needs to the sensorily registered conditions of the world. It is the sensory maps and the behavioral instructions that change fast, not the needs. This is not so in mental guidance, however, where the problem is to coordinate the fast changing sensory and other cognitive inputs with the succession of desires and other posited goals. The solution to that problem takes the form of mental scripts of goal situations, or *goal scripts*.

People, possibly most social animals, are natural teleopsychologists. They cannot help but see their conspecifics and themselves as being goal directed, and in particular, animated by beliefs and desires. As I suggest in the next chapter, this is because we are so programmed, for good bioevolutionary reasons. I note now that antecedently all organisms are teleocognizers, while humans are also teleocogitators. The difference is this. It has been a basic tenet of my argument, that all animals, us included, cannot help (because so programmed) but frame the situations encountered as goal situations and approach the evolutionary or immediately practical problems to be solved to satisfy goals as goal-related problems.[3] Whereas all animal teleocognizers are

[3]This is similar in spirit to the observation made by Hume and developed by Kant and later by psychologists such as Michotte that we are primed to construe physical interactions among objects, or successions of events, as causal in that we project causation onto such interactions and successions.

programmed to guide themselves to their goals, humans and possibly some species of superior apes also evolved a cogitative, not just representation-producing "computer" interposed between stimuli and responses (to paraphrase Fodor, 1990a, p. 208). The argument of this chapter is that the cogitative computer is programmed teleopragmatically to script goal situations and reason with such scripts. The scripting of and reasoning about goal situations require more cognitive sweat, as it were, and individual initiative than is involved in forming and transforming representations (a production task), for there is more access to various sources of current and stored data, more room for individual experience, and more demand for contextual and goal-sensitive adjustments of cognition and behavior.

The teleopragmatics of cogitation need not result in anarchic improvisation, as is often believed. On the contrary, a close look at the facts suggests that cogitation is managed through a disciplined sequence of tasks such as framing goal situations, representing goals, choosing solutions to the problems posed by goal satisfaction, and still others. As a matter of bioevolutionary history, it seems that most of these tasks are carried out by preset and largely dedicated programs that operate spontaneously. The account of goal scripting proposed here is not the only option, although it is a plausible one for any system that shares the objective constraints on human cognition such as limited long-term memory; a much more limited short-term memory and attention span; access to a variety of sources of data; ambitious and changing goals; incomplete inputs that force reasoning and decision programs to operate inductively and uncertainly; and, so forth.

I should note that although both the production and cogitation tasks are inductive, given the poverty of the evidence relative to what the programs need for their outputs, the difference is that the computational execution of the production tasks results in representations of distal affairs (computational induction), whereas the teleopragmatic execution of the conceptualization and cogitation tasks results in scripts of and reasonings about goal situations (cogitative induction).

A summary of the tasks required for goal scripting:

(7.1)

- Represent specific goals and sequences of goals.
- Frame a goal situation (context).
- Identify the problems posed by the satisfaction of the goal.
- Select and background the relevant data, relative to the problems.
- Make or exploit assumptions about how the given data fit the context and bear on goal identification and goal satisfaction.
- Consider explicitly, implicitly, or by default alternative solutions to the

goal problem that are consistent with the data, the context, and the assumptions.

- Activate some measure or standard of probability, plausibility, relevance, cost-benefit, and usefulness for grading the alternatives solutions, and choose one (or abstain and start again).
- If necessary, acquire new data in order to reach or further examine a solution.
- Summarize the goal script or the solution to a goal problem as output in a form utilizable by further cognitive executions of subsequent tasks (reasoning, memory storage, etc.).

This is, quite schematically, a suggestion about how the cogitative mind does its goal scripting. Often a goal script suffices to secure guidance. Yet goal scripting by itself is not the only business of cogitation. We script goal situations in order to script still others because we normally handle a goal by anticipating or formulating intermediate goals first, and so forth. This latter exploit requires reasoning. (7.1) is a schema for goal scripting, not for reasoning. The distinction will be developed in section 4. Now we explore the notion of goal script.

The task of goal scripting often involves representing new goals and not merely recognizing given goals and rehearsing one's cogitative responses to them. When the mental goal is to posit a goal for, say, behavior, the mental goal consists in forming a desire that posits a behavioral goal. This is what we do, for example, when we plan ahead: We desire to form intentions—as in desiring to form a plan for a trip—and we satisfy the former by forming the latter—the plan itself satisfies the desire that led to it. A goal script is conative when, as in this example, the goal scripted is the formation of a goal; a goal script is cognitive when the representation of a goal is already available and the scripting effort focuses on data, alternatives, and the other tasks evoked by (7.1). My analysis at this point does not discriminate between cognitive and conative scripts but will do so, to some extent, in section 5.

(7.1) is meant only as a general frame of reference. The real work is in the details one fills in by specifying the rules and instructions for the programs handling each component task. Its generality notwithstanding, (7.1) suggests that goal scripting is (a) local in scope, because the tasks handle only a goal situation at a time; (b) conceptually adjusted, as the level of abstraction and detail of the concepts used is adjusted to fit a goal situation; (c) incremental, as the articulation of the script proceeds through the execution of limited information tasks; (d) ephemeral, because an individual script of a goal situation occupies the cognitive resources only for a brief period; and (e) inductive, as goal situations and the problems they pose are normally scripted on the basis of incomplete evidence and uncertainty, which invite alternatives and force choices. These properties reflect constitutive constraints posed by the information tasks of goal scripting. The discussion of several versions of cogitation and their illustrations in the next sections also identify some of the regulative constraints that reflect the competitive pressures of time, costs and benefits, reliability, and relevance.

Goal scripting and reasoning about goal situations require, and could not have evolved without, a calculus of representation or language of thought that presupposes programs for forming and transforming representations. I treat these as production programs. For the purposes of my discussion, I do not have to assume that the mental calculus of representation is necessarily symbolic and formal, as opposed to having a connectionist or some other encoding and processing format. Furthermore, the programs handling this representation calculus are not tied and are, in fact, antecedent to a natural language. One can envisage systems (of which superior apes could be a biological version) that script goals and reason about them in a representation calculus but not in a natural language. Aside from innate concepts and learned categorizations (if any), their representation calculus will owe its semantics to the production programs of vision and sensory–motor coordination, and their cogitation will tap these resources to do its job.

The access to a natural language and its syntax and semantics is bound to modify the character of the datal and conceptual structures involved in goal scripting and reasoning, and thus the form in which the cogitation tasks are executed, but not the nature of the tasks themselves. A human may represent a goal state in English in the form of a sentence expressing a desire, whereas an ape may simply visualize a goal state or symbolize it in some other form; the subtask is the same, its program executions are not. Likewise, humans may identify or describe a goal script in English, with or without the help of commonsense psychological concepts such as belief or desire, whereas an ape may simply index a goal script in some other form, again visually or iconically.

When one accesses a natural language during goal scripting and reasoning, and particularly when one linguistically indexes or describes a goal script or reasoning, or during reflection and evaluation of their outputs, one necessarily buys into the semantics of that language. That semantics need not be the same as the semantics of vision, sensory–motor experience, or mental imagery and need not be sensitive to the teleopragmatic innards of cogitation. This is why a natural language description of a goal script or reasoning, peppered with commonsense psychological concepts and attributions, need not reveal the nature and sequencing of the tasks involved. This is also why I hesitate to use the commonsense language of propositional attitudes (beliefs, desires, etc.) in the analysis of goal scripting and reasoning, even though, when properly translated, a goal script may often amount to forming an intention or fixing a belief; reasoning may amount to moving from beliefs to other beliefs or intentions. (Because the commonsense language may easily mislead, the reader is begged to follow stoically the stipulational jargon adopted here under polemical duress. Relief from jargon is only occasional, like rest areas during a long driving.)

3. THE PROXIMATE HAND OF TELEOLOGY

Cogitation is proximately teleological, thanks to the preeminence of the informational pull of conceptualization, goal scripting, and reasoning over the psychosemantic push of the representations that animate the scripting. More precisely, cogitation is run teleologically because its programs have the task of adjusting continually to (i.e., tracking the key properties of) a goal situation, and that adjustment has functional preeminence over the causal work of the underlying production programs that feed it with representations. Through goal-adjusted conceptualization, access to various sources of data, and the goal scripting tasks envisaged in (7.1), the cogitation programs are designed to fine-tune and combine representations to provide the information needed to handle a particular goal situation. Neither the fine-tuning nor the specific articulation of the representations (i.e., which conceptual paths were taken, at what level of detail, which alternatives rejected and choices made, etc.) can be explained by the inputs that caused the representations, the computational manipulations of the representations, by the semantic properties of the representations, and the causal impact of these properties under the rules of the calculus of representation.

The contrast here is reminiscent of that noted earlier (in chap. 2, section 7) between the goal-driven task of temperature stability and the alternative programs (perspiration, vessel dilation, glandular activity, etc.) that execute the task relative to a context, the condition of the organism, the state of the other programs, and so forth. The task of cogitation is teleologically determined in the same sense, and so is therefore the design and the work of the programs for conceptualization, goal scripting, and reasoning. The temperature stability programs traffic in energy exchanges, and the cogitation programs traffic in information; yet both traffic in what they do teleologically because the tasks they are designed to execute are sensitive to the goals of the system and allow for alternative executors that are available in or best fit a goal situation.

Within cognition itself, one may look at the same contrast by means of an analogy. The calculus of visual representation, sketched in the previous chapter, makes available to cogitation the representation of a scene, just as the calculus of linguistic representation makes available to cogitation the description of a state of affairs or event. Informationally, however, cogitative perception normally focuses only on a particular segment of the scene or on an increment in the changes of scenes because only that focus may remove an uncertainty, sharpen an identification, or help with a decision. Visual attention accomplishes such a segmentation or incrementation. (We will have an extended illustration of this gambit in the next section.) Similarly, cogitation may pick up only a segment or increment of discourse to extract the information of interest for reasoning or imaging or some other task. In conversation there are subprograms such as cleft constructions or intonation contours that help marking, thus calling attention to, the flow of relevant information across the datal structures (utterances) that encode and represent it semantically. A cleft construction (e.g., "It is Guillaume that ate the scholarly book") is pragmatically utilized to specify the information of interest (that it was Guillaume and not somebody else); the semantic information about the state of affairs itself remains the same with or without the cleft emphasis. One must be prepared to accept the same story for cogitating systems (superior apes?) that have access to a calculus of representation, but not to a natural language. Their attention and emphasis programs would be different, but the tasks they execute would bear a functional resemblance to ours.

The general point, to be amply illustrated in the next sections, is that in cogitation, whatever the specific modality, representations are simultaneously or sequentially read for information that can be intelligibly individuated teleologically, relative to a goal pursued by the execution of goal-sensitive tasks, and not relative solely to the sensory inputs and subsequent representations that encode semantic information. This reading for or extraction of information is done by cogitation programs. Whatever their specific rules, these programs are capable of picking up the relevant information relations from the representations that participate in a goal script.

Recall (from chap. 3, section 3) that our analysis looks at information relations in terms of sequences of causal interactions among input, fulcrum, and uptake structures. Such triadic sequences operate at every level of ontological complexity, beginning with the physical, and take a functional turn at the biological level. With each ascent in complexity in guidance and cognition, the programs involved need be sensitive only to the form in which data are encoded, categorized, and utilized at that level of complexity. That is the trick of cognitive evolution. The functionally top-most forms of encoding, categorization, and utilization define what counts as the operative input, fulcrum, and uptake structures, hence as the cognitively effective information at a given level of processing. A cleft clause in conversation (e.g., "It was Guillaume who . . .") may encode the cognitively effective information in a goal situation, even though, necessarily, that requires successive layers of lower level tokenings of myriads of other information relations, functional and then physical. With this background reminder to help, the claim now is that in mental cognition the information that is cognitively effective for cogitation is the one whose form is shaped in and across goal scripts at that level of teleopragmatic complexity and not merely at the underlying and contributory levels of data processing, whether these latter levels pertain to vision or some other calculus of representation. This claim has a teleological foundation because its truth conditions reflect the configuration of the tasks of cogitation.

The claim has an implication for the much debated question of mental causation. I argue that it is the teleopragmatics of goal scripting and reasoning and not the underlying computational work of assembling and manipulating representations that functionally drives our cogitation. My argument has consistently focused on the types of information tasks that must be managed if cogitation is to be possible, while assuming that only the programs designed or evolved to handle those tasks could be causally efficacious by being functionally effective in handling the right information. The causal efficacy of these programs must be determined by their functional efficacy, or else everything involved in cognition, from elementary particles up, is causally efficacious in some sense. This being clarified, for mine is not an account of the programs themselves, I assume that the cogitation programs are functional by virtue of how their applications obey the instructions and constraints that are geared to execute the tasks suggested in (7.1).

I also assume that the teleopragmatic duties of the cogitation programs are reflected in the design of the control architecture that initiates new cogitation processes and behaviors whenever the right information is in. Although I have sketched the tasks whose execution configures the right information in cogitation, I have no idea of the form in which that information is encoded and summarized to be recognized and acted upon by the control architecture. If this is any consolation, a vast and evolving literature notwithstanding, I do not think that the psychosemanticist is better off on the matter of mental or cogitative causation. The reason it looks as though the psychosemanticist is better off explaining mental causation is because of the doctrinal policy of reducing utilization tasks and programs to their production counterparts. The causal–functional work of the latter is, so far, understood better than that of the utilization programs. Yet the reduction itself is a mistake I denounce and deplore many times, particularly in chapters 9 and 10.

Talking of critical delineations, I should warn the reader about differences between our account and other accounts of cogitation that look teleopragmatic but really are not. Although I have voiced sympathy for the teleological spirit of early work in cybernetics and for its theoretical imagination of seeing organisms as only one version of goal-directed and self-guided systems, my notions of cogitation in general and goal scripting in particular are not those of an internal model of the environment favored in the cybernetics literature. The notion of internal model remains too psychosemantic and reflexive for my taste, amounting almost to a copy or analog theory of cognition, and so do some recent refinements of Craik's notion of mental model (Johnson-Laird,

1983; McGinn, 1989) and even the more abstract and procedural version of mental model proposed by Holland et al. (1986).

The teleopragmatic format proposed here also bears a resemblance to the familiar model of hypothesis formation and testing in decision making and scientific inference. That familiar model has been utilized in the analysis of mental affairs by pragmatically minded philosophers and psychologists of cognition, language, and science. I am thinking not only of early pragmatists, such as Peirce or Dewey, or of Popper. There exists, more recently, a vast and specialized literature on the nuts and bolts of the pragmatics of cogitation ranging from the psychological and AI literature on problem solving and decision making to that on the pragmatics of communication, inductive inference, and the practices of explanation.[4] Fodor (1975, 1983) advocated a similar hypothesis-formation-and-testing model of thinking and used it to identify some critical limitations for a cognitive–scientific understanding of thinking, on which more in the concluding sections of chap. 10.

The key difference between my account of goal scripting and these important inductive theories is that the latter assume a sort of overarching psychosemantic task of thinking whose outputs must be veridical representations of the world. In Fodor's work, for example, the inductive travail of thinking appears to be much like that of forming a visual image or assigning grammatical structure: cogitation is viewed as production of representations. I do not see goal scripting and reasoning as resulting in representations of anything, semantically speaking, but rather as complex inferential strategies for extracting and organizing the information needed to handle goal situations.

It is true that I have indicated (as the last task in the goal scripting scheme 7.1) the need to summarize a goal script in a form that can be utilized by subsequent programs for various purposes. Although that summary could, and is likely to, be a representation of some sort, possibly with procedural import, playing a functional role in subsequent cognition (say, in memorization or activation of control), that role is for internal purposes, as it were. The summary is not a representation of the world or of a particular action or of the goal itself and therefore is not cognitively effective in that sense. I have shown that the representations of goals, actions, or other external states of affairs are formed as distinct and earlier moves in the goal scripting game outlined by (7.1). The tasks involved in their formation are different from those involved in the manufacture of the summary representation. I return in more detail to

[4]Two important monographs offer comprehensive surveys on the inductive pragmatics of cogitation. One is that of Holland et al. (1986), which generalized a good deal of psychological and AI work, the other that of Sperber and Wilson (1986), which focused on linguistic communication but had many insightful things to say about cognition in general.

this matter of summarizing goal scripts for internal consumption when I discuss (in section 5) mental attitudes such as believing.

4. COGITATION BY DIFFERENT MEANS

It is time now to put some flesh on the skeletal description of goal scripting in (7.1). The objective of this exercise is: (a) to recall and bring together some familiar facts in order to establish the teleopragmatic character of mental guidance; (b) to show that the information that guides to goal does not map systematically into the conceptual and semantic dimensions of the representations utilized to fix that information; and (c) to urge a reconsideration of mental attitudes, which has important implications for the cognitive–scientific explanation of mental cognition (see chap. 10).

Perceiving

"Our acquisition of knowledge by visual means is incremental . . . . [T]his is an extremely important but apparently overlooked feature of [epistemic] seeing." So wrote Dretske (1969, p. 93) in a splendid analysis of perception. His thesis, translated into our idiom, is that the task of perception is cogitative in that it coordinates the constantly updated visual and memory data with inferences that generate the beliefs servicing desires and plans in a goal situation.

The production (i.e., representation-generating) model of vision and the introspective as well as commonsense reports of perception have long been the standard analytic tools with which philosophers examine the work and outputs of perception. These tools are not very good at exploring the work of cogitative perception and individuating the information it makes available to further processes. The culprit is the psychosemantic tasks attributed to perception: perception as production of veridical representations. That is the task of vision. Perception is the uptake of vision, the utilization of its outputs. The fact is that the information fixed in perception is not encoded exclusively either in the visual image or in our conscious sampling of it and is certainly not revealed by ordinary reports of perception.

If I say I perceive something, the psychosemantic analyst is inclined to center the analysis around the content question of what I am said to perceive in commonsense terms. This is the wrong way to go about analyzing perception or any form of cognition, for that matter. It is wrong in general, because commonsense pronouncements may have little to do with scientific truth. It is also wrong if one does not have answers to such questions as what commonsense psychology does, what is the relation between its reports of perceptual contents and the datal structures handled in perception, or the relation between such reports and introspection. (Because most philosophical theories of perception don't bother with such distinctions and questions, I don't bother with these theories either.) Later in this chapter and in the next two, I criticize the content approach and suggest that commonsense psychology does not offer a principled description of the tasks and cogitative work of perception or other forms of mental cognition.

I should note that the cogitative tasks of perception neither entail nor exclude, as do those of vision, the influence of goals, various utilities, and memories. The influence depends on the goal situation and its task demands, and on how the cognitive work of the visual and mental programs are parsed.[5] Because perception is essential to behavioral guidance, one can expect it to have a degree of automaticity and modularization higher than other forms of mental cognition. In particular, one can expect the fixation of perceptual beliefs and their functional uptake to be fairly regimented and often mandatory. This being acknowledged, I proceed to motivate and illustrate the notion that the information tasks of perception are cogitative and that the perceptual programs are shaped by the guidance nature of these tasks.

Here is an example adapted from Dretske (1969): I want to see whether the water that Catalina said is in the pot is boiling. I go, look, and see that it is. To understand what information is being fixed by my perception, one should ask what information tasks are executed in my perceiving what I do in that context. How does my perception help me find whether the water is boiling or not? This is an uncertainty problem. Its solution is to establish which state of affairs obtains. Assumptions must be made, the informational labor divided, task responsibilities assigned, and complexities of tasks allocated. The familiar game of guidance is now played internally, mostly in the perceptual mode.

I begin with the division of informational labor. Data are needed to handle my goal situation. To get them, several information tasks must be executed by distinct but cooperative programs—some by vision, others by memory, still others by inference. The task for vision is to represent the new data about the state of the liquid. My vision executes the task by forming and categorizing the representation of a colorless liquid in the pot that is in an agitated state. The memory retrieval task is to select and provide the relevant background (nonvisual) data to which the new visual input can be added. So I retrieve the memory data that the liquid is water. These are data acquired earlier by hearing what Catalina was saying. Time now for an assumption: As I have no reason to doubt the given data, the task demands of my current goal situation do not require that I question whether the liquid I see is water or not. Vision

[5]Dretske's (1969) analysis was extremely good at locating and illustrating this division of labor and of epistemic responsibility between vision and perception, although he did not draw the distinction the way I do.

informs me that it is, but that, in the current context, is not vision's task. The water issue is settled by assumption.

My perception in the context is local and incremental, as it progresses from the liquid identity (water) to one of its properties (boiling). The concepts activated are as detailed or rough as needed by the question I must answer and the properties they access as many or few as needed for categorization. The choice between the initial alternatives (boiling versus not boiling), now settled by the new data, was made on the basis of further assumptions (i.e., what people say is generally true, what Catalina says is always true, what people see is generally what is in front of their eyes), with their measures of plausibility and probability shaped by past experience, measures that catch our attention when things go wrong. Despite the rhetoric of my presentation, all that takes place cognitively in this and so many other cases of perception is quick, spontaneous, unreflective, yet invariantly responsive to cogitation tasks such as those surveyed here.

Recalling the generic character of my discussion, note that the design of any perceptual system sharing the constraints on and the tasks of ours is likely to embody many of the program features sketched earlier. In other words, the programmer of such a system could look at my revision of Dretske's account, or at other such proposals, for suggestions as to how to write an appropriate program for cogitative perception. Contrary to mainstream philosophical trends, the programmer is not advised to look at the psychosemantic analyses of commonsense reports of perception for a similar inspiration, unless she wants to program commonsense perception talk and not perception itself.[6] The two have little in common. The aggregation of the information tasks of perception, and the dynamics of their program execution, as revealed by my story, are very unlike the static and pedantic commonsense report that I see the water is boiling or whatever. In the normal flow of discourse some of this dynamics is somewhat recovered. This is because discourse and communication are themselves forms of utilization of data for guidance to goal. It is the psychosemantic analyses of commonsense reports (of the sort '*S* believes or perceives that *p*'), when taken to describe cognition, which obscure our understanding of cogitation tasks and of the corresponding programs.

Remembering

Like perception, memory reconstruction, as opposed to spontaneous memory retrieval, is an area of cognition where there has been reluctance to acknowledge the execution of cogitation tasks. It is introspectively manifest that attempting to reconstruct a situation from memory often requires handling

[6]In fact, I argue in the next chapter, even the latter aim cannot be accomplished on the basis of the standard philosophical literature, but that is another matter.

the same cogitative tasks as those involved in perception or reasoning. There is: a goal situation (recalling a past event); a context that generates it (say, somebody asking a question); a problem to solve (how it happened or what happened); data to assemble and assume through a division of labor between perception (current input) and memory (other connected things we remember); some competing reconstructions compatible with given data; an (informal) evaluation procedure with standards of plausibility and vividness; reliance on further general assumptions (that we remember something if we saw it, that we generally remember well); and so on. As they get executed by specialized programs, these tasks guide recollection.

Just as perception relies on vision to manufacture its representations, which it then utilizes to manage its cogitative tasks, so memory reconstruction relies on memory programs to produce representations, which it then utilizes to complete its reconstruction tasks. And as the computational programs of vision execute part of the information tasks of perception, so those of memory execute in part the tasks of reconstruction. Recent research on memory shows systematic incremental interferences with what is being recalled if, for example, the given data are locally altered in some fashion. Significantly, the alteration in question goes unnoticed by the subject because it occurs as given or assumed data, which are generally outside the scope of attention.[7] This phenomenon has its communicational counterpart when speakers stress some part of the utterance as new data (the focus of the utterance) while backgrounding the rest (the topic). It turns out, as in memory recall, that incremental changes in the background data are not noticed by the hearer as his attention is focused on the new data (Clark & Clark, 1977, chap. 3). In general, the contexts where the properties of noticed-because-focused-on and not-noticed-because-assumed are displayed are those in which cogitation tasks are executed.

The reconstructive form of recall is a wise solution to the storage problem. It would be uneconomical, if not impossible, for memory to store the immense variety of representations needed to specify so many scripts of goal situations and much easier to generate such scripts by manufacturing the required representations on a need-to basis. This is not to deny that memory contains

[7]Loftus (1980, pp. 46–47) reported an experiment where subjects are shown the film of a traffic accident and are then asked misleading questions about their background data. Asked later to report on what they saw in the film, the subjects include the misleading information. Loftus' comment is, "this seems to happen because the information in the questions, whether true or false, can become integrated into the person's recollection of the event (which was visual), thereby supplementing that memory." This result can be generalized: The outputs of the execution of cogitative tasks, whatever the modality of execution, are not reliable indicators of what is going on cognitively when one perceives or recollects something. Consequently, theories of the outputs, whether commonsensical or more sophisticated, cannot be good theories of cognition.

dogmatic dossiers where data are stored as received. Still, such dogmatic dossiers, like the routine programs of reasoning or belief fixation, simplify and standardize the manufacture of mental scripts rather than store the contributing representations.

Another reason why memory is unlikely to store full blown representations of mental scripts is that memory copies decay rapidly into schematic and shallow simplifications of the originals. It is common observation that soon after one reads or hears a sentence, one tends to forget its actual wording, grammar, intonation, even cogitative context, yet retains a summarizing representation of its meaning for a longer time. Nevertheless, a summarizing representation of meaning is not mental information but rather the schematic scaffolding on which to hang and parse such information in a particular context of cogitation. It takes grammatical features such as emphasis, passive versus active constructions, cleft constructions, intonation, prior text, and surrounding context to shape the information conveyed by a sentence. The fact that these information shapers are not themselves stored is good indication that the information they shape is not stored either.

The neuroscientific evidence for reconstructive memory is also supportive. Neuroscientists have been aware for a while that the brain processes information on many parallel channels. Recent experimental evidence has shown that, for a variety of tasks, the recall programs tap a large number of widely distributed locations where data are stored. These observations point to a parallel to what Fodor (1983) said about the outputs of the production modules. Fodor called those outputs "shallow" in the sense that only their syntactic and semantic features are computed. It is, in my terms, the execution of cogitation tasks to manufacture the information that guides to some goal or solves some problem. There may be some reverse process by which memory programs strip representations of their cogitative ambiance and store them in a shallow form for later utilization. When a particular goal situation needs to be scripted, our mental programs mix the shallow outputs generated by the production and categorization modules with those stored in memory. The result is mental information.

Communicating

Animals communicate a lot. For most of them, though, communication is a strictly codified affair. Bees dance to communicate where the food is, how far from the current location of the swarm, how good it is, how effortful it is to get it, and the like. This information is encoded in dance patterns. The scout bees are programmed to code it this way and the other bees to decode it and behave appropriately. This communication game is innately set up and requires no spontaneous individual contribution, certainly no heavy thinking. The bee communication program, which is a data production program, allows for variable responses to context, and even for regimented alternatives when the sensory evidence is incomplete or poor, in which case back-up programs are activated, or when several food sites are competitively contemplated, in which case a sort of democratic contest takes place to settle the issue.

This latter accomplishment is not unlike that of vision having to "decide" between alternative readings of a scene (rabbit or duck) or having to fill in details in a poor and ambiguous picture, and also not unlike that of the language module having to settle syntactic ambiguities. In all these cases, the inductive algorithms involved do not require the execution of any cogitation tasks; the algorithms are part of the programs executing production and categorization tasks. The poverty or fragmentation of the input motivates the computational induction involved in the (modular) production of visual or grammatical representations. Computational induction is different from the cogitative induction involved in the utilization of representations in that the task of the former is psychosemantic and is executed by generating a veridical representation of some state of affairs, whereas the task of the latter is to handle a goal situation by utilizing representations in creating an appropriate goal script.[8] Animal communication relies on reflex or computational induction if it has access to computational resources, whereas human communication generally relies on cogitative induction. To give a flavor of this truth, here are a few examples.

Suppose that in an appropriate conversational situation you ask the famous Sutton why he robs banks and get the answer that this is where the money is; or ask the equally famous Grice where the closest gas station is and get the precise, short, relevant, and informative answer that it is on the second street to the right. Both ordinary reflection and psycholinguistic research show that in understanding what is being communicated, one executes some of the cogitative tasks discussed throughout this section (Clark & Clark, 1977; Sperber & Wilson, 1986). The goal of communication is typically to get or impart information, and as a result, to influence some attitude or behavior; there is a context, made visible by prior discourse or by some event shared by the communicators, that makes the information communicated relevant. Some data are backgrounded by the hearer as given (from memory, context, things already said), and suitable assumptions are made (for instance, that Sutton needs money and has a problem finding it; that one needs a gas station to buy gas to run the car, etc.). Alternative interpretations of what is communicated are considered explicitly or by default; some relevance and

[8]Sperber and Wilson (1986) made a very good case that human communication requires cogitation—inference, as they call it—as opposed to mere decoding, which, in our terms, would be a production–categorization rather than utilization task.

plausibility measures help in choosing the appropriate interpretation; the result is then packaged in an output form that can be integrated in the flow of communication as well as that of further reasoning.

Communication also makes clear that typically what is communicated (the information fixed in communication for definite interlocutors in definite goal situations) is not necessarily and not likely to be what is represented (meant or referred to) by a particular utterance. The former is a matter of utilization, the latter of production of representations. If, arriving at your house, I say that I haven't eaten since early morning, I am not only imparting a literal meaning that individuates (truth-conditionally) a state of affairs. I said what I did in a cogitative (thoughtful) frame of mind, adopting a certain attitude and having certain expectations. You, in turn, must execute some cogitation tasks to recover from my utterance not only the literal meaning but also its pragmatic intention because the latter reveals my attitudes and expectations and therefore guides your behavior toward me. In saying what I did I have revealed certain implicatures, to use Grice's term, which must be reconstructed by executing appropriate cogitation tasks. To figure out what I meant by what I uttered, it suffices that you compute the grammatical and conceptual structure of my utterance. To figure out what I said (the proposition expressed), you need to attach the literal meaning in question to the actual facts of the context of my utterance and thus recover the truth conditions of my utterance. These are basically production and categorization tasks. But that is still not what I communicated to you by using the utterance with that meaning and proposition (Sperber & Wilson, 1986; Recanati, 1989). The information communicated also includes implicatures, assumptions, and attitudes. To identify them, you need to execute a number of cogitation tasks under various constraints, including the ones made famous by Grice: Be as informative as is needed; be relevant; tell what you are justified in believing to be true; be brief, orderly, avoid obscurity; and the like. Communicative animals are designed by evolution to obey such maxims; humans are too, but we also have cogitative choices.

Reasoning

So far I have surveyed modalities in which representations are utilized inductively and pragmatically to script goal situations. Typically, these modalities work in mutual interaction. And, almost as typically, they end up servicing a still further teleopragmatic modality that handles such tasks as problem solving, decision making, planning—in a word, reasoning. The cogitative picture of reasoning is subjectively accessible when one watches herself deciding and planning on a course of action or working one's way toward an intellectual position, explanation, the next chess move, verbalizing how to get the stubborn cat home, step by patient step.[9] What is accessible is normally deliberate, not spontaneous reasoning.

Perceiving, imagining, or communicating, by themselves or in combination, are primarily modalities of scripting specific goal situations, whereas reasoning consists in calculating one's way through sequences of goal situations scripted perceptually, communicationally, or in some other fashion. Reasoning operates on and with goal scripts. If reasoning itself results in a script of a goal situation, as it often does, it is after having scripted prior and intermediate goal situations. Perception, recall, and communication work teleopragmatically because they script goal situations relative to the demands of the context, by interacting with other cognitive modalities and having access to their data bases. To that extent, their inductive manipulation of representations is pragmatic and cognitively penetrable. The same is true of reasoning. The difference is one of tasks. That translates into a difference in computational resources and their domains of application.

Whereas perception integrates current input with available memory data under some appropriate categorization, reasoning operates on the resulting integration itself, as goal script, and in fact operates on several such integrations. Perception or memory recall rely on programs that integrate representations to extract the information needed to script of a goal situation. The outcome of goal scripting is a mental attitude (thought, belief, desire, plan). Reasoning requires programs for metarepresentation. Reasoning operates on or with mental attitudes. Belief or thought fixation is an outcome of goal scripting; inferring one belief from several others is a case of reasoning. Yet, I hasten to add, I do not want to phrase the analysis in such commonsense psychological terms because their official semantics does not and is not meant to capture the innards of cogitation, which is precisely my intention. The next section explains this caution. Just as a perceptual or belief description in commonsense English is unlikely to reveal the work of goal scripting involved in forming a perception or belief, so a description of reasoning in commonsense English is unlikely to reveal that and how reasoning works with goal scripts.

Reasoning is meta-representational or rather meta-scriptic in that it ranges over goal scripts. Think of chess playing as a classic though impoverished example of reasoning: Current perception and mental imaging provide the raw or first level cogitative material in the form of goal scripts for specific moves that are anticipated; reasoning is the second level calculation and evaluation of optional sequences of individual goal scripts in terms of further

[9]There is a vast professional literature on reasoning, from cognitive psychology to formal decision theory, philosophy of science, inductive logic, and artificial intelligence, which contains many important insights and models. For representative monographs and surveys, see Levi (1967), Fodor (1975), Bogdan (1976), Hintikka (1976), and Holland, et al. (1986).

implications, costs, benefits, probabilities of certain developments, and the like. The politician reasoning about her next moves in parliament or the philosopher thinking how to answer a counter-argument illustrates the same pattern.

Given the difference between goal scripting and reasoning, one can imagine systems capable of perception, memory recall, or even imagination, as forms of goal scripting, but not of reasoning. The reasoning tasks require resources for meta-representation that simpler goal scripters may not have. It is possible that those resources depend on the evolution of superior intelligence and a calculus of representation, such as a natural language, which is publicly and externally accessible through conventional symbols. In other words, one should be open to the possibility of first-order goal scripters and second-order reasoners as cogitators. I assume that humans are of the latter sort, although many of the things to be said next about mental attitudes are true of exclusive goal scripters as well.

5. MENTAL ATTITUDES

If my account of the tasks of cogitation is plausible, then, at the cognitive level, the programs involved must be regarded as teleopragmatic rather than psychosemantic, for the tasks they carry out concern goal situations and do not merely represent facts about the world. Individual representations employed in a goal script may be, and many are, the outputs of programs executing semantic tasks of production or categorization. For example, a representation involved in a goal script may be the image of an object, while another may be the memory of an event. Both types of representations may have a semantic function in the script: to represent and thus make certain facts available to the agent's thinking. Yet the semantic information conveyed by these representations is only part of the script the agent constructs to handle a goal situation, hence only a part of the pragmatic information fixed by the script. As a result, the semantic information delivered by representations singly or collectively is rarely if ever sufficient for an agent's knowledge in a goal situation.

Another implication of my account (previewed in chap. 3, section 4) is that the teleopragmatic information provided by a goal script typically is not encoded in a single and isolated datal structure. Nor is that information typically encoded and stored durably as long lasting datal structures. Except for the most routinized contexts of guidance, mental cognition is shaped and run by goal scripts and reasoning chains that make the information available to further processes on an occurrent, need-to, and short-term basis.

As noted earlier in this chapter, the reason neither individual nor durable datal structures convey the information shaped in a goal script is that the execution of cogitation tasks requires the extraction of information from a variety of sources through the brief activation and aggregation of sensory and memory data, and the concomitant backgrounding of assumptions, default alternatives, data from previous scripts, and so on. There is no way in which this cumulative information can be encapsulated by an individual and durable datal structure. Some elements of a goal script, such as assumptions and default alternatives, may not even be instantiated datally anywhere in the system. They resemble the uncognized ecological assumptions built into or assumed by the design of any organism; yet, like the latter, the former are needed to explain proximately the informational configurations at work in a goal script. Once a particular script has done its work, it's gone. One may keep track of it in some form (say, that of a summary), but that form no longer contains live information—that is, information in an *occurrent* sense, which, according to the argument of chapter 3, is the only sense there is, and certainly the only sense in which information can be functionally efficacious. The utilization programs are designed to manipulate representations in forms that fit particular goal situations. As the goal situations change constantly, so do the representations and the scripts they animate.

These features of cogitation force a rethinking of the conception of single and durable mental states with functional significance in cognition and behavior. The most affected are the notions of thought, belief, and desire, stylishly called by philosophers *propositional attitudes*. A propositional attitude is said to contain an attitude part and a content (proposition) part. The standard view is that the notion of attitude (believing, desiring, thinking) identifies either the type of relation an agent has to some data or the type of data processing. The attitude is typically analyzed either in terms of the causal or functional role of the data or in the (operating system) terms of underlying dispositions, storage facilities (e.g., a belief or desire box). The notion of content is meant to identify the data so attitudinized, either in semantic terms (propositions, objects and properties, situations, possible worlds) or in terms of expressions in a natural language or some other (e.g., inner) code.

It is common observation that organisms have desires and act to satisfy them by forming beliefs about their situation in the world. The problem is to accommodate this observation into my frame of analysis without importing either unwanted assumptions of commonsense psychology or the biased philosophical reconstructions of the commonsense notions, typically, in the form of psychosemantic theories of propositional attitudes. The conspiracy between a misconstrual of commonsense psychology and a biased philosophical agenda can be detrimental if not fatal to understanding mental cognition. Not only does commonsense psychology appear to posit principled types of individual and durable states at work in our cogitative heads, but philosophical fashion has it that these types are the very same propositional attitudes concocted by philosophers as reconstructions of the commonsense wisdom. As a result, the propositional attitudes are realistically projected on the cognitive mind in the form of functionally efficacious processes and states produced by appropriate programs.

I think that this conspiracy should be resisted. The mental attitudes of cogitation should be distinguished from the propositional attitudes of commonsense psychology as having different domains of application. I examine in this section only the mental attitudes, while leaving for the next chapter the genuine but still unanalysed commonsense psychological notions of propositional attitudes. When confusion is imminent, I characterize the former as cogitative and the latter as commonsensical. I begin my analysis of mental attitudes with some technical distinctions.

I introduce the notion of internal *goal indicator* to capture the tasks involved in goal identification and in marshalling the processes aimed at goal satisfaction. I distinguish three types of goal indicators: goal promoters, goal allocators, and goal informants or representers. The notion of *goal promoter* defines the tasks that induce or motivate or otherwise determine organisms to pursue and satisfy their goals. The programs that handle these tasks are mostly physiological; we taxonomize them as urges, instincts, needs, wants, affects, pleasures, and the like. *Goal allocators*, such as moods and emotions, have the tasks of calibrating and adjusting the organism's attitudes and responses to the various behavioral, social or internal challenges (de Sousa, 1984; Tooby & Cosmides, 1990).

Finally, the notion of *goal informants* (or ends-in-view) define the task of providing information about goals, either in a cognitive mode, as *beliefs*, or typically in a conative mode, as *desires*, or, when the contemplated action is also factored in, as *intentions*. For simplicity, I take desires to cover the domain of intentions as well. A goal informant typically is indexed by a representation whose job is to summarize the conative information shaped in a goal script. If this is understood, then a goal informant can also be called a goal representer. This nuance must be understood because, as noted previously, most often a desire comes to represent a goal as a result of a conative script or reasoning. Only basic goals lock automatically, hence noncogitatively, into fixed desires but then those fixed desires merely express goal promoters or allocators. Generally, however, desires are more complex pragmatic creatures. Given this analytic background, the following is a suggestion for a teleopragmatic account of *mental attitudes*.

Desire and Belief

Desires come first because, like all organisms, humans are goal-directed, and desires either inform about goals (goal informants) or else express goal promoters, such as needs and drives, or even goal allocators, such as moods and emotions.[10] In the informing posture, desires project real or possible outcomes of cogitation (finding a solution to a problem), of action (eating something or reaching a destination), or of social initiative (quiet in the neighborhood or, almost as difficult, world peace). In the expressing posture, desires give a goal promoter (e.g., a need) a representation adequate to a specific situation and action. The representation of the need, which need not be linguistic, is such as to effect an alignment of the need to the agent's cognitive condition and possible actions. For example, thirst as need for liquid, can be represented by a desire for not too cold soda, given data about what is available, past experience with very cold or flat beverages, and so on.

Central to the notion of desire is the alignment of an internal goal indicator (representer, promoter, or allocator) to an actual or possible action or plan for action in a given situation. Getting such an alignment is the task executed by our conative goal scripts and their desire programs. The task cannot be executed without information about the goal situation and the agent's position in it. This is where beliefs come into the picture. A belief attitude can be construed as the output of belief programs whose task is to align the representation of a goal (desire) to the conditions of the world and of action, as revealed in the script of the goal situation by input, memory, and reasoning. Phrased in task talk, beliefs coordinate desires (the agent's primary teleology) with the conditions of the world and the actions mentally scripted by the agent.

How should one individuate desires and beliefs? Assuming this is a metapsychological, not commonsense, question, one must go back to goal scripts, and regard a belief-fixation program as being involved in the execution of several scripting tasks (call them belief tasks), such as selecting and backgrounding data relevant to a goal situation, making or exploiting assumptions, considering alternatives, grading their plausibility, looking for new data if needed. It would matter for their individuation whether the beliefs and desires result from mere goal scripting, as they do in perception and often memory recall or simple communication, or from executing more complex and extended reasoning tasks through a sequence of goal scripts. I suppose that, strictly speaking, plans and intentions must be reasoning-based desires, just as hypotheses or conclusions must be reasoning-based beliefs. Whether the attitudinal programs work in simpler goal scripting or more complex

---

[10]A fellow teleologist, Colin McGinn (1989), put this point very well: "beliefs exist in order to help organisms satisfy their desires, and hence their needs. . . . [D]esire is the more basic propositional attitude, theoretically and developmentally. And desire is where teleology gets its initial grip on minds. Accordingly, artificial intelligence [and all the sciences of cognition, I would add] should start with desire and work out from there to thought. Intentionality begins with wanting, I suggest, not with thinking. To simulate [and understand, I would add] intentionality properly you need to simulate the entire biological system in which it is found, not attempt to slice off the cognitive part and hope to find real intentionality in that part considered by itself "(p. 155).

reasoning environments, the question is how to identify and describe their work.

The predicament is particularly obvious in practical contexts where goal scripts guide action. Consider the case of simulational and nonpropositional models (Johnson-Laird, 1983; McGinn, 1989) where a verbal description of what is believed cannot possibly capture the actual execution of the belief tasks or the outcome of that execution. How does one conceptually parse and put in words what data are assumed and/or backgrounded and what alternatives are contemplated and rejected, when, for instance, I imagine and reason about my jumping the fence, avoiding the bush, and climbing the wall to rescue my postmodernist parakeet? And what about goal scripts that involve a discursive execution of cogitation tasks, or contexts where, literally talking to oneself, one must decide one course of action over another?

We can summarize part or even the whole work of the belief programs in some symbol intended for private consumption (the final task of goal scripting in 7.1) such as storing the output of the belief programs in an appropriate memory file for further use in learning or transfer to other scripts of similar goal situations. The summary can also take the form of some sound bite intended for public consumption (belief reports) such as referring to, talking about, reconstructing, or evaluating the work of some belief program. The public report may even index the private summary and share with it some functions, such as memory storage. This being acknowledged, I deny that a private summary or public report can capture an identifiable datal structure that does the belief work in a goal script and is functionally efficacious, qua belief, by virtue of what it represents. I deny, in particular, that what the private summary or the public report describe is what the technical notion of propositional attitude is all about. A belief in a goal script is no simple datal structure to be individuated by a propositional attitude report, although that report may portray the work of belief programs for various purposes. I made earlier the same point about desire.

One such purpose may be the public reconstruction of one's goal script. For example, the attribution that she believes that her car was parked around the corner may be used to reconstruct her mental script of the situation, in particular the belief ingredients of the script: what she assumed generally; what she assumed specifically; what she remembered; what alternatives she ruled in and out; and so on. These reconstructions are important when one justifies the attribution or explore its implications. Such an attribution is different from burdening her with the precise mental tokening of the attributed content clause (that the car was parked around the corner) in the form of a specific datal structure with the functional duties of belief.

This is not the only counterintuitive feature of my notion of belief, in case the reader's intuitions have been excessively trained by commonsense psychology and psychosemanticism. Another feature, already evoked by my argument, is that the notions of belief and desire identify occurrent, ephemeral, and script sensitive types of mental patterns. This is because goal scripts and reasonings are manufactured in particular contexts of cogitation, relative to particular goal situations. It follows that in the absence of cogitation there are no tasks to be executed and hence no desires and beliefs programs at work, none whatsoever in my sense of the term. And if no such programs are at work, then no beliefs or desires exist as datal structures with functional jobs.

What about the sense in which one has durable and context-invariant beliefs and desires, so many of them? One is reminded of the question, asked in chapter 3, section 4, whether information is stored durably in some individual structure (DNA, audio tape, whatever). In terms of the notion of information I propose the answer is negative. But before we apply the answer to the question at hand, about beliefs and desires, further disambiguation is in order. Am I asking a commonsense psychological question or a metapsychological question? Neither question, I take it, is about believing and desiring as mental programs or capabilities, as opposed to particular program outputs, which are now being examined. For if the former were intended, then surely one has enduring and context-free program capabilities to attitudinize (i.e., acquire, background, and assume data, measure their probability, and other such tasks) and act on mental information.[11] These are no different from other program capabilities. Humans have, for example, durable program capabilities to register and react to pain, or to form mental images; nevertheless, these durable capabilities are exercised only intermittently, in appropriate conditions. Pain registration and reaction to pain or mental images are occurrent or performance outputs generated by the respective programs. Ordinarily, we do not store pains or reactions to pain or mental images durably. Moreover, the occurrent properties of the pain or image depend essentially on the context of their instantiation and on the interactions with the outputs of other programs. This is why a look at a particular program would not reveal everything about its output (pain, reaction, image), particularly in cogitation where the context of instantiation or the interactions among programs are not preprogrammed. The same is true of believing and desiring. One believes and desires by necessity, occurrently and briefly; the programs are intermittently active and fine-tuned to the context of operation (goal situation).

But when there is the need for durable beliefs, as it must be, aren't the specific contents attitudinized the same way, for a long time, perhaps a lifetime? Isn't commonsense right about my having believed for a long, long

[11]Notice that the commonsense psychological notion of attitude, like my notion of belief or desire program, is a summary of several subprograms or capacities. Strictly speaking, there is nothing specific and homogeneous in an organism's cognition that would be picked up by the notion of attitude.

time that 2 + 2 = 4, that the sun rises everyday, or that my deaf grandmother always prepared superb papanashi? The question now is not whether commonsense is right about these durable beliefs (surely it is), but rather what exactly it is right about? No doubt, I remember these facts and many others. Therefore, I must have stored their representations in my memory in some form—so far so uncontroversial. I have no idea how this is done, and in what form it is done, nor has commonsense. It isn't obvious, in particular, that the data in question are stored in the very form that I recall and report them now. What is obvious is that whenever the cogitation context requires that I recover the information that 2 + 2 = 4, I do it on the basis of my memory data, no matter how the data are stored and retrieved. There are two claims being made here. One acknowledges that the occurrently manufactured information to the effect that 2 + 2 = 4 is recovered from durable memory data. A different claim is that what I believe, when asked whether 2 + 2 = 4, is (type) identical with the memory data from which I manufacture an answer in an appropriate goal script. The former claim is true; the latter is not.

Before examining and defending these answers, I hasten to note that 2 + 2 = 4 is not a very good example. It is used so often, almost as an intellectual reflex, particularly by philosophers, that it would not be surprising if, for economy, our memory stores the inscription in question in the right conceptual file, and recovers it automatically by accessing the file. A good number of datal structures, visual and linguistic, might be stored either in a nearly explicit form or else recovered fast from some efficient storage system, perhaps similar to that of the visual and sound shapes of words. I don't discount the possibility that such memorized structures are stored in a special belief box or address or are filed with an appropriate label signifying [BELIEVE WHAT FOLLOWS or WHAT IS STORED NEXT], or something along these lines. The information believed was once manufactured and learned in a context of cogitation (e.g., in the third session of arithmetic in kindergarten), then attached to such a label or address, and filed forever in a doxastic dossier specializing in storing dogmas. A good deal of learning would have to depend on such dogmatic procedures of storage and retrieval. Because they dogmatize information, such procedures would count as attitudes of some enduring sort. Does it follow that what is stored in a dogmatic dossier is the belief that 2 + 2 = 4?

Almost, but not quite. For even if a procedure like [ALWAYS BELIEVE that *p*] is explicitly stored in my dogmatic dossier, it is still stored as a virtual rather than active sort of belief. Let us say that a belief is virtual if the datal structure is stored in a dossier or at an address where the contents, when activated, are always believed *as* stored. This sort of belief is virtual because it is unactivated and hence functionless. If activated, the virtual belief becomes real when it is cognitively instantiated on the mental space of cogitation where, given its dogmatic credentials, and assuming other things to be equal, it goes automatically in an active belief position. This means, operationally, that a number of program instructions for the normal belief tasks involved in goal scripting, such as backgrounding and assuming data, selecting alternatives, and evaluating the datal structure under consideration, are told that all is well and shouldn't bother. Even then, the cognitive reality of a virtual belief emerges only in active cogitation, teleopragmatically.

Yet the context of cogitation can still make a difference, even for virtual beliefs of the dogmatic sort, when other things happen not to be equal. Suppose that the competing alternatives range over new and wild candidates, or that the plausibility comparisons change, or that new assumptions are entered. If, to take a Cartesian hint, the alternative of Satan's manipulating my mental representations becomes serious, my virtual belief that $2 + 2 = 4$ may be up for reevaluation when it shows up for active duty. Virtual beliefs must struggle to become functional beliefs in an actual cogitation, and the outcome is not necessarily preordained.

The standard view of belief, attempting to combine the requirements of commonsense attributions (such as long standing beliefs with fully specified contents) and those of psychology (datal structures functionally active in cognition and behavior), is thus confronted with a choice: The datal structures may be stored as virtual beliefs, in which case they have no functional efficacy, no interaction with anything; otherwise, they become actual beliefs only when doing occurrent work in a goal script, in which case their information and functional impact are shaped teleopragmatically by the execution of the inductive tasks of cogitation and not solely by what was stored in memory.

Tacit Belief

Most durable beliefs are not stored and do not work this dogmatic way. Let me approach their condition from the standpoint of what philosophers have come to call tacit belief (Lycan, 1986). Do I believe that 465 is larger than 2 or that a house is larger than a chair? Now that I ask myself the questions and quickly go through the cogitative moves required to script an answer mentally, I determine that, yes, I do. Did I believe these truths two minutes ago, before I asked myself the questions? Or fourteen years ago? Did I believe them explicitly? Not likely. I do not recall that the representation that 465 is larger than 2, in this or any other form, was ever copied by my memory because it was never sent there. I had never thought of it before. And even if I once formed it, I trust an efficiency device in my memory discarded it after a while, as it probably does with most occurrent representations.

Do (did) I believe that 465 is larger than 2 implicitly or tacitly? What would that mean? That I believe it as a potential but never represented (never stored) implication of some basic truths of arithmetic whose representations I store in my dogmatic dossier and thus virtually believe? This won't do. First, it is not theoretically wise to extend the notion of belief to unrepresented logical implications of stored datal structures for the simple reason that something unrepresented cannot convey information while our notion of belief is intended to conceptualize an attitude to actual information. As I've shown, even something represented is not enough, just by being represented, to convey information in cogitation. Second, even if I decide to extend belief tacitly to unattended logical implications, as many philosophers urge, I should acknowledge that the decision is motivated on syntactic and semantic grounds, which do not necessarily reflect the teleopragmatic constraints on mental information.

Syntactic and semantic constraints underdetermine the mental information that is attitudinized as belief. I can, for example, communicate different items of information by shifting the emphasis in an utterance whose syntactic form and semantic values remain the same. I can say, "Guillaume ate the *book*," meaning that our postmodernist parakeet choose the book this time, as opposed to the table or anything else made of matter; I can say, "Guillaume *ate* the book," as opposed to dropping on it, which is another habit of hers. The emphasis opens up different informational spaces where the tasks of cogitation (new and given data, assumptions, competing alternatives, etc.) are differently executed. Yet in both cases the syntax and semantics of the utterance stay the same, which is as it should be, given that the fact represented remains the same; my cognitive interest in it, given the information it conveys in different contexts, varies.

On most occasions, one is not interested in representing facts as such but rather in having their representations convey information relevant to a goal situation. If the notion of proposition or content is technically intended to capture the representation of facts, as I think it is, then this is further evidence that the notion of propositional attitude is not the right explication of cogitative belief. The notions of logical implication or logical closure, sensitive to syntactic structure, the facts semantically represented, and the truth values of representations, are too coarsely grained to track the information associated with our chains of beliefs and goal scripts generally (Dretske, 1969, 1972; Bogdan, 1985a, 1986b).

There is a vast linguistic and philosophical literature on the topic of stress or emphasis and its pragmatic, as opposed to syntactic and semantic, parsing of the information conveyed in discourse (Clark & Clark, 1977; Dretske, 1972; Sperber & Wilson, 1986; Bogdan, 1987). I think the pragmatic parsing reflects how one scripts and reasons about goal situations. The pragmatics of communication reflects the teleopragmatics of mentation. When construed solely as syntactic and semantic creatures (representations of facts), beliefs convey as much information as do unemphasized and decontextualized strings of words, which is very little information. Commonsense psychology is concerned with how beliefs and other attitudes represent facts and with the logical implications of beliefs, including those of tacit beliefs; this concern shows that its notion of belief does not describe mental cognition and the information it handles and has other functions than a realistic psychological taxonomy and explanation. If, as I suggest in the next chapter, the commonsense psychologist is mostly interested in how the world is, given what an informant says or how he behaves and what follows from that, then it makes sense for her to focus on the informant's representations of the worldly facts. The semantic interest is warranted in this case; yet, by the same token, the semantic interest, captured by the notion of content, betrays indifference to how cogitation works and how goal situations are actually scripted by the informant. If the commonsense notion of belief is construed semantically, then surely belief is not cogitative belief.

How, then, should one think of my current cogitative belief that 465 is larger than 2? Simply as the convenient and canonically formulated summary of the information occurrently manufactured and scripted in the context of cogitation generated by the question asked a few paragraphs ago. What about my alleged belief that 465 is larger than 2 before I entertained it? The answer is more like that about dogmatic and virtual beliefs. Before entertaining it, the representation that 465 is larger than 2 was not a belief in any cognitively robust sense that relates an attitude to mental information, where the notion of attitude paraphrases the program instructions that configure the information in question. This is not to deny that on the attitude side of the belief equation there may be a special class of dispositions (subprograms) to recover from stored datal structures and to manufacture a type of mental information that is automatically attitudinized (treated "believingly") solely by virtue of how it was recovered and from what sort of data, without appeal to other data. Whereas the virtual belief that 2 + 2 = 4 was stored as such in a dogmatic file, the tacit belief that 465 is larger than 2 is retrieved by dogmatic means, deductively. This hint of analyticity is all I can see in and recover from the notion of tacit belief.

I sum up my discussion of mental attitudes by answering an objection that the philosopher is very likely to raise. "Haven't you given us all along," she would say, "an account of belief fixation but not of belief itself, of what it is to believe or to have a belief?" The genesis of a belief may be teleopragmatic but that is surely different from the intrinsic nature of belief; likewise, for other mental attitudes. The philosopher would argue that I have given no account of these latter features.

Quite so, I answer. Mine is an account of belief fixation, more exactly, of the belief programs at work in goal scripting and reasoning. And, the account claims, this is all there is to believing, namely, its occurrent and cogitative fixation, even when borderline cases of dogmatic, tacit, and virtual beliefs are contemplated. As far as I am concerned, the objection begs the very question at hand. The objector assumes what she must prove, and I have tried to disprove, namely, the principled distinction between fixing and having a belief. This is a distinction without an explanatory difference. In her talk of belief, the objector makes two presuppositions that are not mine. One is the psychosemantic presupposition that the commonsense psychological concept of belief picks up real datal structures in the head that are functional in virtue of their content (what they represent), in which case, of course, those datal structures would be different from their formation. The other presupposition is that ingredients of the belief recipe such as memory data, input data, items in dogmatic dossiers, and the like, are the beliefs themselves, that is, the outputs of the programs that participate in goal scripting and reasoning. I have argued at length against both presuppositions.

Does it also follow from my account that no two beliefs formed in one head at different times or in different heads are ever the same? It depends. Sameness is an aspect-relative notion. If the belief programs in goal scripting or reasoning produce the same outputs from similar inputs (sensory data, memory data, dogmatic dossiers, and so on), then different belief tokens could be similar—a rather unlikely but not impossible event. If we ask the same question in commonsense psychological terms, then we shift the aspects that count in similarity. For in the commonsense framework, the aspects of interest are robustly semantic (e.g., how is the world, given what the informant believes or how he behaves), and hence much more coarsely grained than their teleopragmatic counterparts. As a result, a similarity of beliefs, commonsensically individuated, is much more widespread, particularly because cogitative idiosyncrasies are deliberately overlooked. I note, preemptively, that when one reflects or talks about his beliefs, and compares them with past beliefs or those of others, he necessarily employs the commonsense psychological framework, which is why a more coarsely grained similarity policy is at work.

The general critical upshot of this discussion is not that humans do not have occurrent and durable, explicit and implicit, or tacit or even virtual beliefs, desires, and other propositional attitudes, as commonsense psychology construes them. Surely, these commonsense notions are on to something that is insightful and explanatory. What I deny is that commonsense psychology gives us the descriptive and explanatory format in which one has, stores, and operates with and on mental attitudes such as beliefs and desires. My objector and I may be speaking two different languages without a translation manual.

6. IMAGERY AND SYMBOLIC ECOLOGIES

There is another, perhaps more marginal yet even more controversial form of cogitative utilization of representations. It is mental imagery. I could have discussed it earlier, alongside other forms of mental cognition, but decided to treat it separately, and speculatively, because mental imagery has utilization properties that raise the more offbeat issues of symbolic ecologies and of cogitation constrained by the medium of representation.

Imaging

Mental imagery utilizes representations in the execution of space-related information tasks, and to that extent it is more than a computational production of imagistic representations. Or so I want to suggest. The suggestion does not prejudge the type of representation, depictive or descriptive, involved in mental imagery. Nevertheless, I focus on the depictive type for four reasons. One is that if mental imagery historically owes some of its mechanisms and resources to topomaps and topographic vision, as is possible, and the latter have depictive outputs, then mental images are also likely to be depictive to a significant extent. A second reason is that the information tasks of mental imagery appear to have much in common with those of topmaps and topographic vision—except that the mental imagery tasks are utilization tasks whereas the latter are production or categorization tasks.

We saw that topomaps and topographic vision are involved in object tracking through space as well as in spatial navigation and possibly object recognition. One engages in mental imaging typically when the mental tasks are defined by problems requiring shape properties and other spatial relations to be made explicit as representations in order to be inspected and manipulated in virtue of their explicit form. It is a fact that such properties and relations are best and most economically read off depictive rather than descriptive representations.[12] If the organism happens to have access to depictive representations, it would be unwise not to utilize them to solve problems about shape and spatial relations.

The third reason why I want to explore depictive imagery has to do with a larger issue: The way mental images depict may reveal something interesting about how humans utilize internal symbolic ecologies to carry out cogitative tasks. Fourth and finally, like perception, mental imagery presents theoretical challenges to disengage the codification (mostly production) from the utilization tasks, when the cognitive execution of both types of tasks is depictive.

To begin with, in what sense is mental imagery a matter of utilization rather than production of representations? Mental images are not representations necessarily produced spontaneously, automatically, and rigidly, once the input is in, as are visual and linguistic representations. Mental images are outputs of cogitation, whereas visual and linguistic representations are

---

[12]I am following Kosslyn's (1990, 1981) recent work and Kirby and Kosslyn (1990).

outputs of production modules. Mental images are often deliberately and slowly constructed, under verbal or thought instructions; they can also be spontaneously articulated under the prompting of memory triggers. In either case, their construction is part of executing some cogitative task, something to figure out in a context, in order to solve a problem. As Kirby and Kosslyn (1990) note, "the generality of imagery as a means of solving problems hinges on the ability to map problems into depictions (p. 336)." Once the mapping is done and the problem solved, the mental image is gone, for gone is the need for it. It is as ephemeral as a judgment or inference or any other executor of a cogitative task, and for the same reasons. Like the latter, a mental image functionally competes for attention with other utilization processes and outputs, in addition to competing for the same visual buffer or short-term memory with the outputs of vision.

Aside from its information tasks of object recognition and object identity recall, which help categorization, mental imagery is involved in more complex tasks such as inspection of spatial relations of an object or scene; the spatial manipulation of objects as in rotation; translation of their position as when imagining in what position the bags will fit into the trunk; spatial comparison as when imagining whether the unnecessarily tall visitor will fit into your small car; simulation of motion as in wondering how a plane refuels another in midair. According to Kosslyn (1990), mental imagery is at work mostly when either the information to be recalled is a subtle, not obvious visual property; or the property to be identified has not been previously considered, labeled, and stored in an explicit format; or finally, the property in question cannot be easily derived from the stored data. These conditions of utilization explain why the imagery tasks are ad hoc and occurrent, depending on what the information problem is in a goal situation. The same conditions also explain why, relative to a task or problem, memory data are utilized in a depictive fashion to find an appropriate solution, the same way memory data are used to find solutions to various other sorts of problems, whether of decision, inference, or belief fixation. All are cases of cogitation through utilization of data.

The imagery programs that execute the tasks must have access to a basic vocabulary of symbols (e.g., points), which are constructively combined into ever more complex representations (lines, curves, shapes, figures, scenes) under rules of spatial juxtaposition. The semantics of depictive representation is defined by visual resemblance (Kirby & Kosslyn, 1990). This, again, is not that different from vision. Imagery and vision share not only key information tasks but also, as Kosslyn (1990) suggests, "some of the same processing mechanisms used in recognition, navigation, and tracking" (p. 76). Yet, whereas it is conceivable that vision is not representational (in the sense that compiled transducers could do what computational modules do, as speculated in chap. 6), it is close to inconceivable that mental imagery is merely compiled. How could I form an image from what you say, and then modify it as you change your instructions, if the underlying generative mechanisms were more like complex transducers or fixed compiled link-ups? How would that work?

What do these comparisons with vision tell us about mental imagery? The difference may be one of production (vision) versus utilization (imagery). What is special about mental imagery is that it produces representations as part of its utilization tasks, the way reasoning produces new linguistic representations as part of its utilization tasks. I can refine this suggestion and say that mental images simulate what visual representations are caused to encode. Yet simulation is not the objective of imagery; it is only the means. The objective is mental problem solving. It may not even matter much how the simulation is done, by what representational means, as long as it carries out the information task for which it was initiated.

In principle, a depictive representation has been said to be better suited than a descriptive one to encode spatial properties. Yet even in its depictive format, the imagistic simulation, unlike visual representation, is schematic, incomplete, sensitive to task and context, cognitively penetrable, and often driven by beliefs, memories, and verbal or thought instructions. This suggests that the simulation is geared to the task at hand and samples as much as is needed to do the job. This also suggests that the imagistic simulation shares with perception and reasoning a local and incremental deployment of representations, relative to some goal, background data, and assumptions contained in the verbal instructions or whatever triggered the process. Imaging seems like another form of cogitation.

There are, however, aspects of imagistic simulation that are more constrained and rigid than my discussion so far has implied. In inspecting a scene I am mentally imaging, in order to go from point A to point B, I must necessarily pass through intermediate points and do so in a certain computational sequence. Such, notoriously, is the story of mental rotation. This does not seem to be a task requirement (level two: cogitation tasks) as much as a matter of how one executes it (level three: cognitive programs). There are dimensions of execution that are beyond one's choice and control. One is stuck with the intrinsic properties of the medium of cognitive execution (representation). Here is an analogy for a task-execution medium conspiracy. Most people who have become bilingual or multilingual later in life, as opposed to early childhood, know that when they reach the cash register in a store and have to count their money, quickly, almost automatically they do it in their first, native language. Switching to another language is bound to mess up things. For the last 15 years or so, I have spoken (accented) English most of the time, have thought, and joked in English, even daydreamed in English; yet when it comes to counting, occasionally swearing, it is back to good old reassuring Romanian. Why? I don't know why, but I have a suspicion that what is going on in such cases is not that different from what is going on when I have to image my way through a space-related cogitative task. It looks like no choice.

This suspicion is worth generalizing, for it points in the direction of design constraints on mental cognition. From an evolutionary point of view, those constraints are likely to reflect durable constitutive and regulative constraints on mental guidance, more so than the shorter lived cogitative tactics one tries to learn.

Symbolic Ecologies

I have noted that mental imagery shares with visual perception not only some information tasks but some architectural resources. This would mean that imagery exploits some of the codification resources of vision to do its own job. Kosslyn (1990, p. 87; forthcoming) talks of the topographic maps on the visual cortex being among the resources thus shared. Such sharing would not only explain why vision and imagery compete for both resources and the same utilization area (the visual buffer), which is why their outputs are necessarily short-lived. It might also explain why, once the imagistic simulation is initiated, certain features of it, such as the relation between processing time involved in scanning an image and the distance to be scanned, have an inevitable deployment, outside our control. Although the information task, having to do with cogitating about some space properties, may invite such executive features of imagistic simulation, there is nothing in the task itself that would exclude its being executed by a cognitive program (say, a descriptive one), which does not necessarily instantiate the same coercive relation between distance and processing time.

So there must be something in the medium itself, in the resources employed for space simulation, that would explain the coercive relation and other architectural constraints on imagistic simulation. In particular, there must be something about the topographic maps and their spatial display that explains why imaging distance requires time. Topomaps were presented (in chap. 5, section 5) as data displays that encode spatial information about position and motion (as change in position) relative to the topological organization of the peripheral sensory space. Various functional processes access and utilize the data displayed by the topomaps in virtue of their spatial organization. The topomaps do not encode distal and specific information about anything in the world, which is why they are not semantic. The topomaps help with certain information tasks (tracking an object through space, sensory-motor coordination) once the semantic values are fixed by other means.

In imagery, the suggestion now is, such topomaps may constitute a sort of *internal symbolic ecology* that permits the simulation of the fragments of the visual world required to carry out a particular cogitation task. The visual buffer (localized in the occipital lobe), where mental images are generated, is known to contain a variety of topomaps capable of supporting imagistic representations of the depictive sort (Kirby & Kosslyn, 1990). The suggestion is that the basic symbols (points, etc.) may be deployed under spatial juxtaposition rules to form images in the internal informational ecology provided symbolically by the topographic maps. The ecology is internal because it is inside our heads; it is symbolic because the topomaps instantiate symbol structures (images), which, relative to a cogitation task, are treated as datal structures for solving a problem, drawing an inference, and so forth.

This suggestion accommodates several properties of mental imagery, not always easy to reconcile, particularly its being and not being under the individual's control. The motivation for symbol deployment is provided by some external input (thought, verbal instruction, or memory item). The output of such deployment of symbols, in the form of an image, is determined by the information task at hand (rotate an object, scan a scene). Both the motivation for engaging in imaging, and the information task executed by imaging something, are pretty much under the cognizer's control, and are influenced by her memories and beliefs—although cases where imagery is prompted involuntarily are also frequent. Once the symbol deployment is launched on a topomap, or set of such, under some information task demands, some of the properties of the imaging are rigidly determined by the medium itself. Codification, at this point, takes over cogitation. Or rather, one must cogitate the way one encodes the relevant data. The scanning of a distance, for example, requires proportionate real time as does the respective tokening of symbols on the topomap. The utilization of the symbolic ecology provided by topomaps for space simulation exacts its codification price just as the exploitation of natural ecologies by simpler minds had its inflexible price.

The suggestion may accommodate the impatient exhortation often voiced by Pylyshyn (1984) and others that what is analog (space-preserving in my example) is merely physical or derived from intrinsic properties of the hardware. Topomaps do have the property of miniaturizing or even making implicit spatial relations in their physical organization, which is why they are appropriate for space simulation; to that extent, they are indeed analog by virtue of a physical property. Topomaps by themselves are not representations. They can analogically support or instantiate depictive representations generated by processes outside topomapping. The representations are depictive because they simulate space relations, and as the simulation occurs on a topomap ecology, it is instantiated by analog means, because the symbol instantiators are physical features of the topomaps and the resulting symbol structures are topographic displays.

To conclude, then, the forms in which information is explicitly coded in a symbolic ecology put their stamp on how that information is going to be utilized in cogitation. Why, then, in some pressuring circumstances, do I execute my simplest arithmetical tasks in Romanian? It is a very old and well tested language, so it must be safe to count in it. More to the point may be the psychological fact that at a critical stage in the development of my counting abilities, the Romanian symbolization system happened to be there to provide the means for a speedy and reliable processing. With speed and reliability worth preserving in carrying out arithmetical tasks, and no other choice during that window of developmental opportunity, I may have bought into some intrinsic features of the medium of overt computation.

In general, for all its new adaptive freedom through cogitation, mental guidance is constitutively bound to exploit whatever symbolic ecologies are available for the execution of its information tasks and is also likely to be regulatively pressed to settle on those internal ecologies that provide speed, reliability, least effort, and other such advantages. In this respect, mental cognition reflects the invisible hand of the guidance equation, which, for various economical considerations, forces any form of knowledge to rely on efficient ecological signs and correlations.

7. SUMMING UP: THE TELEOPRAGMATIC PSYCHE

All forms of guidance have received an ultimate teleological explanation. For the first time, the argument of this chapter has brought teleology to bear on the proximate work of mental cognition. I have not made this proximate move in simpler forms of knowledge because their information tasks were managed by programs that, once evolved and frozen into the organism's design, did their work under causal–functional constraints. The work of the programs has a goal-directed motivation, because it contributes to guidance to goal; but it is not goal-directed because it does not posit goals and does not script patterns of guidance to them. In premental guidance, the goals of the organisms are preset by evolution and rarely initiated individually. The job of the programs is to convert sensory stimuli into the right behaviors; the conversion can be done by causal–functional means alone.

Cogitation is a different guidance game with its own teleopragmatic rules. Some of the tasks, such as desiring, planning, problem solving, are intrinsically goal-directed, which is why their execution could not be explained exclusively in causal–functional terms. This is not because the programs do not work causally, by executing myriads of functions, for they do. The proximate teleological difference, in their case, has to do with the fact that the programs have the job of setting and resetting their own parameters teleologically; this is accomplished by positing or reacting to end states to be causally brought about in some functional way, contemplating several alternative ways of doing so, choosing one and correcting or changing it, if it doesn't work, and terminating the process when the end state is instantiated.[13]

The proximate difference that teleology makes to understanding cogitation has had two major implications that are discussed and amplified in the concluding chapters 9 and 10. One implication is that the explanation of mental cognition and its outcomes (thoughts, plans, actions), although compatible with physical and neural causation, is essentially goal-sensitive, not cause-sensitive. Under the causal impact of the environment, humans have and/or posit goals, pursue, and are guided to them by causal–functional means. But how we choose the goals and handle them conatively and cognitively is not causally predetermined, as is in simpler organisms. This is why, wisely, the commonsense explanation of cognition and behavior is primarily teleological or outcome-oriented and only secondarily attempts, when necessary, to reconstruct which causal–functional path was chosen by an agent in the pursuit and satisfaction of a goal. The next chapter addresses this matter, albeit too briefly. How cognitive science can handle or mishandle such explanations is a topic we worry about in chapter 10.

Another major implication, following from the first, goes against the idea that the cogitative mind has only psychosemantic tasks, and that semantics runs its programs. A psychosemantic task consists in causally converting the registration of the way the world is into an appropriate behavior. Because, as I have shown, such causal moves play only a secondary role in the game of cogitation, after the teleopragmatic rules has been set up, it is no wonder that a systematic mismatch can be found between semantic (production) and mental (categorization and utilization) tasks, between the respective forms of information relations, between semantic force and pragmatic efficacy, and between what datal structures represent and the information needed to categorize and script goal situations. This is why mental information is not semantic, and why it cannot be functionally efficacious in virtue of just being semantic. The properties in virtue of which the information in a goal script is functionally efficacious are not type identical with the properties in virtue of which the component datal structures are semantic. This is a difference reflected by the programs involved, and is due in turn to a difference in the information tasks they execute. The task demands under which representations are formed and manipulated are semantic, for they are geared to recovering and assembling specific and distal aspects of cognitive and behavioral interest, whereas the task demands under which goal scripts are formed are teleopragmatic, because they are geared to guidance in particular goal situations. Given that teleology makes a proximate explanatory difference to

[13]This is why some writers (Woodfield, 1976) thought that only a goal-positing cognition requires teleological explanation. I think this view unnecessarily restricts teleology to proximate forms of explanation and acknowledges goal-directedness only when manifested by programs.

understanding cogitation, not production programs, and that most of cognitive science is dedicated to the study of the latter, whose tasks are eminently psychosemantic, it is no wonder that teleology is invisible to cognitive science, to the detriment of the latter.

Cogitation is teleopragmatic not because it generates messy and context-dependent interactions of mental states, which is the popular but only symptom-bound view, but because, antecedently, it concerns the satisfaction of goals, the alignment of actions to the conditions of the world and of the agent, the removal of uncertainties, and other such exploits that are not semantic, even though semantic relations are respected in their pursuit. Humans cogitate teleopragmatically because, as self-guided agents, we care about more than how the world is. Mental pragmatics is no joke; it is the real thing; or, if you like, is the joke evolution played on us by programming our brains to run a miniaturized form of goal formation and guidance to goal.

8 Social Guidance

Most of our individual knowledge is obtained by social means, in social contexts, and a good deal of it either depends on, or contributes to, social knowledge and the collective satisfaction of goals. This being a fact of life for social species, evolution must have installed programs that enable them to handle the information tasks of social guidance. Animals react to the world and perceive such reactions, goal-directedly. Social animals extend this reaction to their conspecifics and perceive them as part of their goal and guidance situations. Advanced social species frame conspecifics not merely as animate parts of their goal situations, but also as agents, hence as goal-directed and goal-guided systems.[1] The social animal therefore is a natural (commonsense) teleologist capable of framing and recognizing individual and social goals and also a natural (commonsense) psychologist capable of figuring out how conspecifics view goal situations and satisfy their goals and how the conspecifics' goal situations and satisfaction plans can be factored into one's own. The latter capabilities for social calculation are thought to have mutated into the programs involved in reasoning (in the sense of the last chapter).

Although this is not the place for a systematic inquiry into social knowledge, commonsense psychology, and their impact on the design of the cogitative mind, a few words about them will add some significant details to

[1]Put the contrast this way: Animals generally treat each other as goal-directed systems, whereas superior apes and humans treat each other as agents (deliberative, voluntary, intelligent). These treatments need not be conscious; they reflect how animals are programmed to react to and process information from each other.

my account of guidance and prepare the critical ground for a fuller examination of psychosemanticism. In the way it individuates goals and goal-directed processes, commonsense teleology is responsive to the social features of goal-directedness and guidance. This is the point of the next section. Commonsense psychology builds on the teleological individuation by framing actions and goal indicators in formats designed to convey information about other agents, their goal situations, and their worlds. This is what section 2 shows. On the critical side, according to section 3, looking at commonsense teleology and psychology as specifying interpretational programs that enable social organisms to manage their communal tasks, under constraints similar to those encountered in other forms of guidance, should preempt the temptation to view the two commonsense practices as theories of life, behavior, and mind, respectively, and in particular as props for psychosemanticism.

1. COMMONSENSE TELEOLOGY

Social species need social guidance to goal and must evolve the means to implement it through communication, natural and artificial languages, or rituals of social behavior. The tasks involved in social guidance could not be effected unless the social agents manage to individuate their goals and those of others, and also the internal and behavioral conditions in which goals are posited and pursued. These individuation tasks reflect the fact that agents perceive each other as goal-directed and goal-guided systems, perceive what they do as instantiating goal-directedness and guidance to goal, and also perceive the effects of what they do as goals or implications of goals. These perceptions are embodied in commonsense teleology and are operative in two major goal individuation tasks.

Goal as Outcome

Commonsense teleology often construes a goal as an end or outcome condition (action, state of the environment, state of the body) brought about by internal and behavioral processes to satisfy an antecedent biological or psychological condition. Everyday speech is well geared to this construal. When I say that my goal is such-and-so, such-and-so can describe an action to be performed (e.g., my goal is to run), or a state of affairs brought off by performing the action (e.g., getting home), or a psychological condition to be in (e.g., enjoying something). These are different goals, individuated by the external aspects of the outcome state. There are no fixed descriptions that individuate goals-as-outcomes because the outcomes matter differently in different contexts (i.e., my goal may be individuated as simply running, in a context, or as running very quickly and scared, in another, and so on). The notion of goal as outcome assumes that some antecedent internal state (a need or desire) indicates or represents the goal and joins other mental states to bring it about. The assumption is backgrounded, and the focus is on the outcome. I schematize this individuation gambit as follows:

(8.1) [input → internal states (conative + cognitive) → action] ⇒ goal

The assumption is contained between the brackets; → refers to the goal-directed processes that are assumed, whereas ⇒ refers to those explicitly identified. (8.1) individuates only the outcome of an action, not its cognitive and conative antecedents, because the commonsense narratives and explanations that employ it focus solely on outcomes and their repercussions.

Goal Internally Indexed

To describe and explain the psychological state of an agent, given the way the world is or could be, or predict the state of the world as a result of what an agent might wish, think, or do, common sense needs another individuation task centered on internal goal indicators. To do its job, the task must range over a longer stretch of goal-directedness and consider features of the internal indicators of goals. On this new individuation formula, a goal is the object of an internal indicator or the referent of an internal state picked up by the indicator. In attributing to one the desire to write a book on Dracula's influence on deconstructionism, the notion of desire picks up an internal goal representer and identifies the writing of the book as the goal represented.[2] I schematize this individuation task as:

(8.2) [input → internal goal indicators/representers] ⇒ action ⇒ goal

(8.2) is the task whose execution brings commonsense psychology into the picture because the individuative antecedents of action and goal satisfaction are internal cognitive and conative states. (The formula (8.1) assumes those internal states but does not need them to individuate goals.) It is worth noting that even with a more comprehensive individuation of goals, by appeal to psychological states, commonsense teleology remains practical and

---

[2]Common sense often describes this relation as goal satisfaction: Someone's goal is to write the book; the writing of the book satisfies the goal. This description of the goal invites the popular idea that goals are internal and their satisfaction conditions external. If, in adopting this reading, I want to emphasize (Bogdan, 1988a, 1988b) that goals have internal springs, that we have goals because we have desires and intentions, and we have the latter because . . . until we reach the genes, then the emphasis is the right one. Nevertheless, I think common sense is committed to the externality of goals as socially identifiable targets of cognition and behavior. This is a commitment I assume here.

atheoretical. (8.2) is no better than (8.1) in ultimately explaining why conation, cognition, and behavior, are goal-directed, and how they handle goals. Common sense assumes goal-directedness and uses goal indicators as goal individuators. Commonsense psychology also goes in the other direction, and uses goals and behaviors to individuate goal indicators (beliefs, etc.). This two-way individuation traffic is informative rather than explanatory. Far from being a criticism of commonsense teleology or psychology, this is a comment on their pragmatic wisdom. The individuation tasks (8.1) and (8.2) are designed to pick up patterns of relations that identify goals and chart in context their antecedents and repercussions.

Such is the job of commonsense knowledge, generally. The commonsense teleological notions reflect our practical conception of ourselves and others as goal-directed agents and categorize the features that mark goal-directedness in behavioral and social contexts, just as our commonsense physical notions reflect our relations to things, space, or motion, in terms expressing our practical interest in them. When robots are designed to do what humans do, one thinks of the commonsense physical tasks they must accomplish (behavioral navigation, handling objects, etc.) the way human tasks are construed. The suggestion now is to look at commonsense teleology and later, psychology, in the same spirit: If one thinks of designing a social species of goal-directed and goal-guided robots to do a lot of things together, it makes (task) sense to program them to individuate each other's goals either in the external and publicly accessible terms of how the world (context, behavior, its effects) looks, as (8.1) does, or in the internal terms of the agent's prior psychological and behavioral states, as (8.2) does. With a network of individuative relations thus in place, the robots, like humans, extract information about one part of the network (e.g., actions and their goals) in terms of other parts of the network (e.g., internal goal representers). The knowhow for the latter task originates in commonsense psychology.

2. MAKING SENSE OF OTHERS

Commonsense teleology has the task of framing goal-directedness and individuating goals. Commonsense psychology has the more specific task of setting up and figuring out the values of the equation of social guidance where other agents are informants about something or other. To get an intuitive sense of how this works, imagine the commonsense psychologist, the interpreter, describing another agent, the subject, as having seen the enemy. This is not a scientific description of the subject's vision. The interpreter describes an aspect of what the subject perceived in terms of a property or relation of interest to the interpreter in his goal situation. Describing what she saw as the enemy informs on some aspect from her past, identifies a current reaction, anticipates her future posture, indicates a condition of the world, things of that sort. (The notion of "enemy" does not belong to the vocabulary of theories of vision, and its use is a clue that the commonsense conceptualization has other objectives.) All these are aspects of interest to the interpreter. The attribution that she saw the enemy summarizes the information needed by the interpreter for handling his goal situation (mere curiosity or plan for action). The summary may be used to anticipate what she did or did not do next or to infer what happened to the enemy, or the like.

This attribution game is equally visible in our descriptions of actions. If I say that his movements were tense, I am not really describing bodily motions in scientific terms. My description implicates properties that are not part of his motion, for example, his antecedent state of mind, the effects (even distant) that might follow from his motion, and so forth. The choice of the concept 'tense' to individuate the quality of his movements makes such information bearing implications available to explanation and inference. The concept tense activates a number of connections, such as being nervous or tired or on guard, which allow certain predictions or retrodictions about the subject and his world. Or to turn a much discussed, metaphysical example into a commonsense psychological truism, how does one know that flipping the switch is or is not the same action as turning on the light, as far as the interpreter is concerned? We know it is the same action, as viewed by the interpreter, if she chooses to describe it in terms of its effects in a wider context. Portraying the flipping of the switch as turning on the light emphasizes, and (in that context) informs on, an antecedent state of mind (intention) responsible for the physical motion of the finger as well as an intended effect of it (light in the room). Actions, so conceptualized, are the creatures of commonsense psychology.

The same is true of how commonsense psychologists construe and describe people's thoughts and beliefs. If I say, of some people, that they believe that wars are wrong, I cannot plausibly describe either the cogitations leading up to their individual beliefs or the workings of the implementing architectures, for both are likely to differ vastly from person to person. As interpreter, I am in no position to do it, and why should I? The whole point of my attribution is to ignore the cogitative and cognitive idiosyncrasies of the subjects in order to abstract and summarize a common feature of their cogitative outputs in terms designed to inform on their position on the matter, predict certain reactions, or explain their past histories. The further such a summary extends informationally in various directions, the more useful it is in helping the interpreter manage his tasks.

Why do commonsense attributions work this way? Why do they single out aspects of interest to the interpreter while shunning the details of the subject's psychological condition? Think of KICM. What is the knowledge problem in this case? Humans are a social species made of agents. Our commonsense teleology instructs us to see each other as goal-directed and goal-guided systems. Given that a good deal of our guidance is social, we treat others as informants. To do this, we need a suitable method of extracting and interpreting the information they convey. The extraction and interpretation must be sensitive to the commonsense teleological truth that the informants are themselves goal-directed and goal-guided. This means that normally the information they convey about something of interest to the interpreter must be isolated and recovered from whatever the informants are doing in their own goal-directed and goal-guided ways. The tasks of retrieving that information and making it available and useful to the interpreter are the information tasks of commonsense psychology. Those tasks define the evolutionary rationale for commonsense psychology (Bogdan, 1991b).

We saw all sorts of organisms treating ecological events and correlations, including conspecifics and members of other species, as informants about their goals and surrounding goal conditions. A magnetic field informs a bacterium where the oxygen is; a song tells the female finch that the male is approaching; the male finch's approaching and singing tells the cat that the female finch may be there, too. Organisms rely on ecological and biological informants, and so do we. When we regard conspecifics as informants, from the experts (such as scientists and doctors), who have information lay people don't have and don't understand, to the mundane (such as friends, people in the street), who inform on one or another matter of interest, we treat them as tools in our social ecology doing an informational job for us.

Yet there is a dramatic difference between how we treat conspecifics informationally and how other organisms do it, a difference we found in communication as well, and for the same reasons. Our commonsense psychology and our communication share the formidable cogitative challenge of having to make sense of the information provided explicitly and/or implicitly by intelligent agents. The worker bee left behind does not have to be intelligent to figure what the scout bees, just returned from their food location mission, are communicating through their dance. The scout bees are programmed to dance as they do, relative to the situation encountered, and the worker bees, too, are programmed to decode the transmitted message appropriately. (If there is any sweat involved here, it was evolution's, in the past.) The bees simply play their assigned scores. Even for animals that learn how to treat conspecifics as informants for specific classes of goal situations, once the learning is over, the resulting interpretation program is compiled and fixed forever; no reason to labor one's imagination every time an informant does its spiel. Not so in the human case, not at all.

Human communication and behavior express intelligent cognition, and to that extent can be full of surprises. Intelligence allows for individual improvisation in a particular goal-situation, as opposed to enduring species adaptation to a fixed class of goal situations. As a result, individual intelligence poses a tremendous Interpretation problem for the utilizers of social information: how to make sense of the expressions (utterances, actions, gestures, various implicatures) of a conspecific's cogitation. The solution resides in the fact that the interpreters themselves are intelligent cogitators and can improvise the right interpretations and adapt them to the context. (Compare: If you are a bee trying to interpret a human, you are in trouble, because you don't cogitate, you only encode information, and your interpretive program is exclusively for decoding conspecifics in standard situations. You can't cogitate your way to an on-the-spot interpretation of an intelligent informant.)

The informed speculation presents the interpretation problem and its solution in terms of an evolutionary arms race: The nascent intelligence of the informant (particularly, the ability to plan ahead, control reactions, deceive) selects for an increased intelligence of the interpreter, if the latter is to stay ahead of the informant, which in turn selects for new tricks in the informant's intelligence, and so forth. At the end of this process, so far, lie not only our current ability for commonsense psychology but, apparently, the very powers of reasoning that drive our cogitation (Alexander, 1989; Astington et al., 1988; Byrne & Whiten, 1988)

Given the interpretation task, what an intelligent interpreter needs by way of programs is a battery of attribution concepts and rules in terms of which she can cogitate (reason) to a reading of the information of interest conveyed by an intelligent conspecific in a context of guidance to goal. Commonsense psychology provides that battery of attribution concepts and rules. The suggestion, then, is to construe commonsense psychology, not as a pop logos or protoscience of cognition, as is frequently done, but as a biosocially shaped practice evolved to ensure social guidance. Its interpretation tasks are: (a) extracting from conspecifics information about them, their cognitive and/or behavioral condition, and/or about the world, or (b) extracting from the world information about conspecifics; or finally, (c) sharing information with conspecifics in communication, cooperation, and conflict. The practice appears to be based on an innate competence that enables us to "read" each other's psyche and behavior in order to individuate the information needed to handle goal situations.

If commonsense psychology is an interpretational practice involved in social knowledge, one should expect it to reflect constitutive and regulative constraints on guidance. It does. The division of informational labor is present in almost all contexts of social guidance (experts and laypeople, people who communicate, those who cooperate in an action, etc.). Because the imparting of social information is situation-specific, all the parties tend to follow such constitutive constraints as the (Gricean) rules of economy, locality, and incrementality, assuming some information as given, focusing on the new, implicitly or explicitly considering relevant alternatives, and the like. Furthermore, informants and interpreters operate with information under assumptions to the effect that informants normally inform reliably, cooperatively, and so forth. There is even an ongoing reallocation of complexity of the information tasks involved: The more informative the informant, the less the interpreter has to know in a given respect, and can focus on other aspects of her goal situation; when the informant is less informative, new tasks kick in.

On the regulative side, the attributions of mental attitudes tend to be as informative, relevant, and economical as the context requires. Seeing her running out of the building, I use the perceptual evidence, other facts about the situation, and some general expectations, to attribute to her beliefs and desires in terms that tell me something about an earlier condition of her in the building, and whatever else matters in that context. My attribution is not about to include irrelevant facts about her and is commensurate with the context. If she seems scared, then my interest is heightened and the attributions become more fine-grained and precise than if she were casual. One recognizes counterparts of Gricean maxims: Make your attributions of propositional attitudes as relevant, detailed, fine-grained, and informative as the situation demands.

3. THE INCOHERENCE OF THE PROPOSITIONAL ATTITUDE

Suppose that commonsense psychology is in fact a tool employed in social guidance, not a descriptive prototheory of the cognitive mind, and that its categories individuate the information of interest to an interpreter (the content part) relative to the psychological or behavioral condition of the subject (the attitude part), and not principled types of datal structures and programs. This would have the beneficial effect of breaking the illegitimate marriage between commonsense psychology and psychosemanticism and weakening the case for psychological Newtonianism generally. This is a critical dividend I need in the next two chapters, whence this critical section.

Many philosophers of mind and cognitive scientists regard a psychosemantic construal of propositional attitudes as doing justice to commonsense psychology. The psychosemantic construal is motivated by the notion that attributions of propositional attitudes are causally explanatory: We attribute beliefs, desires, and other attitudes in order to explain and predict cognition and behavior causally. Because the commonsense explanations are often successful, it follows that the propositional attitudes must individuate internal types of causal–functional structures and processes. It is by virtue of being explanatory constructs of the causal–functional sort that propositional attitudes do a psychosemantic job.

The problem with the psychosemantic notion of propositional attitude is that it is incoherent. When a propositional attitude is individuated semantically, its content, a token of a semantic type, cannot be as such psychologically real and functionally efficacious, and hence cannot be used in a psychological explanation of the causal–functional sort; when an attitude to mental information, in the sense of chap. 7, is individuated as psychologically real and functionally efficacious, it is underdetermined by its semantic coordinates and is not functional by virtue of those coordinates. A propositional attitude cannot be both psychologically functional and semantic; its semantics cannot be functionally efficacious. This conclusion follows from the argument of chapter 7 and the points made earlier in this chapter, and also from methodological solipsism (Fodor, 1980) and the two-factors view of propositional attitudes (McGinn, 1982).

Viewed from my angle on commonsense psychology, a content attribution (say, her belief that the cat is lost) has the task of individuating the information of interest to the interpreter (e.g., that her cognitive and behavioral condition informs on a state of the world in which a cat is lost). The interpreter's task of figuring out the subject's cogitation (e.g., her cogitative belief that the cat is lost) is quite different from the first attribution (her commonsensically individuated belief that the cat is lost), for now he must individuate her goal scripts and attitudes. The latter individuation cannot pick up a proposition as a semantic unit because (as chapter 7 argues at length) there is no such proposition that would characterize her goal script in the semantic detail that reveals the script's functional efficacy. The content individuation (as a practical summary of the information of interest) in an attribution of propositional attitude may be semantic, and most often is, but is not mental (i.e., functionally efficacious as cogitated or teleopragmatically). According to psychosemanticism, the content individuation is both mental and semantic, which, according to me, it cannot be.[3] The incoherence of the psychosemantic notion of propositional attitude suggests that a realist construal of commonsense psychology, as a descriptive account of the causal–functional nuts and bolts of the mind, is wrong. The realist construal misrepresents not only mental cognition, but also the biosocial objectives of commonsense psychology.

---

[3]If my sketch of commonsense psychology is on the right track, it does no good to attempt to naturalize the commonsense categories and axioms on the assumption that what is naturalized are the internal organization and operation of cognition. Some mind naturalization projects (Fodor, 1975, 1987, 1990a; Dretske, 1981; 1988) officially operate under this assumption. Fortunately, quite often, these philosophers are naturalizing genuinely internal features of cognition (vision, perception, concepts), which they mistakenly (but often harmlessly) taxonomize in commonsense terms.

PART 3

IMPLICATIONS

9 Psychosemanticism

The teleonaturalization of the cognitive mind runs counter to the prevailing winds in philosophy of mind and the foundations of cognitive science, where the reigning paradigm is that of psychological Newtonianism. I take the latter to be a way of thinking, rather than an explicit doctrine, animated by the notion that the cognitive mind is a complex body in causal motion, functionally autonomous, whose design can be ultimately explained causally by natural selection, and whose program operations can be proximately explained by a functionalized version of causal explanation. Within philosophy of mind most of the work on behalf of psychological Newtonianism is done by psychosemanticism and its central notion of content. These final chapters turn critical and identify the pluses and minuses of psychological Newtonianism and psychosemanticism. The conclusion is that in the areas of teleological difference, the ultimate explanation of forms of cognition and the proximate explanation of mental cognition, the numbers do not add up to a viable alternative to a teleoevolutionary story. This chapter focuses on the psychosemanticism of content, whereas the next chapter explores the prospects for the psychoNewtonian understanding of mental cognition.

The psychosemanticism of content has been challenged from various quarters. Some have urged a retreat to the nonsemantic properties of mental programs (Fodor's (1980) methodological solipsism; Stich's (1983) syntactic theory of mind). The two-factor theorists maintain that the semantic and functional dimensions of content don't fit (McGinn, 1982). And in the background, are echoes of the early attacks on the mentalization of meaning, the linguistic cousin of content, from Wittgenstein and Quine to Dennett and recent externalists such as Putnam and Burge. Undeterred, the psychosemanticists do not want to abandon the larger territory of biocognition and see no other alternative but content as the natural basis from where semantics can run the psyche.

The psychosemantic naturalization of content is not a homogeneous enterprise. In terms of my analysis, I see three possible interpretations of what the content theorists are up to: content as information task; content as occurrent representational state; and, content as program. Each interpretation has some pluses but mostly minuses for the psychosemantic project.

1. CONTENT AS INFORMATION TASK

The psychosemantic notion of knowledge has two dimensions, the semantic relation to the world and the functional efficacy of its internal relatum. This notion of knowledge has shaped two key research areas in philosophy of mind: (a) the possibility and nature of semantic cognition or its intentionality, as it is often called, or, in Fodor's (1987) terms, "How can anything manage to be about anything?" (p. xi); and (b) the possibility and nature of the functional potency of semantic cognition: How can something, by virtue of being about something else, be functionally efficacious and cause anything?[1]

[1]There have been philosophical theories concerned only with answering one of the two questions, without much concern for the other. Such theories are not psychosemantic. Plato and Descartes, for example, were much more interested in the metaphysics and epistemology of mental states than in the psychological explanation of cognition and behavior, which is why they could place very strong normative constraints on semantic knowledge and pretty much ignore how cognition could meet them so as to steer behavior appropriately. Their KCM analyses indicated an epistemic rather than psychological semanticism. Since Frege, a number of theories of intentionality and meaning have also attempted to answer the aboutness question with an eye to metaphysical or epistemological or purely logical requirements, without bothering much about semantic causation and its psychological innards.

In all these prenaturalist traditions, a strongly normative notion of knowledge conspired with metaphysical assumptions of idealism and dualism and an indifference to psychological explanation to force the KCM analysis to come up with the notion of an immaterial mind. This is in part why the modern scientific revolution and its Newtonian ideal of mechanical explanation could not extend to the study of cognition and mind and make it into an exact natural science—in spite of the favorable Zeitgeist and the documentable fact that most elements of such a science (a right understanding of logic (Leibniz), grammar (Port-Royal), mental symbols (Hobbes), innate cognitive programs (Descartes), mechanization of thought processes (Descartes, Leibniz)) were already in place (Bogdan, 1993c). This development had to await the 20th century when the emerging sciences of cognition adopted a descriptive and information-based notion of knowledge (content) happily married to the notion of a material mind. For materialists, psychosemanticism is also important metaphysically: showing that the material mind can causally encode and process semantic information provides a materialist solution to the problem of intentionality.

The answers to these questions have been taken to offer a definitive and ultimate explanatory profile of the cognitive mind.[2]

To get into the spirit of psychosemantic naturalization as a source of ultimate explanations, here is Dretske (1989) as a guide:

> Suppose I give you a design problem. I want a system S that will do A when, but only when, conditions C obtain. Make me something that will behave this way. This is a common enough problem in engineering problems. I want a device that will turn the furnace on whenever the room temperature gets too low. . . . This kind of problem is also common enough in nature. Reflexes and other rigid . . . patterns of behavior . . . is nature's solution to this same design problem. When the object being touched is hot, withdraw. Fast! When a certain silhouette, the kind a hawk makes, appears in the sky, freeze, run, or hide. . . . We also encounter a similar problem in simple learning situations: How does one get the pupil to say 'oak' (not 'maple' or 'pine') when shown the distinctive markings of an oak tree?
>
> In very general terms, the solution to the Design Problem is always the same—whether it is the deliberate invention of an engineer, the product of evolutionary development, or the outcome of individual learning. The system S must embody . . . some kind of internal mechanism that is selectively sensitive to the presence or absence of condition C. It must be equipped with something that will indicate or register the presence of those conditions with which behavior is to be coordinated [THE ABOUTNESS PROBLEM]. . . . Once this requirement is satisfied, all that remains to do in solving the Design Problem is to harness this indicator to effector mechanisms in such a way that it produces output A when (and only when) it positively registers the presence of condition C. The only thing left to do . . . is to make the indicator of C into a cause of A. . . . [Nature] converts, by means of natural selection, sensory indicators into behavior switches [THE FUNCTIONAL EFFICACY PROBLEM]. (pp. 6–7)

Let us say, for starters, that the cognitive (indicator) state registering C and causing A as a result is a content-instantiating structure or content state. A content-instantiating structure is involved in the cognitive execution of an information task defined by a content relation. A content relation can then be

---

[2]In support of this account of the research agenda of psychosemanticism, I should note as a revealing socioprofessional fact that two of the most distinguished and influential mind naturalizers of the psychosemantic persuasion, Fodor and Dretske, have divided their labors so as to tackle the two research questions separately and in bookish detail. Fodor's *Language of Thought* (1975) can be regarded as outlining his theory of the functional mechanics of the mind, as an answer to the second question, while his more recent books, *Psychosemantics* (1987) and *A Theory of Content* (1990a) are concerned with the first question about semantic aboutness. Dretske went in the other direction and first dealt with aboutness in his *Knowledge and the Flow of Information* (1981) before turning to the second question in *Explaining Behavior* (1988).

construed as a mapping of a semantic relation into a functional role. A content structure is part of the instantiation of such a mapping. Psychosemanticism views content literally as the moving force of cognition and behavior, the causal vehicle of semantic information, the little map that steers in virtue of what it represents.

Note the level distinction in my characterization of the dimensions of content: The content relation itself, the mapping, specifies an information task, the content structure, or state, specifies its cognitive execution by some program operation. In Dretske's story, the design problem defines the content relation, whereas the sensory indicators that become behavioral switches count as content structures (executors). Many psychosemanticists are aware of the level distinction and intend to use the notion of content to describe only semantic information tasks, irrespective of the cognitive architectures involved in their execution. Fodor (1987), an influential member of the psychosemanticist politbureau, issues an ukase about how to look at content as a psychosemantic task:

> [T]hough protons exert causal control over "protons" via the activation of intentional mechanisms, a naturalistic semantics doesn't need to specify all that. All it needs is that the causal control should actually obtain, however it is mediated. . . . For purposes of semantic naturalization, it's the existence of a reliable mind/world correlation that counts, not the mechanisms by which that correlation is effected. (pp. 121–122)

We can take this reading of the Fodorian thesis and regard content relations as characterizations of information tasks, of the local and domain-specific sort. In that case, the notion of content is a philosophical paraphrase of a cognitive–scientific account of those tasks. This may be the healthy core of the psychosemantic notion of content. The latter can be cashed in scientific terms but at the cost of a narrow and specific domain of application, basically, that of production and categorization tasks. If, however, this notion of content is generalized to the organism's entire knowledge task, then its narrowness and domain-specialization prevent it from ultimately explaining how that knowledge is possible (the argument of this essay); and if it is generalized only to utilization tasks, it also fails to explain proximately how cogitation works (chap. 7).

I should note from the outset that the description of any information task is bound to pick up at a lower implementational level a causal mapping of some condition of the world (being interacted with) into an uptake condition (inside the organism). This follows from my definition of information, which portrayed an actual information relation as obtaining whenever there is a causal conversion of an interaction condition into an uptake condition through the reorganization of a fulcrum structure (chap. 4, section 3). The execution of any information task requires a solution to the design problem of how to get an interaction to produce an uptake. Any biological task faces the same design problem. What is special about semantic information tasks is not the nature of the interaction condition but the design constraints on the fulcrum structures because their reorganizations must yield a cognitive or behavioral uptake that bears a systematic relation to selected aspects of the world revealed by the interaction.

Narrowly framed, Dretske's design problem is the right information problem to consider. By narrow frame I mean from condition C to its registration by S and the immediate uptake of that registration. This is the narrowness of domain-specific and local information tasks studied by the vision or learning theorist interested in particular production and categorization programs. These mostly psychosemantic programs contain rules that configure the types of fulcrum structures that convert registrations of S into some cognitive uptake, say, visual discriminations. The programs emerge as cognitive solutions to the design problem for such a conversion. If the conversion is psychosemantic, then in its narrow frame it can be construed as instantiating a content relation.[3]

Since it describes a semantic information task, the notion of content could provide a more ultimate explanation of the possible programs able to execute the task. And once the real program has been singled out, on empirical grounds, its operation and outputs can be explained proximately in the causal–functional terms. The analysis of production modules (vision, language) is full of such two-step analyses. Mutatis mutandis, I have argued, the same is true of simple bacterial cognition. Its key information tasks were to convert registrations of some external chemical condition (sugar) into a cognitive uptake (comparison, integration). In terms of Dretske's design problem, there is the presence of sugar as the C-type condition and the registered values of its concentration, or perhaps the integrator's intake, as the A-type condition.

No matter how one paraphrases such information tasks or content relations, from bacterial to visual cognition, they are operative within narrow limits. These happen to be the limits where, at the executive level, there are stable and systematic linkages, or proximate arrangements among input

---

[3]In an earlier paper (Bogdan, 1989a) I criticized Fodor (1987) for too thin and analytic an account of psychosemantic naturalization, similar in spirit to the conceptual analyses of seeing or knowledge. I took Fodor's analysis to bear on the success conditions of cognitive programs, in contrast with what I expected to be a thicker, more substantive account of what makes these programs cognitive (semantic, in particular). I will rephrase the diagnosis by saying that Fodor's analysis bears on what I call semantic information tasks or what he calls content. The analysis is too thin and incomplete as it fails to motivate the reason for, and the role of, semantic tasks in the larger picture of guidance.

interactions, internal programs, and their functional uptake. When implemented, such proximate arrangements secure the tight structure-to-function bonds with which evolution disciplines and modularizes cognition, animal and human. Where such arrangements exist, one can say, of the programs installed by evolution or architecturally compiled through learning (to map registrations into uptake reactions by tokening appropriate fulcrum structures), that they instantiate content relations. In so doing, the programs convert semantics into functional causation.

So construed, then, the notion of content is a philosophical paraphrase of the cognitive–scientific notion of information task. At the executive level, there would be content programs whose rules have the job of projecting semantic into causal relations. At the implementational level, content states would be datal structures that are functionally efficacious in virtue of the semantic (or generally, hook up) information they encode. There are as many types of content relations as the information tasks it takes to produce and categorize stimuli. Miniaturized and sophisticated as they are in vision, sensory–motor coordination, or memory, these relations are accessible only to the sciences of cognition, and cannot be taxonomized and explained in philosophical or commonsense terms.

More important, these content relations do not add up to any cumulative or totalizing content relation, a sort of global semantic information task, as psychosemanticism would have it. There is no unitary cognitive program to execute such a task and no single output (the content state) to encode its work. As I have had many occasions to note, the knowledge of any organism is articulated by many distinct information tasks, some of which have a registrational or hook up role, while others have comparison, integration, recall, control, and utilization roles. In humans, we are also talking of cogitation. I do not see how an account of the coordination of these information tasks and a consideration of the tasks executed ecologically, all necessary to specify the cumulative content of an organism's knowledge, can emerge from a psychosemantic account. And I have not seen any such account.

But perhaps this is not what the psychosemanticist has in mind. Perhaps the psychosemantic notion of content is a philosophical concoction that tries to marry the cognitive–scientific notion of information task to the commonsense notion of propositional attitude. I think that would be an unhappy if not impossible marriage. Housed, as it should be, in the utilization area of cogitation, which commonsense psychology cares about, the resulting notion of content turns incoherent because it is torn between different tasks and defined over incommensurate vocabularies. For, on the one hand, according to chapter 7, the information tasks of cogitation are not psychosemantic, whereas, on the other hand, according to chapter 8, the notion of content operative in commonsense attributions does not describe internal information tasks.

2. CONTENT AS STATE

At the other end of the spectrum lies the most popular psychosemantic notion of content, that of content as state or structure. There are many reasons why psychosemanticists would want states to be content carriers. Qua physical structures, states encode information and are causal, whereas, strictly speaking, information tasks are neither; states covary or correlate with or represent their semantic targets, and states can be specific in correlating with or representing their targets in ways in which neither information tasks nor the executing programs can. Target specificity is important because this is how we think commonsensically of thoughts and beliefs (as being functional by virtue of representing specific targets), and psychosemanticism is very much indebted to the vocabulary, interests, and explanations of commonsense psychology.

The semantic specificity of content states is of considerable interest to the psychosemanticists concerned with the simplest forms of cognition. Their problem is to have the analysis determine the precise and unique content of animal knowledge in ways comparable with the commonsense determination of the content of human knowledge. What, they ask, is the content of the frog's cognitive state when it registers a fly in motion? What is the content of the bacterium's cognitive state when it indicates sugar or oxygen? What does the dog believe when he sees a bone?

I think that the notion of content presupposed by these questions is, again, close to being incoherent, as it attempts to square commonsense with science. We resort to precise and unique content assignments when we attribute to each other thoughts, beliefs, and other mental states.[4] Our commonsense attributions of content have a precise and unique focus for reasons that are not necessarily generalizable to animal cognition. One reason is that our cognition has the conceptual and linguistic sophistication that allows a refined and precise semantic focus, which other forms of animal cognition do not have. Another reason is that, as content attributors, we have not only the means but the interest to specify the contents attributed in great detail, even if the specification may have no systematically descriptive force with respect to what is going on in a human or animal head.

---

[4]Not accidentally, it is the mind naturalizers holding a realistic, mind-descriptive view of commonsense psychology, who are excessively preoccupied by the assignment of precise and unique content to animal cognition, no matter how simple (Dretske, 1986, 1988; Fodor, 1990a; even Millikan, 1986, 1989 from time to time). And it is no accident either that Dennett, who has long advocated a nonrealist, nondescriptive view of commonsense psychology and an indeterminacy view of content, has noticed how a realist notion of commonsense psychology drives psychosemanticists and even teleologists into the unique content assignment for animal cognition (Dennett, 1987, 1991b).

If we play the commonsense game of attributing precise and unique contents to animal cognizers, then, at best, we are playing a metaphorical game.[5] We have no introspective or commonsense idea of what it is for other organisms to experience or represent something or what it is they specifically and uniquely experience or represent. If one plays the scientific game with the same attribution rules, one gets nowhere. There are no concepts and attribution methods in the candidate sciences (genetics, evolution theory, biology, animal psychology) to appeal to for such a task. Nor, generally, is there any interest in science for such particularized phenomena.

The effort to specify the content of a state, precisely or not, raises an even more troubling methodological problem. It is the problem of informational isolation. It shows up twice: First, because, being trilateral, an information relation requires more than a state to be instantiated and specified; second, because very few information relations, even when trilaterally considered, suffice to do the job (causation by semantic covariation) required by the psychosemantic notion of content. The problem is manifest in the widespread tendency to specify the target of an organism's knowledge from its sensory states in terms of some systematic relation (causal, covariational, nomological, functional) between those states and external objects (Fodor, 1990a, chap. 3; Dretske, 1986, 1988; Israel, 1988; Enc, 1982). I find the exercise hopeless. First of all, a single state wouldn't do as an information carrier. How many states would it take to specify a content? It is known from the analysis of vision that it takes a lot of layers of (representational) states to pick up the various features (contours, shades, texture, etc.) needed for object individuation. When is the content state assembled? When some concept applies? That is no longer a sensory state. And what if no concept applies but there is enough of a convergence of features (say, smelly, dark, small, moving), yet less than a definite object, to activate control and behavior? What sort of content would that be?

The suggested determination of content in terms of sensory states is also hopeless because there are indefinitely many causal and nomological relations between sensory states and sundry distal realities. Our retinal registrations covary systematically not only with features of light but also with patterns of electro-magnetic activity, atmospheric pressure, temperature, and so on. Light itself carries information from (by covarying with) a large variety of ecological features, of which only a few are relevant and useful to an organism. How do we make the selection of what the organism knows? This brings up a third point.

---

[5]As a commonsense psychologists, one is likely to take the behaviorist stance toward animals, look at their behavior, with its environmental causes and constraints, factor in what is known about our own cognitions and behaviors, and come up with hypothetical content attributions and explanations. That is not a rigorously descriptive model of animal cognition.

Looking at the senses only is not going to help delineate an organism's knowledge. Recall the magnetic bacteria. The magnetosomes respond only to values of the surrounding magnetic fields; that is the only information they have. Magnetic fields in turn respond only to magnetic poles (or any magnets); that is the only information they have. (We can replace information by causation and still get the same fragmentation.) How does one determine what the bacterial senses sense? Is it magnetic fields or magnetic poles or what the latter correlate with, namely, oxygen-free waters? Recall that these need not be the only correlations across various physical domains. Magnetic poles also correlate with dark and cold waters, bacteria-shunning fish, sunken ships, etc. On several occasions I have played the paleocognitive game to emphasize the ecological indeterminacy compatible with a purely sensory architecture.

Fodor noted the indeterminacy (1990a, pp. 70–75), and so did Dretske (1986). Dretske's move to add functional complexity to the sensorium is a move in the right direction, as it made the sensorium compatible with fewer proximal and distal alternatives. It is not enough, though. What is the rest of the organism's cognition doing? What are the other post-sensory proteins doing if the sensors were enough for bacterial knowledge? Why would the stimuli be compared, integrated, and memorized? I showed that in simpler organisms knowledge has little to do with what is sensed. This is why one must consider not only production and categorization tasks but also utilization tasks (Dennett, 1969, 1981; Millikan, 1984, 1989). But in doing this one must abandon the hope of finding a single sort of state that does the entire work.

It is worth pointing out that, unlike the philosopher or the commonsense psychologist, the scientist would be inclined to factor noncognitive parameters, such as needs, affects, habits, emotions, fears, and others, into her empirical hypotheses about the sorts of distal objects and events systematically tracked by the organism's knowledge (Dennett, 1991b). The point is not that knowing what the frog eats or dislikes would reveal what it registers and categorizes; the point, rather, is that such noncognitive parameters illuminate the overall functional design of the organism, relative to a variety of selection pressures, and thus clarify the manner in which various tasks and resources fit together adaptively. That, in turn, allows the scientist to figure out the organism's goals (e.g., flies to catch and eat, for the tongue is good only for flies, and so is the stomach), the statistics of their distribution in the environment, the selective significance of errors, and so on. Based on these data, an analysis of the organism's cognitive architecture would reveal major goal-specifiers (moving dark spots), and may even hazard the regulative speculation about the worth and survival value of the teleonomic or teleosemantic precision of the organism's cognitive architecture.

In the human case the presence of explicit goal representers (desires, plans) helps considerably in the theoretical endeavor of identifying goals and finding out how the cognitive programs triangulate goal-revealing properties

(McGinn, 1989; Millikan, 1986; Papineau, 1987, chap. 4). Particular program outputs (states) take the form of sentential or imagistic representations that do a lot of precise and uniquely targeted semantic triangulation on their own. This production and categorization accomplishment, remarkable as it is, is not sufficient to run mental cognition. When the utilization scripts of the latter kick in, no particular content state can do the work expected by psychosemanticism.

In sum, in both animal and human cognition, one cannot make a content specification in terms of some determinate state. All one can do is attempt to figure out a complex guidance equation and determine which different tasks are carried out by which programs with what particular results (outputs, applications) in determinate contexts. A content determination, if one is needed, is at best a convenient summary, couched typically in commonsense terms, of a complicated scientific narrative.

3. CONTENT BY EVOLUTION

A recent and vigorous trend in mind naturalization attempts to explain the semantics of cognition in terms of evolutionary accounts of its contents. Millikan (1984, 1986, 1989) and Papineau (1984, 1987) provided explicit instances of this trend, and so have, to a lesser extent, Dretske (1986, 1987), Matthen (1988), McGinn (1989), and others. I call this family of accounts evolutionary semantics. It is not quite teleosemantics in my sense, for their teleology is only half-hearted or, better, half-legged, in that it shuns genetic goal-directedness and invokes only natural selection as ultimate explainer.

Evolutionary semanticists talk of content as having the evolutionary function to represent something or other in the environment. Such talk is ambiguous. It may be state talk or program talk. In the latter case, programs are identified in terms of their typical applications but the explanation goes the other way, from programs to applications (specific output states). This is the mechanism–program sense in which, for example, Millikan (1986) talked of desires: "the most obvious proper function of every desire . . . is to help cause its own fulfillment. For it is reasonable that the mechanisms in us that manufacture desires (not, of course, any specific desire) have proliferated because the desires they produce are sometimes . . . relevant to our flourishing and eventually reproducing" (p. 63).

Mechanisms and programs for believing or desiring have of course an evolutionary history precisely for the reason noted by Millikan. The evolutionary ploy must be more specific than that to deliver content; it must consider definite classes of mechanisms and programs that explain definite classes of contents. This ploy works for modular programs with an uniform evolutionary history. Such, for example, is simple animal cognition, where the production, categorization, and utilization programs evolved to cope in a reflex manner with domain-specific information and behavioral tasks. When one says that the animal's cognitive output states have the evolutionary function of indicating this or that, because of similar past performances sanctioned by natural selection, one is in fact describing the invariant function of modularized programs. Their applications are rigid and standardized (Normal, in Millikan's sense). Knowledge of the tasks and of the selective pressures on them ultimately explain the program; knowledge of the axioms of the program and of the conditions of its standard operation identifies the program applications (states) in a context. As a result, there is a proximate program subsumption that is causal–functional.

Two things to note, though. The subsumptive explanation is not from natural selection and past performances to current (content) states, for that would not work, because natural selection does not work on occurrent states. The ultimate explanation, rather, is from natural selection to programs, whereas the proximate subsumptive explanation goes from programs and the conditions of their normal operation to specific applications (output states). It is programs, not current performances (states) that explain the success of the past performances sanctioned by natural selection. The other thing to note is that this explanatory transition works only if the programs still operate on the domains, and in the standard conditions, for which they were initially selected. If either of the latter had changed, it would be much harder if not impossible to determine content from an evolutionary story.

That is the case of cogitation. Many of its utilization programs have acquired new domains of application (the culture of writing, for example, is much less ancestral than the selection of most cogitation programs), and their work is underdetermined by the ancestral production and categorization programs. There are, of course, the routine programs of mental modules. They are stereotyped and domain-specific because they evolved to manage specialized and imperative information tasks such as kin recognition, social exchange, or predictions of conspecific behavior (Cosmides, 1989; Cosmides & Tooby, 1987; Tooby & Cosmides, 1990). The routine programs can be as standardized as sensory–motor programs. Even when inserted in the flow of cogitation, they do what they were naturally selected to do eons ago (a face that expresses extreme danger stops our thinking dead in its track while an appropriate ancestral routine takes over). I take it that when evolutionary semanticists talk of the function of cognitive states as being that of detecting or discriminating something, they may be thinking of states that are typical outputs of such modular programs.

The fact that cogitation relies on mental modules does not entail the uniform standardization of its outputs (goal scripts). Mental modules rarely handle only the ancestral tasks for which they were selected and rarely operate on their own. Both facts diminish the chances of finding a natural selection individuation of the contents they handle. In particular, the interaction of modules with other programs including other modules is bound to be subject to teleopragmatic constraints. The evolution of cogitation programs shows that their deployments and outputs are not standardized because of new application domains and the teleopragmatic format of application. I return to this topic in chapter 10, section 4.

Yet, often enough, talk of the evolutionary function of content states is not a paraphrase talk of programs. It is literally and seriously about occurrent states construed as datal structures generated by nonmodular mental programs. It is such types of output states that, say evolutionary semanticists, can be explained (Normally) in terms of their past performances and effects. Thus, Millikan (1986) held that, in general, "not only body organs and systems [i.e., mechanisms] but also various states and activities have proper functions . . . lots of states (tokens) have proper functions" (pp. 52–53). She has referred frequently to nonperceptual beliefs as states with such proper functions of their own. This is not a new position. Pragmatists, early and newer positivists and verificationists, many naturalistically inclined, have taken the view that mental states have content as output states, and that their content should be analyzed in terms of some function and its past success. The function may be representing the world or enabling action, and its success is analysed as verification or completion of action.

Taken literally, this position has problems. One notorious problem is that mental attitudes relate to information, and are causal as a result, only by interacting with other attitudes. This is how humans are programmed to cogitate. To put it in terms of cogitation, belief programs require desire and memory programs to do their job. It takes the satisfaction conditions of desires and the truth conditions of memories to fix the informational content of an occurrent belief. This fact drastically reduces the chances of identifying a belief content in isolation. The same fact also threatens the content individuation with circularity because the contents of beliefs are fixed by reference to those of desires and memories, just as the latter may have originated in prior beliefs, and so forth.

Another and more serious problem is the following. Evolution operates only with and on mechanisms and their programs, not their ephemeral outputs, such as individual beliefs, thoughts, mental scripts, or actions. There is even doubt in some quarters that evolution could ever explain even the mechanisms and programs of cognition (Lewontin, 1990). There is also doubt in the same quarters that natural selection can always explain various evolutionary acquisitions, including cognitive, which may have "piggybacked" on genuine adaptations. Yet there is no doubt about the principled inability of natural selection to track and explain the outputs of nonmodular programs. It is this gap between natural selection and nonroutine outputs that warrants Cummins' (1989, pp. 80–84) and Fodor's (1990a, pp. 65–66) charge that occurrent datal structures do not have evolutionary functions—more precisely, do not have such functions other than those of the programs responsible for them (see also Sterelny, 1990, pp. 128–134). So one cannot generally use evolutionary considerations (functions, past performances, beneficial effects, Normal explanations, and the like) to individuate and explain the contents of particular beliefs, desires and other cogitations. Cummins has suggested that Millikan's notion of belief therefore cannot be that of datal structure. The alternative is that her notion of belief is a program notion. Millikan (1986) wrote that the functions of the contentful entities and states are "derived from the proper functions of the mechanisms that produced them" (p. 59). I have shown that this gambit works only for narrow and domain-specific information tasks, with disciplined programs naturally selected in well regimented proximate arrangements. In mental cognition very few programs fit the bill, and they generally fail to characterize and explain specific cogitations.

If Millikan's notion of belief program is that of cogitative belief program (in the sense of chap. 7), then it would not have standardized (Normal) output applications with their history of past successes, except in a trivially weak sense. Suppose that evolution blesses us with such believing programs as: help desires get fulfilled; be true whenever you can; participate in inferences and be as truth-preserving as is feasible; and the like. That seems reasonable, as a general policy for believing, but would not help identifying particular beliefs in specific goal situations.[6]

Mental contents can also acquire their functions by learning (Dretske, 1981, 1988; Millikan, 1984, 1989). Dretske has talked frequently of internal indicators of distal states of affairs being recruited by individual learning to perform control and behavioral functions. Millikan has agreed and extended this analysis to thinking (1984, chap. 1, 1989). This is not a very promising move. Learning remains a poorly understood process, and so does the idea that natural selection has a direct and effective grip on learning strategies or "principles of generalization and discrimination" (Millikan, 1989, p. 292). If the learning strategies are individual, then natural selection has no grip on them whatsoever. If they are durable dispositions (programmed mechanisms) to learn, then we are back to what sort of programs they are, as evolutionary response to what sort of information tasks. In the case of open-ended learning and cogitation programs, that means being back to the program-outputs gap that evolutionary semantics has not bridged so far.

[6]"Unlike bee dances, which are all variations on the same simple theme, beliefs in dinosaurs, in quarks, and in the instability of the dollar are recent, novel, and innumerably diverse, as are their possible uses. How could there be anything biologically normal or abnormal about the details of the consumption of such beliefs?" (Millikan, 1989, pp. 291–292). Quite so.

4. THE PSYCHOSEMANTICS OF THINKING

Psychosemanticism has drawn considerable force and inspiration from the notion that thinking (cogitation) is essentially a semantically constrained manipulation of representations. This notion would reduce cogitation to production and categorization, which is precisely the view opposed in chapter 7. So I am not going to rehearse my alternative and the reasons for it, but rather explore and criticize the sources of the psychosemantics of thinking.

The notion that thinking manipulates representations semantically (i.e., under constraints reflecting semantic information tasks) has received encouragement from many quarters, some philosophical, others technical. Among the philosophical, I note the venerable view of knowledge as true representation, and of thinking as a provider of knowledge; and also the view that thinking operates under rationality constraints that secure logical coherence and truth preservation. The technical considerations concern the implementation of cogitation programs, and the ability of these programs to simulate semantic information tasks. Because the philosophical considerations have been more directly challenged throughout this essay, I want to say a few words at this point about the technical motivation of the psychosemantics of thinking.

The implementation first: Representations are semantic structures generated by specialized production and categorization programs, operating not only in vision and language processing but also, less peripherally, in concept application and memory retrieval. Because cogitation does manipulate semantic representations generated by such programs, it would appear that cogitation manipulates these representations semantically. This appearance may have two sources, both connected with how the utilization programs of cogitation are implemented. One is in the sense of the raw material, the other in the sense of underground work.

The former is the sense in which vision, language, or memory provide the representations (raw material) handled in cogitation. If one maintains that all that thinking does is pick up the raw representational material, originating in vision or memory, for categorization and logical processing, then one has a semantic cogitation, because the latter two tasks are semantic, and the raw material that their programs handle is also semantic. (Chapter 7 provides a direct response to this psychosemantic view of cogitation.)

The underground work sense of implementation is best captured by the hypothesis of the language of thought or of any other form of an internal code (mentalese) that translates and runs higher level cogitation programs such as those for belief fixation, problem solving, or speech acting. It may help to think of the difference between the implementer and the implemented in this case by analogy with the difference between a programming language and the particular task programs it defines and runs—say, between Pascal and a particular modal logic program, or between UVAX and an airline reservation program. The programming language is a formal implementer of the tasks programs, and so is, on this analogy, the language of thought with respect to various cogitation programs. We do not yet have the psychosemantics of thinking, if the language of thought, or another internal code like it, is only a formal and nonsemantic implementer (programming language). Indeed, this may be the most plausible reading of the language of thought hypothesis, because it explains, inter alia, how the cogitation programs are run and how they communicate with other programs across distinct cognitive modalities.

There is a stronger reading of the language of thought hypothesis that makes three further assumptions. One is that the language of thought is already categorized and comes with its own innate semantics. A second assumption is that any cogitation (belief or desire) can be fully translated into a pair <formula in the language of thought plus its operational role>. A third assumption is that the translation offers a principled classification of that cogitation in the vocabulary and axioms of the language of thought. As a result, there is a reduction of cogitation to the language of thought. If the latter is psychosemantic, so by reduction is the former. This reduction must be opposed until the end of time.

To see the fine print of the distinctions and assumptions just surveyed, take Fodor's proposal to the effect that to believe cogitatively is to be functionally related (have the operational role captured by the rules of the language of thought) to a formula in the language of thought. The proposal is open to several readings. It may mean, on the weaker reading of formal implementation, a mapping of the belief relation into an uninterpreted counterpart formula of the underground programming language. It may also mean, on the stronger but still nonreductive and implementational reading (i.e., without the third assumption), a translation of the belief relation into a semantically interpreted formula of the same language.

Assuming the truth of the language of thought hypothesis, both these nonreductive readings are not inimical to the psychopragmatics of cogitation. For, in either case, the claim is that some sequences of formulae, operated on by some form-sensitive processes, implement some higher level properties and configurations by producing and manipulating representations. The key point here, argued at length in chapter 7, is that this underground production and manipulation of representations does not have a final functional say in mental cognition or mentally driven behavior. That belongs to the pragmatic output of cogitation (the mental script of a goal situation, including a belief relation). The implementing (underground) representations have causal powers in virtue of their form and core semantic properties but these powers are exercised only to implement a mental pragmatics. This is analogous to mental imagery using the symbolic resources of topomaps (a suggestion made in chap. 7, section 6). A space simulation task of imagery can be executed only by symbolic encoding on a topomap. One can say that a formula in the topomap code expresses some spatial information and that a relation between two or more such formulae expresses an imaged rotation or movement from A to B. Yet one would not say that this translation of the mental imagery task, which has to do with solving a problem or anticipating an action, into the language of topomapping also effects a reduction. The topomap language does not have the utilization categories and rules of mental imagery; their programs are different.

This multilevel implementation story is familiar. At a lower level of complexity, physical events are causally manipulated in virtue of properties (such as shape or on/off patterns of firing), which implement the language of thought itself; and again we would not say that the physical manipulation, qua physical, functionally runs and thus explains reductively the psychosemantics of the language of thought. If semantic causation can be saved from reduction to its physical implementation, by citing the functional constraints that configure and explain the former but not the latter, surely the same argument can save the pragmatic work of cogitation from being reduced to its implementation by the language of thought. The fact that the representations that work in cogitation have causal and functional powers in virtue of their formal and semantic properties does not entail that the work the representations make possible is itself semantic; for the exercise of those powers may be subject to further influences and is. Physical states have causal powers in virtue of their atomic configurations, yet in implementing a language of thought, the physical states exercise their powers not only in compliance with physical laws; there must be additional functional constraints at work or else the very idea of an implementation does not make any sense.[7]

The other source of psychosemanticitis is the fact that we can simulate production and categorization tasks in our thinking. Consider, for example, the production of the representation a + b = c out of another representation b + a = c under a commutativity rule. This is a logical transformation that executes a semantic information task. The commutativity rule is a semantic constraint, for it says that the truth values of the complex representations assembled under addition are not affected by the order of the component representations. Or look at it this way: You understand the representation of c by understanding the representations of a, b, +, and = under the rule to the effect that the order of a and b around + does not affect the truth value of the complex representation. This is no different from understanding a sentence by understanding its words under a conjunction rule: the latter tells you to understand "the cat and the dog like each other" the same way you under-

[7]Some of the points made in this section appear in Bogdan (1989a, 1993b). The latter was prompted by a spirited defense of Fodor's psychosemanticism by Dascal and Horowitz (1992) against my criticisms in Bogdan (1989a).

stand "the dog and the cat like each other," relative to a prior understanding of the component words. These are executions of production tasks by syntactic means, where representations are assembled out of other representations.

So we know implicitly, by way of the production programs employed, that the order of conjunction or addition does not affect the truth of conjuncts, but learn in logic and grammar classes how to regiment this implicit knowledge in specific utilizations of representations. Not only logic, mathematics, and scientific inference, but disciplined ordinary reasoning depends on this deliberate simulation of production contexts. In such cases representations are utilized to execute semantic tasks, which is why it appears that the utilization (thinking) is essentially semantic (Bogdan, 1990). If one's view is that the job of cognition is to generate true representations of the world and utilize them only by virtue of what they represent, then one is likely to regard the production and categorization tasks, which are semantic, as definitive of utilization (thinking) as well. If one follows this path, then one would also see the programs that execute production and categorization tasks as the ones at work in mental cognition. This, I have argued to exhaustion, is the path to psychosemantic perdition.

Needless to say, human cogitation is often fully dedicated to executing a semantic task such as conjunction, addition, modus ponens, deductive–nomological explanations, what have you. These are cases where utilization emulates production, categorization, and other semantic tasks. Furthermore, in the process of reasoning inside a particular script of a goal situation, one complies with the semantic constraints on thought transitions, even though the transitions themselves have a pragmatic destination. Preserving reference and respecting truth or probability in thought transitions are semantic values worth honoring in scripting goal situations. Psychosemanticism may regard semantic emulation or semantic respectfulness as distinctions without a difference. Nevertheless, the difference is there: It is the teleopragmatic difference.

I conclude this list of psychosemantic temptations by recalling that another sort of semantic intruders in the fortress of pragmatic cogitation originate in the routinized and domain-specific programs of the mental modules that may operate in perception, reasoning, or belief fixation. If these programs operate in an exclusively semantic manner (as in probabilistic inferences from experience or in the mandatory fixation of a perceptual belief about the surrounding spatial layout), then there are some fixed psychosemantic segments within a cogitation cycle. That is not only acceptable because it is biologically inevitable, but often desirable. Even if it turns out that the cogitative mind is modular to a more considerable extent than is now thought, that humans cogitate mostly by slaloming from one modular program to another, and that most of these programs are essentially semantic, it would still be the case, I think, that our cogitation has to construct goal scripts, and that to do so, it must represents its goals, choose, and decide among modular programs, premise relevant data, search for new data, the whole teleopragmatic spiel. The construction itself remains pragmatic, even though some or even most of the rooms it connects may be full of modularized psychosemantic stuff.

10 Prospects for Explanation

This book has praised and found support and inspiration in two recent methodological innovations in the foundations and practice of cognitive science. In historical order, one is the classical top–down (ICM) analysis that recommends an explanatory progression from information tasks to the executing cognitive programs and then to the mechanisms running the programs. The other and more recent is the evolutionary analysis that treats cognition the way biologists treat any organ, namely, as an adaptation. The evolutionary analysis complements and motivates the classical analysis by approaching the information tasks of cognition from the direction of the real selection pressures and of the adaptations evolved to answer them. Indeed, as I show in the next two sections, the evolutionary and classical ICM analyses converge in explaining the main information tasks of biocognition. These are the domain-specific tasks of production, categorization, and routinized utilization, all executed by disciplined, modular programs.

This covers a lot of biocognition but not all. There is also mental guidance, where teleology makes an important proximate difference. Apparently lacking domain-specificity and total modular discipline, mental cognition does not lend itself easily to evolutionary or ICM analyses or combinations thereof. This is the challenge of cogitation, sketched in section 3. Section 4 looks at, but is skeptical about, current attempts to assimilate the explanation of cogitation to either classical or evolutionary accounts. The final section examines the nature and scope of what is proximately explained in cogitation.

1. DISCIPLINE THROUGH EVOLUTION

There is fresh air in the basement of cognitive science. It is evolutionary psychology, an important and much needed effort to align psychology to evolutionary biology both with respect to general methodology and the specific strategies of inquiry. As a general project, evolutionary psychology is not entirely new. Darwin himself pioneered the field with his work on emotions in animals and humans (Darwin, 1872). Psychologists and philosophers have contributed to the field ever since.[1] The more specific and much more recent project that I find particularly promising, and relevant to the argument of this chapter, is the one that combines the methodological insights of the classic ICM method, pioneered by Chomsky and further articulated by Marr (chap. 3, section 1), with the explanation by natural selection. The classical-evolutionary combination, which I will call the evolutionary ICM method, is the best hope so far for a biologically based cognitive science. Because, to my knowledge, the spirit of the evolutionary ICM method has been best motivated and articulated in a series of recent articles by Cosmides and Tooby, I take their work as programmatically representative. In spite of my earlier reservations about the explanatory potency of natural selection, for the sake of my current argument, I assume that potency as limitless and see how far it goes.

Evolutionary psychology complements and legitimizes the classical ICM method in biological terms by providing the starting points of the ICM analysis (i.e., the information tasks of cognition) with an ultimate evolutionary explanation. The reason for the convergence between evolutionary psychology and the classical ICM is crucial to the argument of this chapter. The convergence obtains because the information tasks converged on have properties that make them responsive to natural selection and intelligible to classical cognitive science. The information tasks and cognitive programs that cognitive scientists of the classical persuasion know how to analyze are those that evolutionary psychologists also know how to explain, whence the convergence. These are precisely the information tasks and programs naturally selected for their adaptive effects. This explains the convergence of classical and evolutionary thought on the very tasks that natural selection has a grip on. So goes the argument of the present section. The next section shows how this convergence allows for a standard subsumptive explanation of cognitive programs and their outputs.

Let us begin with the classical perspective. Its favorite information tasks

---

[1]In the philosophical area of mind naturalization, Dennett has been perhaps the earliest and most consistent advocate of evolutionary psychology (1969, 1981, 1987). Among others who have followed this line: Millikan (1984, 1986), Sober (1985), even Fodor (not only in the (wrongly!) self-repudiated (1990b) but also in the still authoritative (1990a, chap. 9).

(sensory-motor coordination, visual and language processing) are domain-specific, well defined, well behaved, tightly constrained, and closed or encapsulated informationally. As noted in chapter 6, the tasks of representational vision consist in calculating distal arrangements in terms of invariant ecological primitives that are recovered from sensory inputs and computed into complex datal structures. These tasks divide into a variety of specific subtasks, such as recovery of form from motion, stereopsis, and many others, which can be formally characterized.

Aside from general assumptions about the world and organisms, the precise formal analyses of such information tasks are not based on empirical studies. Instead, in an a priori spirit, the analyses spell out the possible conditions in which the tasks could be accomplished, and to that extent they describe the intrinsic requirements of the tasks rather than their worldly incarnations. Those intrinsic requirements identify the success conditions for the tasks under analysis (e.g., what makes vision veridical, or sensory–motor coordination effective), and thus offer important a priori clues as to what sort of architectures, in what sort of ecological interactions, can possibly meet those success conditions (P.M. Churchland, 1989; Pylyshyn, 1989, pp. 63–66; Fodor, 1983; Marr, 1982).[2] The programs that carry out such formalizable tasks are stimulus-driven, domain-specific, functionally disciplined, mandatory in operation, and algorithmic as opposed to heuristic or pragmatic; the mechanisms that run the programs are hardwired, brain specialized and localized, and genetically determined. I am talking of cognitive modules.

Adaptive success is what natural selection is all about. What it selects as adaptive is installed genetically in durable and species-universal modular architectures interacting in standardized proximate arrangements with an ecological niche. The classical–evolutionary convergence for domain-specific and modularized cognition is explained by the fact that the success conditions for its tasks and programs are the adaptation conditions favored by natural selection. This point is illuminated by approaching the convergence from the other direction, of evolutionary psychology (Cosmides & Tooby, 1987; Tooby & Cosmides, 1990; Tooby & Cosmides, 1992).

The job of evolutionary psychology is to relate the ultimate explanations in terms of natural selection to the proximate explanations in terms of cognitive architectures through an evolutionary account of the information tasks executed by the architectures. Two evolutionary steps are needed before the analysis can join the classical ICM method; these steps bring

[2]I take it that no optimality standards need to be invoked for the classical–evolutionary fit. The classical analysis simply defines the nature and the success conditions of a task (when it is accomplished, not how well or how efficiently or the like), whereas the evolutionary analysis tracks the conditions in which natural selection rewards solutions (adaptations) that satisfy the success conditions and carry out the task.

natural selection to bear on the information tasks of cognition. The first step provides models of natural selection, fitness, adaptation, and genes (the ultimate tools of analysis), and of the psycho–behavioral phenomena to which the information tasks are relevant (e.g., kin recognition, foraging, social cooperation, etc.). The second step specifies the selection pressures (originating in the ancestral, ecological, social, and informational facts encountered during the evolution of a species) that configure the information tasks in question.

This provides a biologized version of the ICM method. The information tasks are now regarded as adaptation problems for which, eventually, design solutions evolve or don't. The solutions evolved count as adaptations, while the selection pressures and the ancestral conditions during which the pressures operated count as ultimate explanations of the adaptations. The organism's design, including its cognitive architectures, is an integration of specialized adaptations. The information tasks now specify the biological functions of the cognitive architectures, the adaptive solutions selected to execute them.

The next and crucial question for my convergence argument is what sort of information tasks natural selection defines for organisms, according to this evolutionary ICM script. The answer comes in several stages. The first, as articulated by Tooby and Cosmides (1992), describes a paradigm shift toward domain specificity in cognitive science:

> The Chomskian revolution in the study of language slowly began to legitimize the exploration of models of our evolved psychological architecture that did not assume apriori that all tasks are solved by the same set of content-independent processes. . . . Thus, researchers who ask hard questions about how organisms actually solve problems and who focus on the real performance of organisms on natural tasks have had to abandon the idea that the mind is free of content-specialized machinery. Researchers who study color vision, visual scene analysis, speech perception, conceptual development in children, mental imagery, psychophysics, locomotion, language acquisition, motor control, anticipatory motion, computation, face recognition, biomechanical motion perception, emotion recognition, social cognition, reasoning, and the perception and representation of motion, for example, cannot account for the psychological phenomena they study by positing computational mechanisms that are solely domain-general and content-independent. (p. 97)

The next question is whether the domain specificity and specialization of the tasks just listed and others like them makes evolutionary sense. It does, and here are some of the reasons. The domain-specificity of the tasks allows the executive programs to be good at something (not at everything, which would be anarchic, inefficient, and detrimental to survival), and therefore to be fast, reliable, and mandatory in operation. Plasticity and lack of specificity invite combinatorial explosion and the randomness of the search for an adaptive solution. This would not fit into the tight constraints of survival. The plasticity of biological design typically reflects not the open-endedness of equally possible responses but rather a capacity for locally adjusting an already specialized architecture or behavior program to the context. Furthermore, the feedback and regulatory mechanisms that evaluate cognitive and behavioral performances, retaining the good types and discouraging the bad, would not know what to look for and report on, as it were, if the performances were genuinely plastic and open-ended. Learning requires prior constraints and domain specialization or else is impracticable.

The point of these evolutionary arguments for domain-specificity and against domain-generality and unrestricted learning is that "an organism's behavior cannot fall within the bounds of the constraints imposed by the evolutionary process unless it is guided by cognitive programs that can solve certain information processing problems that are very [domain] specific. . . . A cognitive program can generate adaptive behavior only if it can perform [domain] specific information processing tasks (Cosmides & Tooby, 1987, p. 288; see also, Cosmides & Tooby, 1987, pp. 291–302; Tooby & Cosmides, 1992, pp. 97–114; Piatelli-Palmarini, 1989).

Earlier, when looking at the information tasks from a classical angle, I asked which of their features make them intelligible to and formalizable by computational theories of cognition. I want to ask the same question about the same tasks, now looking at them from an evolutionary angle. What is it about domain-specific information tasks that render the programs executing them naturally selectable, given their adaptivity, and also render both tasks and programs conceptually intelligible to evolutionary psychology? I am not asking, as I did a few paragraphs ago, why, or by virtue of what effects, domain-specific tasks and programs are selected for (because fast, reliable, economic, feedback sensitive, etc.). I am asking what intrinsic properties of the tasks make the executing programs to have the effects in question in the first place. The psychoevolutionary answer as presented by Tooby and Cosmides (1992) is essentially logical:

> When a class of situations that a mechanism is designed to solve is more narrowly defined, then (1) the situations will have more recurrent features in common, and therefore (2) the mechanism can "know" more in advance about any particular situation that is a member of this class. As a result, (3) the mechanism's components can embody a greater variety of problem solving strategies. This is because mechanisms work by meshing with the features of situations and, by definition, narrowly defined situations have more features in common. Our depth perception mechanism has this property, for example: It works well because it combines the output of many small modules, each

> sensitive to a different cue correlated with depth. In addition, (4) the narrower the class, the more likely it is that a good, simple solution exists—a solution that does not require the simultaneous presence of many common features. The frog can have a simple "bug detector" precisely because insects share features with one another that are not shared by many members of more inclusive classes, such as "animals" or "objects." (p. 104)

This analysis confirms the coincidence between the success conditions of an adaptation, looked at evolutionarily, and the intrinsic requirements of an information task, looked at classically.[3] What makes an information task classically intelligible and formalizable is what makes the programs and proximate arrangements that execute the task adaptive and naturally selected, hence intelligible to evolutionary psychology. The coincidence, in other words, obtains whenever domain-specific information tasks are executed by stable, systematic, and proximate patterns of correlations among: (a) informationally recurrent features of the ecology; (b) modular programs that register and process them; (c) the programs outputs (datal structures); and, (d) the resulting behaviors. Evolution produces cognitive adaptations whenever such enduring and *systematically adaptive patterns* (*SAP*) emerge ancestrally as, and remain over time, solutions to selection pressures.

So, there is a plausible and convergent ultimate story about a distinguished class of information tasks and their programs. The next step in my argument is to show that such a story also spawns the right proximate explanations that science needs. This amounts to showing that, relative to systematically adaptive patterns, the evolutionary ICM theories can engage in the standard subsumptive explanation. As a result, one can understand why cognitive science explains like the rest of science does, and also understand that, conversely, the facts that make subsumptive explanation possible must be the only facts that are scientifically intelligible. The hermeneutical circle is closed.

---

[3]Convergence could have been reached from a rational design or engineering or teleological rationality direction. This is a direction of analysis that is often followed by the classical analysis. Fodor (1983), after arguing that both theory and evidence show that perception is architecturally modular, thus reflecting the specificity of its information tasks, took the reverse, rational design line, and argued that if vision is to deliver data on distal arrangements from proximal stimulations, it must have specific, tightly constrained, bounded information tasks that are executed only by specialized and disciplined modular programs. There are costs and benefits attached to this strategy: For example, the modular computations are reliable and quick, which is a benefit, but narrow minded and not self-corrective, which is a cost, as both accumulated experience and the inevitable variability of the stimulations are disregarded. Dennett (1978; 1987) was an early and enthusiastic advocate of the rational design angle. He regarded biology as a science of reverse engineering of organisms.

2. SUBSUMPTIVE EXPLANATION

All natural sciences aim at explaining by subsumption under natural kinds and laws. This is the ideal of subsumptive explanation. The ideal is compatible with several forms of scientific explanation and fits the peculiarities of various domains of inquiry. A subsumptive explanation can be deductive–nomological, when we explain from general laws (as in physics or chemistry); it can be morphological, when we explain capacities in terms of underlying structures or deeper dispositions (as in biology or neuroscience); finally, the explanation can be systematic, when we explain the exercise of a function, or a performance, in terms of the cooperation of several mechanisms displaying a competence or program (as in cognitive science).[4] What is important to my argument is that these types of explanation subsume their explananda under types of physical regularities that have some sort of causal–functional relation to the explananda. This means that the subsuming explainers are efficacious in some physical sense and that their physical efficacy is explanatory. So construed, subsumptive explanation is thoroughly Newtonian in the sense of this book.

It is important to see what is not at stake in my argument about the prospects and limits of psychoNewtonian subsumption. What is not at stake is the presence of theories that account for some of the ultimate explainers (genetic programs, natural selection, adaptations, etc.) in general terms and propositions. Even if such explanations were subsumptive in some sense, that is not the Newtonian sense of explanatory physical efficacy. The fact that an account operates in general terms and propositions (is a theory) has nothing to do with how general and recurrent or unique its object is (the Big Bang is unique, so far, yet its account is a theory, and the same is true of the origin of life); and it has nothing to do with whether the object of the theory, whether singular or general, is or is not subsumable under causally efficacious arrangements, dispositions, or mechanisms. Mathematical explanation, qua proof, is deductively subsumptive but not in a causally efficacious sense. Teleological explanation in terms of effects (goals) explains subsumptively but not in a Newtonian sense. This, recall, is not because goal-directedness violates causation (it doesn't) or is not implemented causally (it is), but because the causal work that makes goal-directedness possible and effective underdetermines, and thus cannot explain, what goal-directedness does. Closer to my current concerns, there are theories of selective pressures that explain biological and information tasks but their explanations are not

[4] I am using Haugeland's (1978) classification. For how the systematic or functional explanation works in cognitive science, see also Cummins (1975, 1983).

subsumptive in a causal sense either, notwithstanding the fact that the implementation of selective pressures is causal.

This being clarified, let us see what is at stake in Newtonian subsumption. An explanation from laws, dispositions, or cooperating mechanisms, is required to treat its explanandum as a regular, generic, typical, faceless, unoriginal case of the properties and regularities stated by the explanans. I call this the *requirement of the generic explanandum.* It stipulates that a scientific explanation treat the explanandum as generic. Although each individual fact is different from any other, by necessarily failing to share one or more properties with any other, this difference is treated as trivial by scientific explanation, and ignored. Science is interested in the general and sees only the general in the particular. Science does not care about all the properties of an individual, which render it (logically) unique. This indifference to uniqueness is reasonable; trivial unicity often cannot and need not be explained.

An individual is a generic explanandum whenever, in the same context of space–time–causation, any individual of the same kind, occupying the same explanandum position, gets the same explanation. For scientific explanation, the context is really unique, not its occupier. The context identifies its occupier for the explanans, and in so doing, confers trivial unicity upon it. But the context is not explained. It is the occupier that is explained and then only as a generic representative of its kind. As far as scientific theorizing is concerned, any similarly sized and constituted particle or molecule or crystal placed in the same context behaves the same way. For evolutionary biology, the same is true of any adaptation; for evolutionary ICM theory, that extends to any cognitive adaptation (competence) and its performances.

I showed in the previous section how to get from the ultimate axioms (natural selection, fitness, adaptation, and genes) and an analysis of selection pressures to a profile of the information tasks in the domain analyzed.[5] Once there, the analysis moves in the area of proximate explanation where specialized inherited adaptations (programs and mechanisms) are viewed as internal solutions to the information problems posed by the selections pressures. If there is a cognitive adaptation in the form of a specialized program (competence) for a domain-specific information task and also a theory of the

---

[5]Of course, I maintain that without goal-directedness the axioms of ultimate explanation are incomplete, and that without guidance to goal, the selection pressures are not sufficient to explain the forms of, and the constraints on, information tasks. The cumulative effect of these arguments is to deny that a causal (Newtonian) subsumption going from natural selection to selection pressures to adaptations to proximate mechanisms can tell the story of life and cognition. This being on record, the more limited objective of this chapter is to acknowledge and motivate the ability of the subsumptive gambit in explaining domain-specific (modularized) cognition, while questioning its ability to do the same with mental cognition.

program, then the cognitive scientist can explain any particular program output (performance) by causal–functional subsumption in a context.

Why is subsumptive explanation successful in such cases? Recall that a domain-specific and modular program is a cognitive adaptation only if it executes its information task in a systematically adapted pattern (SAP). Adaptations are naturally selected for having exploited regular and durable features of an organism's ecology in systematic interaction with durable and functionally significant features of the organism. This is why adaptations count as solutions to general and recurrent problems posed by the environment. So the answer to my question is that it is these regular, recurrent, general, durable aspects which, reflected in a SAP, secure the explanatory subsumption.[6]

The subsumptive success of the explanation reflects the subsumptive work of the adaptation itself: A SAP in general, its cognitive component in particular, are selected precisely because they allow a general and enduring type of response, with well tested beneficial (fitness ensuring) effects, to current goal situations; such situations are treated as generic instances of the ancestral problem the SAP has evolved to solve. If the current situation fails to be such an instance, the cognitive program, constitutive of a SAP, would not kick into operation. If enough detail about the goal situation is specified, it may become trivially unique, but that is not what the program was selected to handle. The subsumptive explanation does not care for such detail, for it is calculated to track the application conditions of the program in question as a generic instance of a larger SAP.

The nature of the SAP adaptations and the subsumptive range of the modular programs themselves explain why classical–evolutionary cognitive science, being focused solely on modular and domain-specific competencies, is only marginally interested in cognitive or behavioral performances, and rarely for their own sake. Because the contexts of performance do not matter essentially to subsumptive explanation, modular and domain-specific performances can be treated in isolation, often in an artificial, even silly manner. Such treatment is reasonable. As Fodor (1983) put it, "The conditions for successful science (in physics . . . as well as psychology) is that nature should have joints to carve it at: relatively simple subsystems which can be artificially isolated and which behave in isolation in something like the way they behave in situ. Modules satisfy this condition" (p. 128). This downgrades any special significance of real life (in situ) performances. This is because even in situ there are no informational interferences to be factored into the explanation.

---

[6]"Long-term, across-generations recurrence of conditions-external, internal, or their interaction-is central to the evolution of adaptations. . . . For this reason, a major part of adaptationist analysis involves sifting for these environmental or organismic regularities or invariances" (Tooby & Cosmides, 1992, p. 69).

Cognitive modules have evolved to respond only to generic instances of a SAP in an informationally autarchic manner. This makes the contexts of modular and domain-specific performances, in which SAPs are instantiated, trivially unique and scientifically uninteresting. The competence is the law, the particular performance only a law-abiding and generic instance of the causal efficacy of the competence, and the psychoNewtonian style of subsumptive explanation is doing very well, indeed.

3. THE CHALLENGE OF COGITATION

What about cogitation? Fodor (1983) made the infamous suggestion that cognitive science is intrinsically unable to explain cogitation. Here is how he formulated the charge:

> Fodor's First Law of the Nonexistence of Cognitive Science: . . . the more global (e.g., the more isotropic) a cognitive process is, the less anybody understands it. *Very* global processes, like analogical reasoning, aren't understood at all.
>
> . . . [T]here seem to be no way to delimit the sorts of informational resources which may affect, or be affected by, mental processes of problem solving. We can't, that is to say, plausibly view the fixation of belief as effected by computations over bounded, local information structures. A graphic example of this sort of difficulty arises in AI, where it has come to be known as the 'frame problem.'
>
> . . . [In mental processes] it may be *unstable, instantaneous* connectivity that counts. Instead of hardwiring, we get a connectivity that changes from moment to moment as dictated by the interaction between the program that is being executed and the structure of the task at hand. (pp. 107, 112, 118)

The reader recognizes in the last quotation features of cogitation emphasized in chapter 7. Finally:

> While some interesting things have been learned about the psychology of input analysis—primarily about language and vision—the psychology of thought has proved quite intractable.
>
> . . . [G]lobal systems are per se bad domains for computational models, at least of the sorts cognitive scientists are accustomed to employ. Modules satisfy this condition [the *in situ*-isolation similarity of performance]; [cogitating] systems by definition do not. If, as I have supposed, the mental cognitive processes are nonmodular, this is very bad news for cognitive science. (pp. 126, 128)

Fodor's diagnosis underscored the explanatory prospects and limits of classical and evolutionary cognitive science. At least, this is how I see it.[7] My reconstruction of Fodor's diagnosis divides into three problems of explanation. The first concerns the information tasks of cogitation, the second the programs that execute the tasks, and the third the specific mental scripts of goal situations. I construe Fodor's diagnosis to imply that the subsumptive Newtonian strategy fails to solve all these problems.

Earlier in this book, mostly in chapters 7 and 9, I suggested some reasons why, in its psychosemantic incarnation, psychological Newtonianism cannot provide a coherent and plausible theory of the information tasks and cognitive programs involved in cogitation. Against this background, I want now to examine some explicit or implicit (i.e., reconstructible) psychoNewtonian responses to my reconstruction of Fodor's diagnosis, and show why they fail to solve the problems raised by the diagnosis.

4. ASSIMILATION

The Newtonian response to the challenge of cogitation is likely to be assimilationist by construing the tasks of cogitation in terms of those of production and categorization, which I lump under the concept of codification, or other domain-specific tasks and their modular programs.

Classical Assimilation

Let us consider the first assimilation ploy. If cogitation is reduced to codification, then its tasks can be shown to be semantic. This psychosemantic turn would allow psychoNewtonian subsumption to handle the second (program explanation) and third (performance explanation) problems posed by Fodor's diagnosis because, as I have shown, classical cognitive science knows how to translate the semantics of information tasks into the psychological causation of programs. (This is, in effect, what the syntax-over-symbols and connectionist paradigms do.) This assimilation ploy is responsible for the notion that cogitative judging or belief fixation are programs for recognition and categorization, or that inferences are programs for truth-preserving computations, or that communication is a program for encoding and decoding meanings.

If successful, the assimilation of cogitation to codification would allow for the formulation of psychosemantic programs laws, often called intentional laws, in terms of which proximate subsumptive explanations of particular cogitations and behaviors can be deployed. It is ironic, if not somewhat

[7]This is not how Fodor explained the matter. What follows is my diagnosis of his diagnosis. Moreover, Fodor's diagnosis concerned specifically the classical computational view whereas my reconstruction is going to be more general.

inconsistent, that Fodor has been pessimistic about the ability of cognitive science to understand cogitation programs, yet optimistic about the subsumptive work of psychosemantic or intentional laws in proximate explanations. True, he has admitted that the intentional laws are constantly qualified in their application by ceteris paribus conditions, but he has blamed the need for such conditions on the undeniable fact that the intentional laws, being nonbasic, must be implemented by mediating mechanisms. The latter are known to break down or fail to work or be implemented by alternative mechanisms (Fodor, 1990a, chap. 5).

I think Fodor is right about the implementing mechanisms running cogitative programs under variable and often suboptimal conditions but wrong about the idea that intentional laws govern cogitation and wrong about the ceteris paribus conditions. The ceteris paribus conditions, far from being mere features of the implementing mechanisms, reflect the way in which cogitation works when confronted with changing information tasks posed by the succession of new goal situations. Cogitation is intrinsically ceteris paribus, which is why ceteris paribus qualifications must be part of any proximate explanation of cogitation and cogitation-run behavior.

The psychosemantic reading of intentional laws is itself assimilationist. A closer look at Fodor's examples reveals that the intentional laws are either of production or categorization, or else of logical discipline, hence of routine tasks. Fodor's favorite instances of the former are linguistic, phonetic and grammatical, and occasionally visual. The latter typically have the form of a belief attitude tracking some logical law (as in 'if you believe that P, and believe that P entails Q, then you believe that Q, ceteris paribus'). The intentional explanation is meant to subsume proximately any instance of cogitation under an appropriate intentional law or combination of such laws. The subsumption is psychoNewtonian because the laws are assumed to characterize causally potent program dispositions and regularities.

The problem, as presented in chapter 7, is that these are not genuine and normal examples of spontaneous cogitation. Fodor needs to dress his intentional laws in ceteris paribus clothes, not so much because of what the implementing mechanisms do or do not do, but because his intentional laws do not constrain fully the work of cogitation. The task of the cogitation programs is to model goal situations, not to produce and categorize representations, or to run some logical entailment, or to ensure the logical closure of thoughts or beliefs. It was shown in chapter 7 that cogitation programs do not work spontaneously under intentional (psychosemantic) laws alone. If only the latter can render mental cognition scientifically intelligible, then mental cognition is not intelligible to a psychoNewtonian analysis guided by intentional laws. It was shown in the concluding section of the previous chapter that either in a raw material or underground work sense, the reduction of cogitation to codification does not work.

The assimilation of cogitation tasks to those of production, categorization, or modular routines, has had detrimental implications for cognitive science. These implications are seen in the psychological study of spontaneous reasoning as deductive or probabilistic inference and its AI simulation, also in the study of language processing and communication. Criticisms in the foundational literature (Bogdan, 1990; Clark & Clark, 1977; Sperber & Wilson, 1986) and Fodor's own lament indicate that one cannot profitably think of cogitation the way one thinks of codification. If cognitive science is conceived of as a science of codification, then one must stare helplessly at the problems raised by Fodor's diagnosis. For not only have the tasks and programs of cogitation been misconstrued, but, as a result, there is no answer to the third and proximate explanation problem, because the programs of cogitation, unlike those of codification, are not psychosemantic or intentional. The mental scripts do not simply convey meanings and preserve semantic values, which is why they cannot be subsumed under—because they are not fully determined by—psychosemantic programs exclusively geared to meanings and semantic values.

Assimilation by Evolution

Could evolution vindicate the assimilation of cogitation to codification by favoring a psychosemantic mental design? It could, says one suggestion (P.M. Churchland & P.S. Churchland, 1983, p. 14), if mental design is shown to have evolved either like, or out of, the design for codification. The latter was "calibrated" by evolution to "measure, via the excitable cells, certain features in the environment." For the mental design one must assume that evolution calibrates, not registration patterns and associated motor responses, but learning strategies. On this assumption about mental design, P.M. and P.S. Churchland (1983) concluded: "Here then the job for neurobiology and neuroethology is Herculean but the bets are that the story for complex organisms will be built on the more basic story of calibrational semantics for simpler organisms, following the steps of evolution itself" (p. 14).

Let us grant that evolution calibrates the mental design of cogitation the way the Churchlands said it does. (We can even throw in a bit of neural Darwinism, which Dennett anticipated [1969, chap. 3], to speed up the process.) The question is what evolution is expected to calibrate in mental design, what sort of learning strategies. If the answer is learning and applying concepts, or forming representations of various situations, we are back to the assimilation of cogitation to codification, and the arguments proposed earlier against this reductionist move.

Another option is to view the cogitative mind as having its own disciplined and domain-specific tasks, some psychosemantic, some not, run by an array of modular programs. The tasks in question are regarded as having had major biosocial and practical values at the time the modular programs evolved. Examples are foraging, kin recognition, social exchange, predictions of conspecific behavior, social deception, tool manufacture and utilization, and the like. The programs executing these tasks evolved as task-related adaptations and remain so because many of these tasks are still with us, in a form or another. In addition, some of the modular programs may have been pirated for cogitation tasks other than the ancestral ones. The implication is that we may be thinking in the very forms in which chimps and early humanoids figured out (say) what conspecifics are up to (see papers in Byrne & Whiten, 1988, particularly those by Humphrey & Jolly; also Alexander, 1989; Cosmides, 1989).

Even if accepted, the truth of this hypothesis is still far from helping us with cogitation. Fodor may have been wrong about the nonmodular organization of the cogitative mind, yet, as I construe his diagnosis, still right about the failure of mainstream cognitive science to explain cogitation at both the program and program application levels. The modularity hypothesis invites us to imagine the possibility that every major feat of cogitation is accomplished by some mental module evolved out of those that dealt with tasks configured in ancestral SAP arrangements. This hypothesis would allow an ultimate psychoevolutionary explanation in terms of ancestral SAP's to reach deep inside the utilization area of mental cognition and explain the modular programs of cogitation. A reconstructive account of an ancestral domain-specific task would provide a basis for the examination of the SAP evolved as an adaptation selected for that task. The SAP in turn would elucidate the functional and possibly computational nuts and bolts of the executive modular programs. Knowledge of the task and of the programs, and of the SAP-type contexts in which the programs operate, then identifies the types of inputs that causally set the programs in motion. As a result, the analysis generates proximate functional explanations of the cogitations routinely produced by such programs. Motivated evolutionarily, this would look like psychoNewtonian subsumption. This I take to be the view advocated by Tooby and Cosmides. Would it add up to a general solution to the problem of cogitation posed by Fodor's challenge?

It is too early to tell whether the modular programs constitute a majority, a very busy minority, or a marginal plurality among our mental programs. The debate is just heating up. For the sake of the argument, let us suppose that cogitation is very heavily modularized. The answer to this question could be positive if cogitation worked in single-track executions of SAP-related tasks—the way visual, sensory-motor, or grammatical tasks are managed. But that does not seem to be the case. Even though I am prepared to admit that mental modules may have evolved to execute as many of the goal scripting and reasoning subtasks as is imaginable, I do not see that either the general form of cogitation (mental guidance) or the current task-specific patterns of goal scripting and reasoning would be explained by an evolutionary theory of mental modularity. Although I do not deny that such a theory could one day tell us much more about cogitation than it does now, I am skeptical so far about the notion that evolutionary accounts of ancestral tasks, SAP's, and their modular programs, are sufficient to answer the problems raised by my reconstruction of Fodor's diagnosis.

Even if one assumes that humans think mainly in ancestral grooves, as it were, each with its own data base and program, the pull of the goal and the unfolding dynamics of goal situations still remain preeminent in the shaping and selection of the patterns of utilization of the modular programs handling goal scripting and reasoning tasks. That would be true even in simpler and fully modularized thinking. Even though the young chimp engaging in a calculative social deception of the old dominant male may be reacting to a typical input and context, we may assume that the chimp often has goals more ambitious than deception. In that case, the chimp's scripting and reasoning maneuvers must be more complicated than his social calculations, and hence the sequences of explanation of the form—context to input to program to program application—are less unique and predetermined in the former than in the latter case. That, surely, is even more so in the case of humans. Just as the chimp's deception round is part of larger goal-driven games (get the desired mate, show ability and guts that will be useful in later alliances, and so on), so our alleged modular calculations in planning the next restaurant outing or the next argument in a debate are local rounds in larger games of cogitation. And just as the young chimp could have abandoned deception for some other tactic (apparent submission or indifference) with the same long term ends, so our thinking may choose different concepts and different modular programs to rehearse its way to some goal. The thinker may appeal to the same cogitative means without employing them in the same configurations, for the same sorts of tasks. We may be thinking in ancestral grooves but in new informational domains, with new tasks. The difference is important.

The modularization of cogitation, whatever its extent, is a matter of means, of how current tasks are executed by ancient architectures. The tasks themselves need not be ancient nor do they need to interact in combinations that have an ancestral adaptive pedigree. Even the most hardened mental modularists would not deny this fact.[8] Such tasks, then, need not have any relevant SAPs to start from. And, without such SAP, the required explanatory sequence of subsumptions from task to context to input to program to program application is lacking. An evolutionary account of the ancestral

[8]"The human entry into the 'cognitive niche' appears to have involved the evolution of cognitive adaptations for improvising novel sequences of behavior to reach targeted goals of certain kinds, and the breadth of applicability of these mechanisms has obviously allowed humans to penetrate new habitats and subsist in new ways" (Tooby & Cosmides, 1990, p. 406).

tasks and the adapted modular programs tells us where the cogitation means come from, why they were initially adaptive, in what circumstances they worked initially, and how. That is quite a lot but still short of meeting Fodor's challenge, as I see it.

Let me make the point in the strongest terms possible. Suppose cogitation is maximally modular: It contains not only modular programs for metarepresentation, goal scripting, and reasoning, but also, more basically, its concepts operate as modules (Sperber, 1993). This, as Fodor would put it, is "modularity gone mad". Yet even a mad modularity would not help the subsumptive evolutionary explanation reach as far as current cogitative performance. Mental modules can and do integrate their work in novel and context-sensitive ways; they can take up new tasks and find new domains of application; they can acquire new data bases that store information and instructions for operation in the form of artificial signs and notations, texts, images, and the like. Equally importantly, a maximal modular architecture is still compatible with the teleopragmatic features of cogitation explored in chapter 7. This means that although the basic units of the central architecture are programmed to work relative to domain-specific inputs and isolated data bases, the occurrent (performance) connections among these units, in some form of goal script or reasoning, follow no modular program and respond only to the demands of the goal situation and the internal condition of the system.

Although architecturally modular, computer systems can engage in holistic, heuristic, and open-ended forms of data processing. As Sperber (1993) noted, "a holistic effect need not be the outcome of a holistic procedure." The question, then, is not how the modules of cogitation have evolved, relative to which original tasks, for that would explain only the basic units of competence. If this is what cognitive science must study, so be it. But then thinking is beyond its reach. As I have noted on a number of occasions in this work and elsewhere (Bogdan, 1983, 1985b, 1986b, 1988c, 1989a), it is true of cogitation that its competence underdetermines its performance, systematically, while its essence resides in its performatory ability to handle goal situations as they come. Unlike Fodor, I take this truth to be compatible with either the modularity or nonmodularity of cogitation or degrees in between. In either version, the truth blocks the ability of evolutionary accounts to explain cogitation in performance. As a result, we are still far from a solution to the third Fodorian problem, the proximate explanation of particular cogitations.

5. WHAT TO EXPLAIN, AND IN HOW MUCH DETAIL?

The problem of proximate explanation begins as a matter of individuation. How close must one come to the particular cogitations to be explained? How much detail is needed to individuate the explanandum? How generic or unique must that explanandum be? The subsumptive explanation in science generally obeys the requirement of the generic explanandum: The assumption is that the explanation has subsumptive force as long as the particular explanandum instantiates the general properties and relations correlated by the laws, dispositions, or rules of the domain.

In addition to the requirement of the generic explanandum, psychological Newtonianism wants the subsumption to mirror causal determinations. We can see why and how an assimilation of cogitation to production, categorization, or modularization complies with the psychoNewtonian demands on subsumption. If we regard a cogitative belief merely as a form of concept application (the representation of an individual under a property), then any specific belief would be subsumed causally–functionally under the properties of the programs for concept application. Whatever else belief might be, the decision to see it only as concept application ensures that any specific belief is a generic explanandum because the concept application programs are general and functionally subsumptive. The only unicity may lie in the particular context of a belief and in the specific input that triggers it, but that is trivial and not in the range of explanation anyway. When the assimilation switches to modular programs, the same is true of the decision to see belief as a spontaneous and rigid acceptance of data (as in perceptual belief) or as a readiness to act relative to input and other states.

The teleopragmatic explanation of a belief is different, although it also appeals to general constraints and properties. I noted (in chap. 7, section 5) that a belief fixation program is involved in the execution of several cogitation tasks such as selecting and backgrounding data relevant to a goal situation, making or exploiting assumptions, considering alternatives, measuring their plausibility, and so on. The belief program applications are subsumed under this teleopragmatic description. The description is mostly about cognitive competence but that is not the competence for production, categorization, or some particular modular performance. It is the competence for goal scripting and reasoning. For most instances of believing, there is no production or categorization task to explain subsumptively the belief program application, and there is no ancestral information task, either, that a specific SAP, containing a specialized belief program, has evolved to execute. As a result, there is no application of the belief program that can be causally subsumed under the program rules, whether of production, categorization or mental modularization. All the belief program says, more or less, is here is a cognition-action situation, structure it goal-directedly, script it in agreement with this set of instructions, reason to other goal-scripts if necessary, and settle upon the solution that best complies with your data and goals.

Even with teleopragmatics, this may be as far as one can or want to go subsumptively, in terms of competence. What else is there to worry about, scientifically speaking? Isn't cognitive science concerned with competence, leaving specific individual performances to the trivial unicity of contexts? Wasn't Chomsky emphatic about his theory of grammar being a theory of linguistic competence, not performance? Aren't production programs and mental modules more like grammar, and cogitative goal scripting and reasoning more like linguistic performances? Chomsky, joined by so many other cognitive scientists and philosophers, seems to think that no science of performance is possible or indeed desirable. The (program) laws of grammar are not those of linguistic communication, which is why, according to this line of thought, no cognitive science of communication is possible. Isn't, then, cogitation more like communication? If so, then why bother with it, from a cognitive–scientific point of view?

To begin with, communication may look arbitrarily variable at the level of performance from the stance of production, grammar included, and categorization programs. Change the explanatory stance, follow a different parsing of the appropriate tasks and the executive programs, and you find a different story of communication emerges (Sperber & Wilson, 1986). I have urged a similar theoretical shift about cogitation, which, after all, is a key engine of communication. This shift responds to the teleological difference, more exactly, to the proximate difference teleology makes in cogitation. Let me illuminate the difference by backgrounding what is common in competence subsumption, whether the competence pertains to production or cogitation. To explain why and how a particular cogitation is an instance of, say, goal scripting is to subsume it under the teleopragmatic competence for cogitation. In terms of subsumption under competence (program) rules, this is no different from subsuming the grammatical structure assignment for a particular utterance under the rules of grammar. In general, subsumption under competence works whenever the input and the program rules standardly determine the output. So far, so common.

Now the difference. The proximate teleological work of cogitation makes a critical difference in that, depending on, and responsive to a goal situation, the cogitator has alternative routes to outputs (goal scripts or reasoned sequences of such scripts) that do not depend exclusively or even standardly on inputs and a particular and fixed set of program rules, as was the case in production and categorization, or in the isolated operation of specialized mental modules. This difference is a matter of competence, the teleopragmatic competence. The human cogitator is designed by evolution to alternate, modify, even suspend internal programs, and influence their operation in response to how a goal situation is framed, relative to past goal situations, anticipations, utilities, and the like. The latter are competence parameters to be factored in to explain why the agent cogitated this way (to a goal script) rather than the other way; why she represented the goal situation in this manner instead of that manner; why she assumed such and such data instead of some other data, and so on. To identify and track the particular programs at work and the causal–functional route of their application, this proximate explanation needs, of course, more than subsumption under a teleopragmatic competence; it also needs the boundary conditions that specify how the competence responded to that particular context of performance. This is true of any explanation. But there is, again, a teleopragmatic difference.

For the sake of pedagogy, let me put it metaphorically. A physical event simply and passively, as it were, falls under the incidence of physical laws. There is nothing in the event as explanandum and its boundary conditions that would determine how the laws apply or select which laws apply. In cognition, the laws take the form of program rules. Yet, what is true of a physical explanation is largely true (mutatis mutandis) of simple cognition and behavior: The sensory–motor laws, or program rules, installed by evolution in a simple mind map the boundary conditions of the context into behaviors in a fixed and invariant manner, without mental interference. Teleopragmatic cogitation is different in that it responds to the boundary conditions of the context, which include not only input data but also whatever the cogitator knows, prefers, anticipates, by selecting not only the programs and subprograms that will do the work but often their modus operandi. This selection, which need not be conscious or deliberate, reflects the design of a novel mental competence, and to that extent it must participate in explanation.

I have emphasized repeatedly that teleology downgrades the work of functional causation. The foregoing is another crucial instance of such downgrading. The competence for cogitation is designed to follow the pull of the goal, not just the push of the cause, and adjust the deployment of the programs that handle a goal situation. That is an internal teleology, not unlike the one we encountered in temperature control: which program kicks in (perspiration, gland secretion, etc.) depends on the current state of the organism, its past efforts, levels of energy, etc. These latter contextual parameters must be factored in the finer grained proximate explanation of which particular temperature control program did what and when, in a causal–functional manner. In the last analysis, it is the causal push of an application of a particular program that proximately explains the output (fall in temperature). But the antecedent individuation of the program selected to do the work requires a contextual probing of the boundary conditions to which the multilateral competence for temperature control is designed to respond. That competence is multilateral because it is so designed teleologically. The same is true of the cogitating mind. Causation is involved in program execution, not in program choice, and not, antecedently, in the system's response to the context.

Note how this is different from proximate explanations in terms of vision or grammar programs (as production competencies) or mental modules (as utilization competencies). These types of programs are computationally—

hence causally and functionally—creative and inductive in handling their tasks and assigning appropriate structures to the data. To that extent, these programs are context-sensitive. Nevertheless, their causal–functional work is uniquely constrained by the general properties (rules) of the competence in question, given the input. No teleology here, hence no alternative functional routes by different programs, and no choices of programs and their mode of operation, given contextual parameters.

The point, then, is that the competence for cogitation has evolved an essential sensitivity to the contexts of its exercise (local adaptations, to put it nonliterally). A lot of essentially unique contextual variation is in the cogitator's head, given its teleopragmatic design, and not only outside. As far as I can tell, superior apes aside, this is not true of the cognition of other species.[9] The question is whether one wants to attend to such essentially contextual variations as which programs kicked in, on the basis of what data, with what repercussions, and so on. If one simply wants to see some competence at work, and look at the explanandum as a generic instance of the competence, then one does not have to come that close. But if, for some reason, one is curious to identify a local adaptation and make sense of it, then the sensitivity of cogitation to the singularity of context must be viewed as essential. This decision puts considerable pressure on the methodology of scientific explanation.

The decision, I suggest, to attend to the context specificity of goal scripts and reasonings is the sense that cogitation may have evolved as an instrument for continuous local adaptation. This, of course, is not adaptation in a strict sense, for it is not genetically encoded, is not sanctioned by natural selection, and may respond to no ancestral or typical task. But, its defenders would say, that is precisely the point (see chap. 7, footnote 1): Cogitation allows us to do things (improvised adaptations) that other species are lucky to do, ever so rarely, by means of genetic variation and natural selection. We want to know how such individual adaptations work and why, and we want to know these things not only for reasons of curiosity, gossip, or relevance to our own life (the stance of the commonsense psychologist). We also have more scientific reasons. Individual adaptations often become habits of thinking and behaving, spread in a community, and acquire social status. Social beliefs and practices, mentalities and institutions originate in individual adaptations. They are worth investigating and explaining. But how?

A troublesome implication lurking in my reconstruction of the third

[9]A clue to this difference may be found in the existence and operation of a declarative memory. Most organisms "remember" by getting habituated to or learning certain regularities. The data are compiled into behavioral categorizations and routines rather than retained in the form of representations of facts and events, which can later interfere with the current manufacture of representations in goal scripting and reasoning.

problem of Fodor's diagnosis was that, in failing to be generic, the cogitative explanandum is unintelligible. Or, differently said, the explanandum remains intelligible as long as it is scientifically subsumable, and lapses into unintelligibility once the subsumption loses its logical grip on it. I hope I have shown that the psychoNewtonian subsumption of particular cogitations fails not because the mental domain is lawless or unruly, which, teleologically speaking, it isn't, although it looks that way from the psychoNewtonian perspective of particular production, categorization or modular programs. The psychoNewtonian subsumption fails because it tries to assimilate the cogitation programs to the latter. Given the alternative combinations of programs rules and constraints, the influence of contexts, and the inevitable ceteris paribus exceptions, that sort of explanation could end up as baroque and singular in focus as its explanandum.[10] The result is either a mere description or else is scientifically unintelligible. But that result follows from adopting the wrong explanatory stance. The matter of the proximate explanandum in cogitation is not unintelligible, and depends on a methodological decision. My teleopragmatic account motivates why things are this way.

It may be helpful to conclude with an instructive analogy from evolutionary biology. The analogy concerns both the choice of the proximate explanandum and, in this light, what sort of science evolutionary biology is, and therefore what sorts of explanations it uses. These are matters worth pondering as one looks beyond the hardcore psychoNewtonian paradigm and tries to imagine future directions of research in cognitive science.

Many biological adaptations are scientifically intelligible although they are not generic and subsumable in any standard causal–functional sense. Evolutionary biologists care about the essential singularities of particular bioadaptations (such as the long neck of the giraffe, the human vocal tract, and hundreds of others). Quite often, they explain such singularities intelligibly but not by causal–functional subsumption. There are very few, if any, causal–functional generalizations that would lock into the nuts and bolts of a singular adaptation. If the interest of the evolutionary biologist is very focused (e.g., why did that species become extinct in those ecological conditions while the other adapted), and the individuation of the explanandum is very fine-grained, then the explanatory subsumption is almost bound to give way to some sort of historical and context-soaked narrative.

Almost but not quite. There is something about how organisms adapt generally that is intelligible and subsumable: teleology. Organisms have and try alternatives in coping with a changing environment. Genetic variations chase goals of various sorts whose satisfaction provides the instrumentalities

[10]In philosophy of mind this was pointed out by a number of authors (e.g., Bogdan, 1986b, 1988c; Morton, 1980; Wilkes, 1981). In AI this issue comes up in discussions of the frame problem (Fodor, 1983).

for maintenance and replication. This teleological pattern bears the mark of intelligibility. It also makes intelligible the fact that the alternative that succeeds, as adaptation, is the one that fits the singularities of an environment. Yet there are no preset causal–functional laws that govern this pattern and illuminate its intelligibility. The story must begin on a teleogenetic note.

The analogy we are chasing is not that cognition is biological, in general, and adaptive, in particular. It is, though not exclusively. But that is another matter. The analogy, at this final moment in my story, is that cogitation is intrinsically teleological and responsive to the contextual pull of the goal. It has alternatives in scripting and acting in a goal situation. If it matters why one alternative was chosen over another, then a causal–functional subsumption will not do. It takes a teleopragmatic account to make the possibility of the choice intelligible, and a narrative reconstruction of the context to explain the particular program choice and even the program operation (assumptions, default assignments, ceteris paribus decisions, etc.).

So far, and at its modest and practical level, commonsense psychology has been better than hardcore Newtonian cognitive science at both tasks. Commonsense psychology has a healthy respect for teleology and narrative reconstruction, which is why it handles cogitation better than standard cognitive science. But this is not because commonsense psychology is a descriptive and explanatory theory of the cognitive mind, for it is not. Rather, it is because commonsense psychology has coevolved with, and hence has become rather finely attuned to, cogitation. The understanding of that coevolution and attunement requires an account of social cognition, as radical and naturalist as that of the individual mind. Except for a few remarks in chapter 8, social cognition is a topic on which little has been said in this book. The project of mind naturalization would be ultimately incomplete without bringing the social mind into the picture.

Glossary*

Architecture: The notion of a *functional architecture* is intended to characterize the ensemble of functional resources that are immediately and systematically responsible for, sensitive to, and therefore explanatory of, the basic processes and structures involved in executing a definite class of tasks, whether metabolic, behavioral or informational. These resources include functionally identified components or systems with their programs and operations. A *cognitive* architecture is involved in the execution of information tasks, and its resources include programs and operations such as storing, retrieving and manipulating symbol or connectionist structures, and the functional mechanisms that run the programs and perform the operations. The relations of immediacy and systematicity cited in the characterization of architecture are needed to exclude a mere implementational reading of architecture. There are plenty of chemical and physical processes that implement metabolic or behavioral or cognitive programs and operations but their laws are simply physical or chemical, not functionally metabolic, behavioral or cognitive (chap. 4, section 1).

Behavioral Categories: Primitively semantic programs for classifications of distal and specific properties that are directly utilized by behavioral routines; single-track dispositions to map data structures into behaviors; in teleonomic cognition there are only behavioral discriminations with proximal or input-bound range (chap. 5, section 3).

---

*The glossary offers brief characterizations of some key technical notions frequently employed, and specifies the section where each notion was first introduced.

Concepts: By contrast, they pick up specific yet fairly invariant or prototypical properties of objects and events and link them with other such properties by means of representations. Concepts have the task of goal-adjusted categorization, meaning that they support cogitation by selecting and linking the right properties in forms apt to handle a particular goal situation (chap. 7, section 1).

Goal-directedness: This is an abstract and global redescription of gene expression through their means–ends phenotypic manifestations, developmental as well as behavioral, individual as well as social; these phenotypic manifestations indicate the manner in which genetic programs implement their properties of maintenance and replication of internal DNA structure; the latter properties as such are not goals of anything, although, for specific species in specific environments, particular metabolic or reproductive states become goals as part of how their genetic programs maintain and replicate their internal organization; metabolic, reproductive and others sorts of goals and goal-directed processes are tools or instrumentalities accidentally evolved by genetic programs in their physical propensity (also shared by crystals and possibly other prebiological forms of matter) to maintain and replicate their internal structure (chap. 2, section 1).

Goal Script: The mental script of a goal situation, or a goal script, is articulated through the joint valuation of a number of parameters of cogitation or thinking such as representing specific goals and sequences of goals; delineating a goal situation or context; identifying the problems posed by the satisfaction of the goal; selecting and backgrounding the relevant data, relative to the problems encountered; making or exploiting assumptions about how the given data fit the context and bear on goal identification and goal satisfaction; considering alternative and competing solutions to the goal problem that are consistent with the data, the context, and the assumptions; activating some measure or standard of probability, plausibility, cost–benefit, and usefulness for grading the alternatives solutions, and choosing one; integrating and representing the solution (output) in a form utilizable by further cognitive processes (chap. 7, section 3).

Information: Defined by three conditions—interaction, reorganization, and effect or uptake; an information relation is instantiated whenever an interaction between two states, S (source) and R (receiver), results in a reorganization of R, which in turn has further effects on other states; information can be material, when governed exclusively by physical laws with no dedicated effects or functional, when also governed by functional regularities and having dedicated effects (chap. 3, section 3).

KICM: The top–down methodology of analysis (from Knowledge to Information to Cognition to Mechanism) that explains functional mechanisms in terms of the cognitive programs they run, the programs in terms of the information tasks they execute, and the tasks in terms of the knowledge (guidance to goal) they secure for an organism in its environment (chap. 3, section 1).

Knowledge: Access to information that guides to goal; having knowledge amounts to being so positioned in a network of information relations so as to initiate a behavior-to-goal routine; this is a goal-relative, information-based, contextual, descriptive, externalist (ecology-sensitive) and nonnormative notion (chap. 3, section 2).

Mental Attitude: Attitudes to, or functional roles of, the pragmatic information configured in a goal script (chap. 7, section 5).

Primitive Semantics: A semantics whose information tasks range over simple and fixed patterns of signs of the external covariations with specific distal properties, which are sufficient in a given ecology to pick up the goals of the system; as a result, the execution of its tasks does not presuppose, as those involved in re-presentational semantics do, the execution of simpler semantic information tasks (chap. 5, section 1).

Psychological Newtonianism: A way of thinking, rather than an explicit doctrine, animated by the notion that the cognitive mind is a complex body in causal motion, functionally autonomous, whose design can be ultimately explained causally by natural selection, and whose program operations can be proximately explained by a functionalized version of causal explanation (chap. 1, section 2; also chap. 9, introduction).

Psychosemanticism: The view that (a) the forms in which information is encoded and processed, as data, have causal or functional efficacy by virtue of how the data hook up with the world and that (b) the job of cognition is to provide the organism with knowledge as information that causes behavior in virtue of what it represents (chap. 1, section 2; also chap. 9, section 1).

Re-presentation: Shorthand for a semantics that secures guidance through a flexible and combinatorially versatile triangulation of goal-revealing properties from internal signs or presentations of other such signs or presentations, with the effect that complex semantic tasks are executed in terms of simpler such tasks. A program generates re-presentations, as datal structures, only if it executes information tasks through which these datal structures are (a) systematically related to specific and distal objects and situations that are (b) semantically analysed in terms of invariant ecological primitives, which are (c) recovered out of sensory inputs and computed in forms that (d) can be categorized and utilized relative to the goals of the organism (chap. 6, section 4).

Systematically Adaptive Patterns (SAP): Stable, systematic, and proximate patterns of correlations among (a) informationally recurrent features of the ecology; (b) modularized programs that register and process them; (c) the programs outputs (datal structures); and (d) the resulting behaviors. Evolution produces cognitive adaptations, in the form of modular programs that execute specific information tasks, whenever such enduring and systematically adaptive patterns emerge ancestrally as, and remain over time, solutions to enduring selection pressures (chap. 10, section 1).

Teleofunction (Systemic Function): A causal relation redescribed in light of the role of its dedicated effect(s) in a larger system of parts and processes; it can only be explained ultimately or teleologically, not proximately and causally (chap. 2, section 5).

Teleonomic Guidance: Guidance to goal (telos) effected by information relations instantiated mostly by ecological laws (nomos) and input-bound cognitive programs (chap. 4, introduction).

Topomaps (Topographic Maps): Data displays organized in ways that can be accessed and utilized by virtue of their (spatial) organization; the maps are *topo*graphic because they encode spatial data about position and motion (as change in position) in terms of the topological organization of the sensory space; they are topo*graphic* because the form in which they encode the sensory and motor data is intrinsically sensitive to, and tracks space organization and motion through space (chap. 5, section 5).

References

Adler, J. (1976, April). The sensing of chemicals by bacteria. *Scientific American, 234*, 33–39.

Alexander, R. D. (1989). Evolution of the human psyche. In P. Mellars & C. Stringer (Eds.), *The human revolution*, Edinburgh: University of Edinburgh Press.

Astington, J. et al. (Eds.). (1988). *Developing theories of mind.* Cambridge, England: Cambridge University Press.

Barkow, J., Cosmides, L., & Tooby, J. (Eds.), *The Adapted Mind*, New York: Oxford University Press.

Barwise, J., & Perry, J. (1983). *Situations and attitudes.* Cambridge, MA: MIT Press.

Beardsley, T. (1991, August). Smart genes. *Scientific American, 265*, 86–95.

Bennett, J. (1976). *Linguistic behavior.* Cambridge, England: Cambridge University Press.

Bennett, J. (1991). Analysis without noise. In R. J. Bogdan (Ed.), *Mind and Common Sense.* Cambridge: MIT Press.

Biederman, I. (1990). Higher-level vision. In D. N. Osherson et al. (Eds.). *Visual cognition and action,* Cambridge: MIT Press.

Bogdan, R. J. (1976). (Ed.). *Local induction.* Dordrecht: Reidel.

Bogdan, R. J. (1983). Fodor's representations. *Cognition and Brain Theory, 6*, 237–249.

Bogdan, R. J. (1985a). Cognition and epistemic closure. *American Philosophical Quarterly, 22*, 55–63.

Bogdan, R. J. (1885b). The intentional stance reexamined. *The Behavioral and Brain Sciences, 8*, 759–760.

Bogdan, R. J. (1986a). The manufacture of belief. In Bogdan, (Ed.). *Belief.* New York: Oxford University Press.

Bogdan, R. J. (1986b). The objects of perception. In Bogdan (Ed.). *Roderick Chisholm.* Dordrecht: Reidel.

Bogdan, R. J. (1987). Mind, content, and information. *Synthese, 70*, 205–227.

Bogdan, R. J. (1988a). Information and semantic cognition. *Mind and Language, 3*, 81–122.

Bogdan, R. J. (1988b). Replies to commentators. *Mind and Language, 3*, 145–151.

Bogdan, R. J. (1988c). Mental attitudes and commonsense psychology. *Nous, 22*, 369–398.

Bogdan, R. J. (1989a). Does semantics run the psyche? *Philosophy and Phenomenological Research, 49*, 687–700.

Bogdan, R. J. (1989b). What do we need concepts for? *Mind and Language, 4*, 17–23.

Bogdan, R. J. (1990). Les sciences cognitives et l'intelligence artificielle face à la barriere semantique (Cognitive science and artificial intelligence facing the semantic obstacle). In L. Sfez and G. Coutlée (Eds.). *Technologies et symboliques de la communication*. Grenoble: Presses Universitaires de Grenoble.

Bogdan, R. J. (1991b). Common sense naturalized. In Bogdan (Ed.), *Mind and Common Sense*. Cambridge, England: Cambridge University Press.

Bogdan, R. J. (1991c). The folklore of the mind. In Bogdan (Ed.), *Mind and Common Sense*. Cambridge, England: Cambridge University Press.

Bogdan, R. J. (1993a). The architectural nonchalance of commonsense psychology. *Mind and Language, 8*, 2, 189–205.

Bogdan, R. J. (1993b). The pragmatic psyche. *Philosophy and Phenomenological Research, 53* (1), 157–158.

Bogdan, R. J. (1993c). L'Histoire de la Science Cognitive (History of cognitive science). In L. Sfez (Ed.). *Dictionnaire critique de la communication*. Paris: Presses Universitaires de France.

Bonner, J. T. (1980). *The evolution of culture in animals*. Princeton, NJ: Princeton University Press.

Bonner, J. T. (1988). *The evolution of complexity*. Princeton, NJ: Princeton University Press.

Braitenberg, V. (1984). *Vehicles*, Cambridge, MA: MIT Press.

Braithwaite, R. B. (1953). *Scientific explanation*. Cambridge, MA: Cambridge University Press.

Brillouin, L. (1962). *Science and information theory*. New York: Academic Press.

Byrne, R., & Whiten, A. (Eds.) 1988. *Machiavellian Intelligence*. New York: Oxford University Press.

Cairns-Smith, A. G. (1985). *Seven clues to the origin of life*. Cambridge: Cambridge University Press.

Casti, J. L. (1989). *Paradigms lost*. New York: Avon Books.

Churchland, P. M., & Churchland, P. S. (1983). Stalking the wild epistemic machine. *Nous, 17*, 6–18.

Churchland, P. M. (1986). Some reductive strategies in cognitive neurobiology. *Mind, 95*, 279–309.

Churchland, P. M. (1989). *A neurocomputational perspective*. Cambridge, MA: MIT Press.

Churchland, P. S. (1986). *Neurophilosophy*. Cambridge, MA: MIT Press.

Clark, A. (1989). *Microcognition*. Cambridge, MA: MIT Press.

Clark, E., & Clark, H. (1977). *Psychology and language*. New York: Harcourt Brace.

Collins, A. (1984). Action, causality, and teleological explanation. In P. A. French et al. (Eds.), *Midwest Studies in Philosophy* (Vol. 9, pp. 345–369) Minneapolis: University of Minnesota Press.

Collins, A. (1987). *The nature of mental things*. South Bend, IN: University of Notre Dame.

Cosmides, L. (1989). The logic of social exchange: Has natural selection shaped how humans reason? *Cognition, 31*, 187–276.

Cosmides, L., & Tooby, J. (1987). From evolution to behavior. In J. Dupré (Ed.), *The latest on the best*. Cambridge, MA: MIT Press.

Cummins, R. (1975). Functional Analysis. *The Journal of Philosophy, 72*, 741–764.

Cummins, R. (1983). *Psychological explanation*. Cambridge, MA: MIT Press.

Cummins, R. (1986). Inexplicit Information. In M. Brand & R. M. Harnish (Eds.), *The representation of Knowledge and belief*. Tuscon: University of Arizona Press.

Cummins, R. (1989). *Meaning and mental representation*. Cambridge, MA: MIT Press.

Darwin, C. (1872). *The expression of emotions in man and animals*. London: John Murray.

Dascal, M., & Horowitz, A. (1992). Semantics and the psyche. *Philosophy and Phenomenological Research, 52, 2*, 395–399.

Dawkins, R. (1986). *The blind watchmaker*. New York: Norton.

Dennett, D. (1969). *Content and consciousness*. London: Routledge & Kegan Paul.

Dennett, D. (1978). *Brainstorms*. Montgomery, VT: Bradford Books.
Dennett, D. (1983). Intentional systems in cognitive ethology. *The behavioral and brain sciences, 6*, 343–355.
Dennett, D. (1987). *The intentional stance*. Cambridge, MA: MIT Press.
Dennett, D. (1991a). *Consciousness explained*. Boston: Little, Brown.
Dennett, D. (1991b). Ways of establishing harmony. In B. McLaughlin (Ed.), *Dretske and his critics*. Oxford, England: Blackwell.
De Sousa, R. (1984). *The rationality of emotions*. Cambridge, MA: MIT Press.
Dickerson, R. E. (1978, September). Chemical evolution and the origin of life. *Scientific American, 239*, 70–86.
Donald, M. (1991). *Origins of the modern mind*. Cambridge, MA: Harvard University Press.
Dretske, F. (1969). *Seeing and knowing*. Chicago: University of Chicago Press.
Dretske, F. (1972). Contrastive statements. *Philosophical Review, 81*, 411–437.
Dretske, F. (1986). Misrepresentation. In Bogdan (Ed.), *Belief*. New York: Oxford University Press.
Dretske, F. (1981). *Knowledge and the flow of information*. Cambridge, MA: MIT Press.
Dretske, F. (1988). *Explaining behavior*. Cambridge, MA: MIT Press.
Dretske, F. (1989). Reasons and causes. In J. E. Tomberlin (Ed.). *Philosophical Perspectives* (Vol. 3, pp). Atascadero, CA: Ridgeview.
Eldredge, N. (1985). *Unfinished synthesis*. New York: Oxford University Press.
Enç, B. (1982). Intentional states of mechanical devices. *Mind, 91*, 161–182.
Fodor, J. A. (1975). *The language of thought*. Cambridge, MA: Harvard University Press.
Fodor, J. A., (1980). Methodological solipsism considered as a research strategy in cognitive psychology. *The Behavioral and Brain Sciences, 3*, 63–73.
Fodor, J. A. (1983). *The modularity of mind*. Cambridge, MA: MIT Press.
Fodor, J. A. (1986a). Why paramecia don't have mental representations. *Midwest Studies in Philosophy, X*, 1–29.
Fodor, J. A. (1986b). Information and association. In Brand & Harnish (Eds.), *The representation of knowledge and belief*. Tucson, AZ: The University of Arizona Press.
Fodor, J. A. (1987). *Psychosemantics*. Cambridge, MA: MIT Press.
Fodor, J. A. (1990a). *A theory of content*. Cambridge, MA: MIT Press.
Fodor, J. A. (1990b). Psychosemantics, or: Where do truth conditions come from? In Lycan (Ed.), *Mind and Cognition*. Oxford: Blackwell.
Fodor, J. A., & Pylyshyn, Z. (1981). How direct is visual perception? *Cognition, 9*, 139–196.
Gehring, W. (1985, October). The molecular basis of development. *Scientific American. 253*, 153–163.
Goodale, M. A. (1987). The compleat visual system: From input to output. *The Behavioral and Brain Scieneces, 10*, 379–380.
Gould, J. L., & Gould, C. G., (1986). Invertebrate intelligence. In R. J. Hoage & L. Goldman (Eds.), *Animal intelligence*. Washington: Smithonian Institution Press.
Granit, R. (1977). *The purposive brain*. Cambridge, MA: MIT Press.
Haugeland, J. (1978). The plausibility of cognitivism. *The Behavioral and Brain Sciences, 1*, 215–226.
Hildreth, E. C., & Ullman, S. (1989). The computational study of vision. In Posner (Ed.), *Foundations of Cognitive Science*. Cambridge, MA: MIT Press.
Hintikka, J. (1976). *The semantics of questions*. Amsterdam: North-Holland.
Holland, J., Holyoak, K. J., Nisbett, R. E., & Thagard, P. R. (1986). *Induction*. Cambridge, MA: MIT Press.
Israel, D. J. (1988). Bogdan on information. *Mind and Language, 3*,123–140.
Jackendoff, R. (1987). *Consciousness and the computational mind*. Cambridge, MA: MIT Press.
Johnson-Laird, P. (1983). *Mental models*. Cambridge, MA: Harvard University Press.
Kirby, K. N., & Kosslyn, S. M. (1990). Thinking visually. *Mind and Language, 5*, 324–341.

Koshland, D. E. (1975). Chemotaxis in bacteria as a simple sensory system. In I. R. Miller (Ed.), *Stability and origin of biological information.* New York: Wiley.
Kosslyn, S. M. (1981). The medium and the message in mental imagery: A theory. In N. Block (Ed.), *Imagery.* Cambridge, MA: MIT Press.
Kosslyn, S. M. (1990). Mental imagery. In D. N. Osherson et al. (Eds.). *Visual Cognition and Action.* Cambridge, MA: MIT Press.
Kosslyn, S. M. (forthcoming). A cognitive neuroscience of visual cognition.
Levi, I. (1967). *Gambling with truth.* New York: Knopf.
Levy, S. (1992). *Artificial life.* New York: Random House.
Lewontin, R. C. (1990). The evolution of cognition. In D. N. Osherson & E. E. Smith (Eds.), *Thinking.* Cambridge, MA: MIT Press.
Lin, E. E. C. et al (1984). *Bacteria, plasmids, and phages.* Cambridge, MA: Harvard University Press.
Llinas, R. (1986). Mindedness as a functional state of the brain. In C. Blakemore & S. Greenfield (Eds.), *Mind and matter.* Oxford: Blackwell.
Lloyd, D. (1989). *Simple minds.* Cambridge, MA: MIT Press.
Loftus, E. (1980). *Memory.* Reading, MA: Addison-Wesley.
Lycan, W. (1981). Form, function, and feel. *Journal of Philosophy, 76,* 24–49.
Lycan, W. (1986). Tacit belief. in Bogdan (Ed.), *Belief.* Oxford: Oxford University Press.
Lycan, W. (1989). *Consciousness.* Cambridge, MA: MIT Press.
Marr, D. (1982). *Vision.* San Francisco: Freeman.
Matthen, M., & Levy, E. (1984). Teleology, error, and the human immune system. *The Journal of Philosophy, 81,* 351–372.
Matthen, M. (1988). Biological functions and perceptual content. *The Journal of Philosophy, 85,* 5–28.
Mayr, E. (1976). *Evolution and the diversity of life.* Cambridge, MA: Harvard University Press.
Mayr, E. (1982). *The growth of biological thought.* Cambridge, MA: Harvard University Press.
McFarland, D. (1983). Intentions as goals. *The Behavioral and Brain Sciences, 6,* 369–370.
McGinn, C. (1982). The structure of content. In A. Woodfield (Ed.), *Thought and object.* New York: Oxford University Press.
McGinn, C. (1989). *Mental content.* Oxford: Blackwell.
Millikan, R. (1984). *Language, thought, and other biological categories.* Cambridge, MA: MIT Press.
Millikan, R. (1986). Thoughts without laws; cognitive science without content. *Philosophical Review, 94,* 47–80.
Millikan, R. (1989). Biosemantics. *The Journal of Philosophy, 86,* 281–297.
Morton, A. (1980). *Frames of mind.* Oxford: Oxford University Press.
Moses, P. M., & Chua, N-H. (1988, April). Light switches for plant genes. *Scientific American, 258,* 88–93.
Nagel, E. (1977). Teleology revisited. *The Journal of Philosophy, 74,* 261–301.
Nagel, E. (1979). *The structure of science.* Indianapolis, IN: Hackett. (Original work published 1961)
Newell, A. (1982). The knowledge level. *Artifial Intelligence, 18,* 87–172.
Papineau, D. (1984). Representation and explanation. *Philosophy of Science, 51,* 550–572.
Papineau, D. (1987). *Representation and reality.* Oxford: Blackwell.
Piattelli-Palmarini, M. (1989). Evolution, selection and cognition. *Cognition, 31,* 1–44.
Pinker, S., & Bloom, P. (1990). Natural language and natural selection. *The Behavioral and Brain Sciences, 13,* 707–726.
Pylyshyn, Z. (1984). *Computation and cognition.* Cambridge, MA: MIT Press.
Pylyshyn, Z. (1989). Computing in cognitive science. In Posner (Ed.), *Foundations of Cognitive Science,* Cambridge, MA: MIT Press.
Quine, W. V. O. (1960). *Word and object.* Cambridge, MA: MIT Press.

Recanati, F. (1989). The pragmatics of what is said. *Mind and Language, 4*, 295–329.
Schopf, J. W. (1988, September). The evolution of the earliest cells. *Scientific American, 239*, 110–140.
Searle, J. (1972, June). Chomsky's revolution in linguistics. *The New York Review of Books*, p. 29.
Searle, J. (1983). *Intentionality*. Cambridge, England: Cambridge University Press.
Shapiro, J. A. (1988, June). Bacteria as multicellular organisms. *Scientific American, 258*, 82–89.
Smith, E. E., & Medin. D. L. (1981). *Categories and concepts*. Cambridge, MA: Harvard University Press.
Smith, E. E. (1989). Concepts and induction. In Posner, M. (Ed.), *Foundations of Cognitive Science*. Cambridge, MA: MIT Press.
Sober, E. (1984). *The nature of selection*. Cambridge, MA: MIT Press.
Sober, E. (1985). Panglossian functionalism and the philosophy of mind. *Synthese, 64*, 165–193.
Somerhoff, G. (1974). *The Logic of the Living Brain*. New York: WIley.
Sperber, D. (1993). The Modularity of Thought and the Epidemiology of Representations. In L. A. Hirschfeld & S. A. Gelman (Eds.). *Domain Specificity in Cognition and Culture*. Cambridge, England: Cambridge University Press.
Sperber, D., & Wilson, D. (1986). *Relevance*. Cambridge, MA: Harvard University Press.
Stabler, E. (1983). How are grammars represented? *The Behavioral and Brain Sciences 6*, 391–420.
Sterelny, K. (1990). *The representational theory of mind*. Oxford: Blackwell.
Stich, S. (1983). *From folk psychology to cognitive science*. Cambridge, MA: MIT Press.
Stich, S. (1990). *The fragmentation of reason*. Cambridge, MA: MIT Press.
Taylor, C. (1964). *The explanation of behavior*. London: Routledge & Kegan Paul.
Tooby, J., & Cosmides, L. (1990). The past explains the present. *Ethology and Sociobiology, 11*, 375–424.
Tooby, J., & Cosmides, L. (1992). The psychological foundations of culture. In J. Barkow, L. Cosmides, & J. Tooby (Eds.), *The adapted mind*. Oxford: Oxford Universituy Press.
Trivers, R. (1985). *Social evolution*. Menlo Park, CA: Benjamin/Cummings.
Vogel, S. (1988). *Life's devices*. Princeton, NJ: Princeton University Press.
Waterman, T. H. (1989). *Animal navigation*, New York: Scientific American Library.
Weinberg, R. (1985, October). The molecules of life. *Scientific American, 253*, 48–57.
Wiener, N. (1961). *Cybernetics*. Cambridge, MA: MIT Press. (Original work published 1948)
Wiener, N. (1956). *The Human Use of Human Beings*. Garden City: Doubleday. (Original work published 1950)
Wilkes, K. V. (1981). Functionalism, psychology and the philosophy of mind. *Philosophical Topics, 12*, 147–168.
Woodfield, A. (1976). *Teleology*. Cambridge, England: Cambridge University Press.
Wolpert, L. (1991). *The triumph of the embryo*. New York: Oxford University Press.

Author Index

A, B

C

D

E, F

G

Subject Index